Feminized Work and the Labor of Literature

Feminized Work and the Labor of Literature

New Literary Perspectives on the Times, Spaces, and Forms of Women's Work

Edited by Emily J. Hogg,
Charlotte J. Fabricius

EDINBURGH
University Press

Edinburgh University Press is one of the leading university presses in the UK. We publish academic books and journals in our selected subject areas across the humanities and social sciences, combining cutting-edge scholarship with high editorial and production values to produce academic works of lasting importance. For more information visit our website: edinburghuniversitypress.com

We are committed to making research available to a wide audience and are pleased to be publishing an Open Access ebook edition of this title.

Edinburgh University Press Ltd
13 Infirmary Street
Edinburgh EH1 1LT

First published in hardback by Edinburgh University Press 2025

Typeset in 11/13 Bembo by
IDSUK (DataConnection) Ltd, and
Printed and bound in the UK using 100% renewable electricity by
CPI Group (UK) Ltd

ISBN 978 1 3995 4133 6 (hardback)
ISBN 978 1 3995 4134 3 (paperback)
ISBN 978 1 3995 4135 0 (webready PDF)
ISBN 978 1 3995 4136 7 (epub)

EU Authorised Representative:
Easy Access System Europe
Mustamäe tee 50, 10621 Tallinn, Estonia
gpsr.requests@easproject.com

MIX
Paper | Supporting responsible forestry
FSC www.fsc.org FSC® C013604

This book is printed using paper from well-managed forests, recycling and other controlled sources

Contents

PART III: THE EMPLOYMENT OF FORM

Figures

Acknowledgments

We are grateful to the Carlsberg Foundation, whose generous funding of the research project Feminized: A New Literary History of Women's Work (grant no. CF20-0554) supported the publication of this book.

Without Ida Aaskov Dolmer, our colleague in the Feminized project, this book is impossible to imagine. For the last three years, the three of us have been engaged in a dialogue about feminization, work, gender, and literature, which has been immensely rewarding and generative. We are so grateful to Ida for her insights, inspiration, and ideas, her support and camaraderie—and also for her practical work in helping to organize the workshop at which this book was developed.

From the outset, we knew that we wanted this book to emerge from a process of close collaboration and feminist thinking together. To co-create it, we invited a group of scholars, most of whom we didn't know and who didn't know each other, to come to the University of Southern Denmark for a two-day workshop. We wanted the event to be an experiment in developing new work collaboratively, and we are grateful to each of the contributors to this volume for participating in this experiment by so generously sharing their work in progress, giving and receiving feedback, beginning expansive conversations about the areas of interest we share, and continuing to work together after the workshop to bring the book into being.

We would also like to thank those who took the time to attend and participate in the workshop at which we developed this book: Rita Felski, Ella Fegitz, Tatsiana Haiden, and Kornilov Konstantin.

To the Center for Uses of Literature, thanks for providing an institutional home for our research, and an inspiring environment in which to discuss the relationship between literature and social and political questions. Thanks in particular to Peter Simonsen, Bryan Yazell, Anne-Marie Mai, Jon Helt Haarder, Camilla Schwartz, and Anita Wohlmann.

We are grateful also to our other colleagues at the Department of Culture and Language, University of Denmark for the research environment in which our project has taken shape. Special thanks to Per Krogh Hansen, Maria Hollemann, Michella Hangård Petersen, and Lone Marianne Villemoes.

Being able to use a poster by See Red Women's Workshop (SRWW) on the cover of this book (as well as to reproduce another in the volume itself) is a great honour. SRWW's work has been so influential and inspirational for us. We thank the collective for their permission, as well as Susan Mackie in particular for corresponding with us and assisting with the practical matters.

At Edinburgh University Press, we would like to thank Emily Sharp for her support of the book, her advice and guidance, and Elizabeth Fraser, for her help and close attention in seeing the book through to publication.

The anonymous reviewers of the manuscript gave us thoughtful, rigorous, and insightful feedback that has greatly strengthened the published text, and we are grateful to them for their attentive readings.

Emily would like to thank Charlotte for the close collaboration on this book. I deeply appreciate your commitment to this project and all of the work you have put into to the volume; our conversations about feminist critique, literature, and culture are a great highlight of my working life. To Mary, Amba and Wendy—thank you for inspiring me to think about this topic in the first place.

Charlotte would like to thank Emily for an inspiring and genuinely collaborative process. Doing this book work together has modelled feminist scholarship in a way I had previously only dreamed of. My unending gratitude also goes to Malthe, for taking on the care work and providing me with the time and means for making this book happen.

Notes on Contributors

Helen Charman is a writer and academic. Her first book, *Mother State: a Political History of Motherhood*, was published in 2024. She is a Fellow, College Teaching Officer, and Director of Studies in English at Clare College, University of Cambridge.

Ida Aaskov Dolmer is a PhD researcher at the University of Southern Denmark. She is part of the project 'Feminized: A New Literary History of Women's Work', PI Emily Hogg, and the research group 'Uses of Literature'. Her PhD dissertation focuses on British women's literature c. 1970s to the present and examines literary depictions of mothering as a form of work as well as the entanglement of mothering with other forms of paid and unpaid work. She has recently completed a semester as a visiting researcher at King's College London and has presented at conferences nationally and internationally.

Lucie Duggan is currently a postdoctoral researcher and PI of the Augustinus-funded research project Reading Women: Karen Brahe and Female Book Ownership (1609–1736). The project investigates the unique library of the early modern Danish book collector Karen Brahe, using digital network analysis to map the texts, contributors, and geographical locations that make up the Brahe collection, revealing the networks of transmission that underpin female book ownership and collecting practices in early modern Denmark. She obtained her PhD from the University of Southern Denmark with a dissertation on the ballad collection of Francis James Child.

Charlotte J. Fabricius is a postdoc with the project 'Feminized: A New Literary History of Women's Work' at the Center for Uses of Literature, University of Southern Denmark. She holds a PhD in cultural studies and works in the intersection of global and digital anglophone literature, comics studies, and feminist critique. She is the author of *Super-Girls of the Future: Girlhood and Agency in Contemporary Superhero Comics* (2023).

Roberta Garrett is a Senior Lecturer in the Department of Arts and Creative Industries at the University of East London. She is the author of *Postmodern Chick-Flicks* (2008), co-editor of *Rachel Cusk: Contemporary Critical Perspectives* (2024) and *We Need to Talk About Family: Essays on Neoliberalism, the Family and Popular Culture* (2016), and author of *Writing the Modern Family: Contemporary Literature, Motherhood and Neoliberal Culture* (2021). She is also the author of numerous articles in peer-reviewed journals and multiple book chapters.

Emily J. Hogg is Associate Professor of Contemporary Anglophone Literature at the Department of Culture and Language, University of Southern Denmark. Her research focuses on contemporary literature's social and political dimensions, especially in relation to precarity, feminization, and human rights discourse. This work has been published in *Textual Practice, ASAP/J, Criticism, English Studies*, and elsewhere.

Christina Lupton is currently Professor of Literary and Cultural Studies at the University of Copenhagen. She has taught at universities in the US and UK and published several books on the history of reading from the eighteenth century to the present, most recently the jointly authored monograph *Reading Novels During the Covid-19 Pandemic* (2022), as well as *Reading and the Making of Time in the Eighteenth Century* (2018) and *Love and the Novel* (2022). Her new project, *Paid Leaves: Writing a Life after 1968*, explores the way different strands of twentieth-century theory have imagined the reorganization of the worker's day and the time to be given to self-representation. She has been the recipient of grants and fellowships from organizations including the Humboldt Foundation, the Leverhulme Trust, and the Carlsberg Foundation.

Leah Misemer is a faculty member at Georgia Institute of Technology where she serves as Assistant Director for the Vertically Integrated Projects (VIP) Program. She has a PhD in English from University of Wisconsin-Madison and specializes in visual rhetoric and popular culture. Much of her published work, as well as her teaching and activism, analyzes and deploys comics' ability to form communities—online, in person, and through printed networks enabled by serial publication. She has published works on comics and community building in numerous journals and edited collections.

Varsha Panjwani is the host and creator of the award-winning *Women & Shakespeare* podcast (www.womenandshakespeare.com) and the author of *Podcasts and Feminist Shakespeare Pedagogy* (2022). Her articles have been published in journals including *Shakespeare Survey* and *Shakespeare Studies*, and in edited collections such as *Shakespeare, Race and Performance*, *Shakespeare and Indian Cinema*, *Eating Shakespeare: Cultural Anthropophagy as Global Methodology*, and *The Arden Research Handbook to Shakespeare and Adaptation*. She is the co-editor of *Re-contextualizing Indian Shakespeare Cinema in the West: Familiar Strangers* (2023) and a special issue of *Multicultural Shakespeare*. She is currently working on a book that examines the vigorous afterlife of the imaginary sister that Virginia Woolf created for Shakespeare.

Leighan Renaud is Lecturer in Caribbean Literatures and Cultures at the University of Bristol, UK. Her PhD research focused on representations of matrifocality in contemporary Anglophone Caribbean literature. Her research interests include Caribbean mothering, Caribbean women's writing, folk, oral traditions in the Anglophone Caribbean, and creative practices of neo-archiving. She has published works in *The Journal of West Indian Literature*, *The Conversation*, and *History Workshop Online*. Her forthcoming monograph, *Motherhood, Mothering and Marronage* examines the representation of matrifocality in twenty-first century Caribbean fiction.

Lindsay Turner is the author of the poetry collections *Songs & Ballads* (2018) and *The Upstate* (2023). Her poetry criticism appears in *Contemporary Women's Writing*, *ASAP / Journal*, *The Los Angeles Review of Books*, and elsewhere, and she is also a translator of contemporary Francophone poetry, philosophy, and social theory. She lives in Cleveland, Ohio, where she is Associate Professor of English and Creative Writing at Case Western Reserve University.

Nicola Wilson is Associate Professor in Book and Publishing Studies at the University of Reading, and co-director of the Centre for Book Cultures and Publishing. She is the author of *Home in British Working-Class Fiction* (2015), co-author of *Scholarly Adventures in Digital Humanities: Making the Modernist Archives Publishing Project* (2017), and editor of *The Book World: Selling and Distributing British Literature, 1900–40* (2016). She has recently completed a history of the Book Society (1929–69) called *Recommended! The Influencers who Changed How we Read* (2025), and is lead co-editor of *The Edinburgh Companion to Women in Publishing, 1900–2020* (Edinburgh University Press, 2024).

Introduction: New Literary Perspectives on Women's Work

Charlotte J. Fabricius and Emily J. Hogg

A woman retrieves a toddler from their bed. She serves her family breakfast. She goes through a day of school drop-offs, cleaning, laundry, food shopping, more laundry, more cleaning, more caretaking. She goes to bed beside her husband. She wakes up, starting over. The smile on her face never falters. She never speaks.

The only person who does speak is her husband, his remark visually singled out through a bright red speech ballon; he tells his colleague/drinking mate, 'My wife doesn't work.' This line of dialogue also serves as the title of the piece, a 1976 poster by See Red Women's Workshop, the UK-based feminist art collective (Figure I.1). The poster draws on the visual language of comics to highlight the repetitive, circular experience of the titular wife. The uniform grid—four panels across, five panels high, each panel labeled with a different hour of the day—suggests the ceaseless rhythms of work that are usually invisible, and yet made visible through this particular form. Several panels are repeated with minor variations, visualizing the repetitive nature of the work being performed. The upper-left and bottom-right panels are identical, apart from the colors being swapped, suggesting an endless cycle of repeated daily drudgery. Time stamps mark the passing of time and their use strengthens the claim that this woman is, contrary to her husband's suggestion, performing work: the time-management logic of factory work or other capitalist production is replicated. Thus, we parse this woman's work through a formal attention to repetition and through markers associated with clocking into a shift job. The notable exception, of course, is that there is no clocking out.

We see, furthermore, the suggestion of these gendered working patterns being passed on. The right-most panel of the top row shows the wife

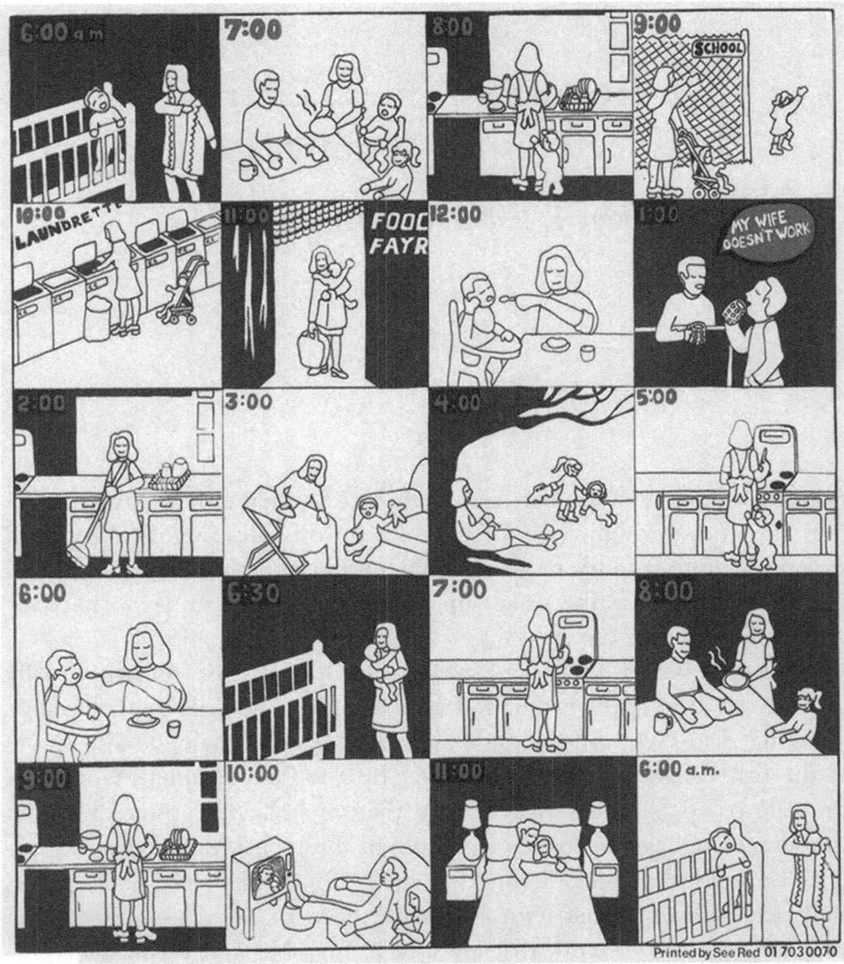

Figure I.1 'My wife doesn't work' 1980 (original version: 1976) © See Red Women's Workshop/Victoria and Albert Museum, London. 79 × 54 cm. Reproduced with permission

dropping off her older child at a place marked 'School.' This child, who is depicted wearing a dress and with long hair in a ponytail, and whom we thus argue is coded feminine, is posed identically to her mother as they wave to each other, suggesting an affinity between them that goes beyond visual similarity. Reading with the suggestion of a ceaseless cycle, the poster leads us to understand that this girl will be expected to grow up and repeat this very pattern.

The central point of the poster—that, indeed, the wife does work, in an endless drudgery of repeated domestic maintenance tasks and sustaining her family—is expressed through the form of comics. The regular grid, the repetition of shapes and panels, the time-stamp captions, the use of contrasting color to signal rhythm and draw our eyes to the 'break' of the husband's remark, are all visual tropes associated with comics. While the comics form lends itself to many disciplinary frameworks, it is included in this collection as one of many forms of literature. This is not to disregard the visual side but rather to emphasize the various uses of form in expressing feminized work. That is: the comics form can, like the poetic and narrative forms discussed in this book, function as a way of drawing attention to the particular characteristics of the types of labor that have conventionally been gendered feminine.

See Red Women's Workshop was an explicitly feminist collective with a clear activist agenda in their work. While 'My wife doesn't work' is a product of the collective's 1970s-era radical feminist sensibilities, it also speaks powerfully across the decades: as an activist poster, it aims to speak a generalizable truth that can foster recognition and rally people to a cause. And although underdiscussed in literary and comics studies, See Red Women's Workshop's visual feminist activism is a clear precursor to the visual literature discussing feminism and reproduction today. We might think, for example, of the word circles that are frequently used by US cartoonist Liana Finck as distillations of feminized work-life, at once representation and critique. In one example, Finck's looping sentence reads 'work to distract yourself from' (Finck, 14 December 2021). Captioning this piece on Instagram, Finck elaborates further: 'Write to distract yourself from life, make cartoons to distract yourself from writing, take on freelance to distract yourself from cartoons, teach to distract yourself from freelance, and focus on life a bit to distract yourself from anxiety over not having enough work.' While gender is not mentioned explicitly in this particular instance, it is pervasive throughout Finck's oeuvre, which is broadly concerned with the feminized experience of artistic work (see Fabricius and Hogg). The 'distracted' mode suggested by Finck gestures toward a rather bleak horizon of unending work but also contains the suggestion that creative work, especially the work of writing, intersects with feminized experience as a way of pausing the drudgery and finding space for expressions of self.

The figure of the middle-class housewife, whose sense of frustrated potential was powerfully articulated in 1960s' and 1970s' feminist texts, from Betty Friedan's *The Feminine Mystique* (1963) to Ann Oakley's *Housewife* (1974), may seem today simply an anachronistic type. To the extent that the ideal was ever relevant, it was primarily relevant to relatively privileged women in the Global North. And haven't even these women left the housewife archetype behind long ago in the pursuit of ever greater educational and career accomplishments? Finck's anxious freelance artist/writer is in some ways very distant from the 'wife' of the See Red Women's Workshop poster, but the recurrence of the circular form across the decades—despite the dramatic changes that have occurred across these decades in relation to the norms and expectations that feminized subjects encounter—suggests that a more complicated relationship between these pasts and presents of women's work exists than a simple narrative of progress would imply.

The theme of women's invisible labor travels and so do the forms used to express it. In the poem 'Circuit,' for example, published in her 2017 collection *Incarnation*, UK poet Clare Pollard describes the embodied (and historically feminized) experience of pregnancy, two-bodies-in-one, as a circling loop. Apart from being the title of the poem, the circuit form is enforced visually in Pollard's text, as the words snake around in a circle on the page, with no clear marking of beginning or end point. From the top, it reads 'as your child twists as your thoughts turn as your blood loops as your hearts churn' (Pollard 23), the verbs describing circulatory movements of turning, churning, looping, even the twisting of the child in utero. The physical labor of carrying two hearts and a foreign body within one's own, having to pump a greater volume of blood, thoughts obsessing over the change that is to come, is literalized as language given a deliberate shape. The linearity of reading, otherwise entrenched in anglophone culture, is subverted by Pollard's poem in a way that recalls both the circularity of the See Red Women's Workshop poster and of Finck's comics. The form chosen by Pollard—the circling text, expressing an experience of circularity—is one that becomes linked up with feminized experiences time and again. As we have demonstrated elsewhere (Fabricius and Hogg), circularity has been utilized by woman artists in different contexts and media to express feminized experiences of work and life.

The continuities between such literary engagements with feminized work are what we seek to explore in this book. The refrain of 'A woman's work is never done,' the tagline of another iconic poster by See Red Women's Workshop and one we discuss later in this Introduction, can be traced back to a seventeenth-century ballad of the same name (see Dowd 2), wherein the singer details her daily household and caring labors. In this sense contemporary ideas about work and gender are embedded in the conditions of modernity itself, and for this reason two of the chapters in this book discuss the early modern period—

either, as in Lucie Duggan's chapter on the Danish noblewoman Karen Brahe, through archival research—or, as in Varsha Panjwani's chapter on Virginia Woolf's *A Room of One's Own*, through considering the ways the period has been imaginatively reconstructed.

Being scholars of English literature and cultural studies, we look to forms of writing produced by women and writers identified with femininity to access narratives of what feminized work *is*, what it feels like, what it *means*. As we discuss further later in this Introduction, recent methods in literary study have been highly contextual, seeking primarily to situate literary texts within the precise moment of their composition and publication. In this book, by contrast, we take a transhistorical and, following the V21 collective (see Coombs and Coriale), strategically presentist approach. By this, we do not claim a vast historical sweep or make any pretense to comprehensiveness. Indeed, our emphasis is, with the notable exception of Duggan's chapter, primarily on the anglophone world of the twentieth and twenty-first centuries. Rather, instead of focusing on the time, place, and provenance of each case study, the aim of the collection is to explore the ways that these texts speak to each other, and to us in our present moment.

We do not advance a singular idea of what constitutes femininized labor; on the contrary, it is abundantly clear that racialization, class hierarchies, and national context all shape the gendering of work in different times and places. But we argue that certain ideas about the work considered appropriate to women are transmitted and transported across contexts and have often become generalized in a globalized world. The book therefore responds to the circulation of such ideas by bringing together texts in different genres (novels, poems, comics, life writing), which come from different locations (including the Caribbean, the UK, the US, Denmark) and which span different moments in, especially, the twentieth and twenty-first centuries. The gendering of work today, we argue, entails the repetition and rearticulation of ostensibly traditional codes of feminine and masculine behavior, as depicted in See Red Women's Workshop's representation of the feminized child's socialization by the mother. All of the chapters' readings therefore place primary emphasis on the way their texts, although inevitably shaped by their particular contexts, also participate in discourses of gender and work that travel beyond any one time or space.

We explore a range of case studies to show how reading for feminized work across contexts and forms can reveal new insights about it as an experience, express its particular characteristics, and, at times, gesture toward a more just organization of the labor required to sustain us. More specifically, the book has two main tasks. We aim to show in transhistorical fashion how literary texts from earlier historical moments can be used to theorize a particular contemporary crisis, the feminization of work, and we also aim to situate very recently published texts within a tradition of literary representations of gendered work. We argue that these tasks are particularly urgent today. While the study of the economic and social conditions in which women's writing takes place has been, since Virginia Woolf's *A Room of One's Own*, an acknowledged theme in literary studies, the relationship between literature, gender, and the broader conditions of contemporary work have been less frequently discussed. The significance of this cluster of topics is suggested by recent work in the social sciences, which has used the term 'feminization' to describe the way that working conditions once primarily associated with women have become more widespread in the context of precarity. Further, as Sarah Brouillette and others have argued, the artist's sense of vocation and passion for her work has provided the model for neoliberal capitalism's ideal worker. Because contemporary labor practices seem to draw upon existing discourses of gender and creativity, there is a need to bring together studies of the conventional category of women's work—both as it is represented in literature and as it shapes literary production—with contemporary theorizations of neoliberal precarity. It is this intersection that is addressed by *Feminized Work and the Labor of Literature.*

Poetics of Feminization

When afforded the proverbial room of one's own and 500 a year, women writers have engaged in the work of writing, editing, circulating, and reading literature, and even in conditions of economic and social limitation, many women have still continued to write. This is illustrated in Tess Gallagher's 'I stop writing the poem,' which is not optimistic but nevertheless imagines a world with more time for the meaningful work of creativity. Gallagher's grief over the loss of her husband, the poet Raymond Carver, is palpable in the poem, yet never explicated. Thus, if read at face value, the poem represents a grown woman doing the work of household maintenance, of care labor, of putting on pause one's creative endeavors to deal with the menial tasks of the everyday: 'there's a shirt, a giant shirt / in my hands, and somewhere a small girl / standing next to her mother / watching to see how it's done' (Gallagher lines 9–12). These meanings linger, even as they are layered beneath the representations of grief and mourning that become apparent when reading the poem in its context of writing. If we remain attentive to the content of the poem, the obvious connection to draw is perhaps not to the celebrated, deceased husband but to the writings of Audre Lorde. In the essay 'Age, Race, Class, and Sex: Women Redefining Difference,' Lorde argues that poetry is an ideal form for women, especially those multiply marginalized by age, race, and class, since it is a form 'which can be done between shifts, in the hospital pantry, on the subway, and on scraps of surplus paper,' requiring the least physical labor as well as fewer materials than prose or other forms of art (116).

The black women of Lorde's writing, too, stop writing the poem. They fit it into the interstitial moments between housework, care work, paid work, the exhausting work of surviving as black women in a white supremacist world. Poetry, to Lorde, is uniquely suited for the feminized experience because it is fundamentally interruptible and requires few material resources, compared with novels or sculptural arts. While Gallagher was a white woman of means and well-connected in literary circles, she remains at the mercy of gender roles: 'No matter who lives / or who dies, I'm still a woman. / I'll always have plenty to do' (lines 1–2), Gallagher reminds us. Her sense of what being a woman entails, however, is not only connected to reproductive work. A few lines later, she muses, 'I'll get back / to the poem. I'll get back to being / a woman' (Gallagher lines 6–8). The enjambement inscribes the multitude of who Gallagher understands herself to be: poet, person, woman. Getting back to the poem means getting back to being a woman but also, at least for a brief moment, getting back to *being*, simply and less defined. While finding a sense of worth and identity in work is a hazardous undertaking under capitalism, understanding oneself through the creative work of writing can provide a space wherein being a woman means more than being confined to folding the shirts of those who left you behind.

There is decidedly less space for 'getting back to being' for the speaker in the black Australian poet Roberta 'Bobbi' Sykes's poem 'The Treadmill of Life,' which bespeaks an experience at once personally specific and gesturing toward the universal. The lines 'Running to'/ 'Running from' are repeated across stanzas in an alternating pattern, evoking the running-in-place of a clearly feminized existence:

> Running from /
> Job to job to job—juggling:
> three part-time workplaces /
> Ever-changing co-workers' faces,
> Names disappearing in the blur of my haste. (Sykes: 31)

These lines give voice to the multiple-shift life of a feminized and, presumably, racialized existence. People are reduced to nameless faces, as they blur past the running speaker of the poem. Sykes' activist investments are clear in the poem's naming of gendered, racialized, and classed inequity, landlords, state institutions, and commercialized spaces; all hostile to the thriving of the speaker. The poem ends with a lamenting citation of the gospel song 'I can't stand up alone' by Martha Carson; a desire to one day stop running and cool one's feet. There is no indication, however, that the treadmill will be stopping any time soon.

This expression of repetition and racialized women's work through lyric poetry can also be observed in 'Woman Work' by Maya Angelou; an African-American woman's version of this experience in both content and form. The rhyming scheme, driving the short lines forward in couplets, echoes the tradition of black work songs. Angelou uses this form to express the feminized work of caretaking, housekeeping, living with the seasons, and the forced labor of cotton-picking:

> I've got the children to tend
> The clothes to mend
> The floor to mop
> The food to shop
> [...]
> I gotta clean up this hut
> Then see about the sick
> And the cotton to pick. (lines 1–4, 12–14)

The poem is situated at once at a specific experience and out-of-time, halfway between to-do-list and nursery rhyme, at once bitter and resigned. The woman owns nothing, the ending lets us know, other than her experiences of the weather, the sensations of the body enduring the changing seasons. This is an experience linked particularly to the black enslaved woman presumed to be speaking these lines but also one that connects beyond that specificity to Angelou's own experience and beyond. A long legacy of black women speaks through Angelou, pushing the poem forward in time from its publication. And the poem also speaks to the seventeenth-century ballad, and the protest poster—texts that differ according to their circumstances but retain affinities across the places and eras they inhabit.

The poems by Angelou and Sykes remind us that experiences of the work women have actually, historically performed cannot be understood monolithically; that racialization, especially as it has existed in different national contexts, has fundamentally shaped the experience of womanhood such that no universal definition exists of the work women do. Our argument in this book, however, is that bringing together different representations can allow us to begin stitching together a patchwork impression of the rhythms, cycles, obstructions, and breaking points of the working conditions that have been conceptualized as 'feminine' and which have, increasingly, become the reality of everyone save the most privileged. That is, while racialization, class, and national context have produced divergent ideas about gender, there are also gendered conceptions of work that have become especially salient in the contemporary global economy, precisely because they are translatable and presumed to be generalizable. By tracking the way these ideas are explored and critiqued in literature, we can gain new insight into the ways feminized work, as ideology rather than as natural female trait, provides the pattern for contemporary labor.

Defining Feminized Work

The See Red Women's Workshop posters were created at a time when 'women's work' was shifting from being something performed mainly in the home to being a combination of unwaged housework and (under)paid work outside of one's own home. While posters such as 'My wife doesn't work' address the women who did not work for pay, the woman of 'A woman's work is never done' is split between housework and factory work, depicted across both spheres of what Arlie Hochschild would later come to describe as the 'double shift' nature of women's work (Figure I.2). This crucial shift prompts a contemporary viewer to consider what is being described as 'women's work' here, and to what extent this historical concept can travel.

Indicating that it is 'never done' places emphasis on the work that takes place after the factory shift has ended, as does the ironic statement that the housewife does not work. This was an important political strategy for See Red Women's Workshop, as it was for the contemporaneous campaign for Wages for Housework, and activist art projects such as *Women and Work: A Document on the Division of Labour in Industry 1973–1975* by Margaret Harrison, Kay Hunt, and Mary Kelly. These efforts aimed for the recognition of what is termed by Marxist feminists as 'social reproduction'—that is, the effort that is expended to maintain the social structure and ensure its continuance (see Bhattacharya; Ferguson)—as work. Given the economic conditions of globalized late-stage capitalism, including gaps in care provision for aging populations, the proliferation of jobs in the service sector,

Figure I.2 'A woman's work is never done' 1974 © See Red Women's Workshop. 51 × 66 cm. Reproduced with permission

and the time-famine characteristic of many dual-income families today, this 1970s' feminist spin on Marxist labor theory has been revitalized by recent scholarship concerned with theorizing the unwaged contributions of women and other minoritized people to the more narrowly defined 'economy.' Our understanding of work is inspired by a Marxist feminist use of the term, which includes reproductive and 'de-skilled' labor, along with paid labor usually undertaken by women. This means work in the most expansive sense of the term, including forms of care work and affective labor, regardless of wage or social recognition (see Gotby). When invoking 'women's work' we mean the types of work and working conditions that have, historically, been associated with women in the Anglosphere. Further, we turn our attention to how these working conditions themselves are 'never done' but come to shape waged and unwaged work alike, for women as well as for workers of other genders.

Thus, while the politics of earlier eras speak powerfully to us today, we use the term 'feminized work' to avoid reinscribing an essentialized connection between particular forms of labor and specific gendered identities. By 'feminized work,' we mean work that has been culturally associated with an equally cultural definition of femininity. We wish to actively counter any notion of womanhood or feminization that relies on binary, ciscentric, white supremacist definitions. While we are interested in women's writing and the working conditions of women historically and today, we are *not* interested in gatekeeping to whom those labels apply. Throughout the book, we have attempted to avoid universalizing proclamations about 'women as such,' particularly when we mean white women, or middle-class women, or cis women in heterosexual relationships. While the efforts will undoubtedly fall short, we hope to inspire continued discussion of gendered work and how feminization impacts the lived experiences of different people in different ways. In a similar vein, we stress that housework has not always, nor for all women, been an unwaged task. If we categorize housework and caring for children as always unwaged and happening in one's own home, we ignore the long history of indentured and enslaved labor, especially as performed by women of color throughout the white supremacist Anglosphere. The work that has conventionally been assigned to women stretches across waged and unwaged work, it has been both housebound and located outside the home.

Therefore, to capture both historical and contemporary gendered notions of work and working conditions, this collection comes together around the question of feminization and feminized labor. In the past decades, roughly corresponding to the rise of neoliberalism and the attendant version of global capitalism, a number of scholars across disciplines of sociology, philosophy, labor studies, cultural studies, and gender studies (to name but a few) have characterized work as increasingly 'feminized'. Donna Haraway's now-iconic 1985 essay 'A Cyborg Manifesto' discusses the feminization attendant to the technological developments and labor restructuring of the 1980s: 'Work is being redefined as both literally female and feminized, whether performed by men or women' (166). Observations of the feminization of the labor force have been present across sociological research disciplines since the 1980s, reacting to shifting gendered labor politics in the anglophone Global North in the 1960s and 1970s, as well as to the gendered, racialized, and classed labor dynamics of globalized capitalism (Jenson et al.; Massey; Standing). The demographic changes were the first obvious signs, and thus dominated in earlier accounts of the trend, as exemplified by the introduction to *Feminization of the Labor Force*: 'at the same time as women's participation rates began to rise [. . . the] increasing economic importance of the service sector and of part-time work meant that there were more jobs in sectors where women had traditionally been concentrated' (Jenson et al. 5–6). The authors argue that these changes allowed more women to enter into paid work but they also meant that women were disproportionately represented among workers who 'were the lowest paid, the least covered by legislative protections, and had the least seniority' (Jenson et al. 6). The contributors to Jenson et al.'s volume consider a variety of national contexts but come to the same overall conclusion: the influx of women into workforces is concurrent with a qualitative change in the nature of work. Thus, 'feminized labor' and the 'feminization' of work characterize at once the changing demographic of workers engaged in paid labor and the types of employment available to them.

Jenson et al. focus primarily on the conditions of employment, tracing the concomitant rise in women participating in paid work and the worsening of security and benefits, particularly for those already marginalized in the workplace. While this disproportionately affects women, they stress, the structural changes affect all workers. This is also the core argument in a 1989 study by Guy Standing, the title of which—'Global Feminization through Flexible Labor'—succinctly sums up Standing's claim. The structural adjustment policies that became the globalized market standards throughout the 1980s, Standing argues, led to deregulation, casualization, and flexibilization of workforces. This had the dual effect of making it more desirable to hire women, whose historical marginalization in most types of work made them more readily accept low wages and insecure, non-unionized conditions, and leading men to increasingly be employed under such conditions too (Standing 1077). Because women 'are most vulnerable to insecure labor status employment' (Standing 1093), the structural adjustments associated with emergent neoliberalism catalyzed, Standing argues, not only increased participation by women in wage labor but also an expansion of such feminized conditions to all workers. While Standing mainly discusses issues of rights and protections, in terms of hours, wages, and social security, he gestures to shifting global patterns of production and technological developments that would, in years to come, exacerbate the effects of feminization.

In the years since, scholars have become increasingly concerned with the qualitative changes not just in working conditions but in the types of labor and labor relations attendant to feminization. The editors of a recent special issue of *Contemporary European History* refer to the 'rapid and substantial increase in the proportion of women in paid work' but focus on three attendant developments in experiences of work, for women and men alike: 'the care crisis, the proliferation of temporary and part-time work and underemployment and the culture of constant work' (Bracke et al. 449).[1] These aspects, it is suggested, are not simply the result of a demographic development. Rather, they reflect a qualitative shift in working conditions and the arena of social reproduction that surrounds them. Thus, contemporary discussions of feminization also argue that the limitless character of the work women do, with its second-and-third shift (Hochschild; Hochschild and Machung), has become a standard experience, if not for all, then for the majority of workers. As argued by Kathi Weeks: 'To the extent that the flexible, caring, emotional, cooperative, and communicative model of femininity has come to represent the ideal worker, women's work under Fordism has arguably become the template for, rather than merely ancillary to, post-Fordist capitalist economies' (38).

It is thus not only the conditions of women's work but also a perceived 'feminine' skillset that has become pervasive, at least throughout the economies of the Global North. As argued by Cristina Morini, 'women seem to represent a model that contemporary capitalism looks at with growing interest, both in terms of the forms of the *administration* of labor (precariousness, mobility, fragmentary nature, low salaries) and in terms of the contents, [. . .] (capacities for relationships, emotional aspects, linguistic aspects, propensity for care)' (42). Although this understanding of feminization has been criticized for treading potentially essentialist waters (see e.g. Adkins; Adkins and Jokinen), it aims to capture a labor market increasingly characterized by 'soft skills,' service work, 'deskilling,' and other forms of immaterial or affective labor. Along with this shift in the content and type of work, proponents of the term also argue that the material and structural conditions of work—part-time or zero-hour contracts, gig work, short-term contracts, the concept creep of 'freelancing', temp work, lack of benefits, and similar structures—also give rise to the comparison with working conditions of women.

The causal relationship between women in the workforce and the perceived feminization of work 'as such' is disputed. Standing posits flexibilization and structural adjustment as the root causes but admits that more data are needed to solidly confirm this hypothesis (1093). While Jasper Bernes has argued that feminization is the result of women entering paid labor in greater numbers (122), Lisa Adkins has, in various venues, criticized the sweeping generalizations of this notion, even questioning the efficacy of the term 'feminization.' Writing with Eeva Jokinen, Adkins argues that focusing on feminization erases the more complex changes to labor, gender politics, and the organization of home and work-lives under neoliberal capitalism (142, 147). Writing in 2001, Adkins argued that the 1980s conception of feminization, which focused largely on the effects of the higher degree of participation in paid work by women, was swiftly becoming outdated. Feminization was transforming, no longer describing a formation of social change in terms of gender, labor participation rates, and policy, but rather an 'aestheticization or culturalization of labor' (Adkins 674). Adkins connects this to claims regarding the feminization of contemporary culture, arguing that, like in culture more broadly, the effects of 'feminization' are affecting people of all genders (674). Thus, while we may not entirely agree in substance, Adkins' critique that 'feminization' no longer has to do only with women dovetails with our current use and understanding of the term.

More than twenty years on from this discussion, feminization has remained a mainstay of sociological critiques of work under late capitalism, although the uses of the term waned in the 2010s, following the scholarly interest in precarity and precariousness (see e.g. Hogg and Simonsen; Korte and Regard; Rys and Philipsen for recent discussion of precarity in relation to literature and popular culture). In literary and cultural studies, the term 'feminization' has, to date, received less attention than precarity, even though it describes a concurrent phenomenon and is similarly associated with the way service economies, flexible employment, and knowledge work have come to dominate the working lives of the middle classes in the Global North.[2] In her prior work, Emily observed recurring claims that precarious working conditions under late capitalism were a new and unprecedented crisis (Hogg and Simonsen 6, 9–10). The literature on feminization vehemently denies this conclusion: in Nancy Fraser's parlance, our current state is simply the latest manifestation of an inbuilt 'crisis tendency' of capitalism (100). Further, as Silvia Federici, Carol Watts, and Angela McRobbie, among others, have pointed out, because precarity and increased feminization happen concurrently, we should attend to the longer history of feminized working conditions. Working all hours for little to no money or recognition, performing emotional labor and maintenance work, and never feeling secure in your rights is not a new and unfamiliar state of being for women. While the rubric of 'precarity' is not an inaccurate description of these working conditions, claiming their novelty ignores decades—even centuries—of feminized work-lives, and their continued exploitation under late capitalism. We counter the claim of novelty by instead stressing continuity and connecting women's work to feminization. If women and feminized persons have lived these working conditions for ages, we should turn to their experiences to figure out other ways of working, surviving, and dismantling the systems that oppress us.

Reading Across Time

Reading comics, posters, and poetry with the aim of making texts speak together across genre, space, and time, as we have done so far in this

Introduction, demonstrates the methodological ethos of this collection. In addition to posters, comics, and poetry, the chapters primarily discuss novels but also include drama, biography, and non-fiction writing such as interviews and correspondence. We consider literature from a variety of contexts, asking what feminized forms of work in and as literature can tells us *now*. Because, as we argue, contemporary conditions of precarity are fundamentally similar to historically feminized working conditions, and because contemporary mobilizations of the notion of feminine labor draw on well-established gendered discourses, we also contend that literary representations and formal explorations of women's work can provide valuable perspectives on our current conditions of life and labor. The chapters in this collection read backwards and forwards in time, entering into conjunctions and allowing concepts to travel.

We and our contributors take inspiration (without committing to doctrine) from the recent turn toward transhistorical reading of literature. Reacting to what Paul B. Armstrong calls the 'contextualizing consensus' (87) and Eric Hayot characterizes as the dominance of periodization (149), transhistorical approaches seek to go beyond Frederic Jameson's exhortation: 'always historicize!' They do not necessarily imply that historicizing readings are fundamentally wrong, problematic, or misguided but rather try to draw attention to what gets hidden from view when these approaches dominate. The aim is not to displace 'history' (as if that were even possible). As Michaela Bronstein puts it, the 'transhistorical [. . .] does not merely oppose the historical; it is its own form of history' (8). Instead, critics such as Bronstein aim to capture the political value and potential of literature beyond—although informed by—the specifics of its production. In her book *Out of Context: The Uses of Modernist Fiction,* Bronstein shows how transhistorical approaches can emphasize literary works' own agency, in contrast to the focus on the structuring power of social context associated with historicist approaches. Her close readings of modernist works show how they seek to imagine and make contact with an imagined future; she interprets their formal features as 'strategies for futureproofing' (Bronstein 19). In this sense she sees modernist writing itself as pushing against the period box in its attempt to speak to future readers. Thus, rather than seeing modernist literature primarily in relation to the time in which it was written, Bronstein investigates the way it reaches out to the future. Importantly, Bronstein elaborates her conception of the transhistorical in relation to a delimited body of literature: canonical modernist texts and the contemporary texts that engage with them. To take a transhistorical approach in this sense is not primarily about considering texts from a wide range of historical periods. Instead, inspired by Bronstein, we see the transhistorical as a *mode* of reading: one which attends to 'literature's gestures toward the past and future' (Bronstein 7). Like Bronstein, our primary focus in this book is on the twentieth and twenty-first centuries, but each of the chapters takes a transhistorical approach by considering its central case in relation to histories of gendered labor or the current interlocking crises of exploitative labor and care deficits described by the term 'feminized labor.'

Transhistorical approaches acknowledge that literature lives beyond its immediate context and that texts affect readers not only in their own time but in the time of reading. As Rita Felski has argued, placing literature in a 'box of history' fails to account for 'what it makes possible in the viewer or reader—what kind of emotions it elicits, what perceptual changes it triggers, what affective bonds it calls into being' (585). The call is thus not to do away with context and historical specificity entirely—indeed, our contributors attend to the circumstances of literary production and contemporary reception in various ways—but to account for the political and aesthetic value of literature today. The V21 Collective advances the notion of 'strategic presentism': the deliberate, theorized attempt to see how the texts of the past can be useful in the present. While 'presentist' is usually a negative term, implying the unthinking and anachronistic reading of the past through the lens of the present, the V21 Collective seeks to reclaim it in their own discipline of Victorian Studies, in order to 'think of the past as something other than an object of knowledge that is sealed off, separated from the present by the onrush of sequential time' (Coombs and Coriale 87). In particular, strategic presentism emphasizes 'why studying the past matters for the present' (Coombs and Coriale 87) by showing how the nineteenth century lives on in the present, and how its concerns, debates and conceptual frameworks continue to shape contemporary life.

The approaches of transhistorical reading and strategic presentism also inform the readings of twenty-first century literature present in this collection. These examples are not imagined to be an 'end point' toward which earlier works are striving—rather, they are placed in conversation with concepts and contexts that precede them, in drawing on the framework of feminization and 'women's work.' In this, we take inspiration from Ann Cvetkovich, whose 1992 study of Victorian sensationalist novels and AIDS activism is guided by the idea that 'Twentiethcentury theory makes it possible to historicize nineteenth-century ideology, and nineteenth-century ideology makes it possible to historicize twentiethcentury theory' (7). This early take on transhistorical reading as a productive conjunction of multiple contexts, concepts, and genres of text demonstrates the timely conclusions that can come from reading beyond the box of history.

As we have argued elsewhere, tracing the forms of feminized work allows us to bring radically unalike literary examples together, explicating their political potential (Fabricius and Hogg). Inspired by the work of Caroline Levine, whose notion of transhistorically repeating 'forms' also inspires Bronstein, we consider 'women's work' to be one of the 'abstract organizing principles that can and do cross contexts' (Levine 638). In the poems and posters discussed in this Introduction, women's work emerges as structuring rhythms of repetition and cyclical patterns, which can alternately serve to bind and provide escape. The valence of feminized labor need not always result in becoming stuck. Rather, the ongoing, never-done nature of women's work can provide an avenue of beginning anew, of becoming unstuck.

Thinking transhistorically allows us to consider how literature might be creatively repurposed and used for imagining, even if not actualizing, a different state of being. Feminized repetition is not the repetition of factory work, contributing to the accumulation of capital. Rather, feminized repetition can take the form of giving and maintaining; the reproductive, housebound work of caring and mending and keeping alive. Focusing on feminized forms thus brings into view a non-accumulative, reproductive model of work, in turn prompting us to rethink work with the aim of non-accumulation, focusing instead on maintenance, reproduction, and care. This work will be repetitive and unfinished but need not be drudgingly dreary or devoid of meaning. In fact, taking the form beyond its context of contemporary capitalism could transform it into a sustainable way of working not toward profit but toward balance.

We ask these questions at a time of widespread feminist protest movements around the globe. The ongoing feminist strikes across South America, born out of the Ni Una Menos protests in Argentina, question what counts as work and who counts as workers. In Verónica Gago's words, 'our refusal to accept the invisibility of all our forms of work' (5) is intimately connected to the fight against gender-based violence. These strikes, along with the Women Life Freedom movement in Iran, the US-based organizing around reproductive freedom, and the Black Lives Matter movement, as well as intersectional feminist fights for sovereignty in Gaza, Sápmi, and Kalaallit Nunaat, are but a few of the contexts that shape our current understanding of how questions of gender, labor, and globalized capitalism profoundly affects everyday lives. Publishing a book of literary criticism in this context has prompted us to ask how literature is used and how can it be useful to us. This echoes what See Red Women's Workshop was trying to accomplish: providing a narrative frame for understanding the working conditions of women and a way for them to change these conditions for the better. While we do not ascribe to the idea that reading a poem in the right way will lead to revolution, we are of the belief that reading and discussing literature can be made to matter beyond the confines of academic inquiry. Literature gives shape to experience and literary analysis allows us to trace those shapes across different contexts, drawing out commonalities and points of difference. As the contributions to this book make apparent, there is a rich history of literary engagement with feminized working conditions with continued relevance beyond the literary realm to present-day political debates about work, fair compensation, and reproduction. While we are scholars and thinkers, we are also teachers and members of communities beyond academia. We hope that our readers will bring these conversations into those contexts, as we strive to do.

Reading this Book

The work of bringing this book into the world has, in many ways, mirrored the themes and concerns at its core. It grew initially out of the research project 'Feminized: A New Literary History of Women's Work,' funded by the Carlsberg Foundation and housed at the Center for Uses of Literature, University of Southern Denmark, for which Emily served as PI and Charlotte as a postdoctoral fellow, along with contributor Ida Askov Dolmer as the associated PhD fellow. The Feminized project prompted us to reconsider the kinds of work undertaken within the academy. The community work of conference organizing, editing, and building connections is disproportionately taken on by women and other marginalized folks in the university. Bolstered by the privileges of a permanent academic position and external funding, as well as by the perceived 'professionalism' that comes along with whiteness and cis-presenting gender identity, we were in a position to push, if but a little, the ideas of how an edited book can be developed. Thus, the contributors to this volume were invited to a two-day workshop, focused on collaboration and peer feedback. In this way, we came together as a group of previously tenuous connections, making community and developing the trajectory of the chapters together. This not only allowed for engaged discussions and intellectual development but also provided a model for what conferencing in person could look like in a world shaped by the COVID-19 pandemic and climate emergency. Within a span of three days in the spring of 2023, a community of feminized scholars considering the feminized work of writing, caring, working, and resisting started shaping this book in earnest. Thus, while the case studies bring together different contexts, time periods, types of texts, and forms of work, they are united by a common goal of understanding the ways that feminization, labor, and literature are entangled. The work of untangling the mess cannot be undertaken by one person alone. This book presents a number of places to begin.

The volume is divided into three sections, one for each of the key themes that organize our case studies. The first section focuses on the labor necessary to produce and circulate literature, the second is concerned with the relationship between literature, feminist activism, and work, and the final part of the book turns to questions of literary form, picking up the discussion we have begun in this Introduction about the capacity of literary forms to depict and question experiences of feminized labor. As a whole the book therefore shows how contemporary experiences of feminization can be illuminated by attention to the past, how entrenched and well-established certain ideas about femininity and labor are, and, in a more abstract sense, how thinking temporality in ways other than the progressive, developmental, or boxy can assist in the attempt to understand the contemporary political challenge of feminized work.

The first section of the book, 'The Labor of Literature,' gathers three chapters on gender and work in the literary field, each of which focuses on a particular emblematic person (historical or imagined). To produce and sustain the institution of literature requires many different forms of paid and unpaid work—writing, agenting, editing, copyediting, publicizing, designing, reviewing, and selling, to name just a few—and these occupations are (like many jobs in other areas) conventionally gendered and differently esteemed. The viral hashtag #thanksfortyping (see Dresvina) showed how frequently men's writing careers have been made possible through women's work as typists, indexers, researchers, and proofreaders—work which might be gratefully recognized in the acknowledgments but is rarely considered integral to the intellectual work it enables. This part of the book therefore contributes to recent discussions in book history, publishing studies, and digital humanities that have sought to show how significant the category of gender is in distributing and valuing the labor tasks that underpin the literary field.

Whitney Trettien uses the term 'bookwork' to describe, first, 'the conceptual labor that springs out of books, pushing off from the material text—the work of reading, composing, annotating, note-taking, thinking, doodling, sharing, orating—and especially the ways these bookish pursuits propel readers back into the world,' (19) and second, the 'actual labor of making a codex—namely, the physical processes of composing type, imposing a sheet, folding bifolia, and binding a gathering of leaves' (20). This framing is useful because it insists on the continuity between forms of labor that have often been distinguished from one another: the work of thinking, reading, and writing, and the physical work of annotating, typing, folding, binding. All the chapters in this section of the book are concerned with the history of women's engagements with diverse forms of bookwork and with the ways that some of these forms of bookwork have been feminized in different times and spaces.

'The Labor of Literature' begins with Nicola Wilson's chapter on Aki Hayashi, employed by the British poet Edmund Blunden as a literary assistant for thirty-five years, whose work as a bibliographer specializing in the Romantics has often been overlooked. Excavating Hayashi's fascinating story, including her move from Japan to England and her relationship (both professional and romantic) with Blunden, Wilson shows how little of Hayashi's labor has been publicly recognized, and reflects on the relevance of her life and work for theorizing contemporary practices in publishing and in feminist bibliography.

In Chapter 2, Lucie Duggan examines a woman's work with literature in another time and place: early modern Denmark. Scholars, including Helen Smith, Valerie Wayne, and the contributors to Wayne's edited collection *Women's Labour and the History of the Book in Early Modern England*, have in recent years sought to draw attention to women's work with books in the early modern period. They add annotation, printing, bookselling, and book-collecting, to name only a few forms of labor, to the established accounts of women's work in this period and bring book-historical accounts of the early modern into dialogue with feminist approaches to early modern women's labor. As argued by Michelle Dowd, the cultural status of women's work underwent dramatic change during the early modern era, through literary representation as well as in women's relationship to literature (2, 12). Duggan builds on such work by developing a case study from the less frequently discussed Danish case. Examining the private library assembled by noblewoman Karen Brahe allows Duggan to not only consider the forms of work entailed in collecting and maintaining a private library in this context, but also the types of gendered work that are attested to in the collection itself, and the forms of labor that are required to bring the collection to the attention of contemporary scholars.

The third chapter in this section, Varsha Panjwani's 'The Labors of Shakespeare's Sister,' also deals with later centuries' engagements with the early modern yet employs quite a different method. While Duggan, like Wilson in Chapter 1, examines the traces left by a real historical figure, Panjwani draws attention to the importance of speculative and imaginative methods in generating new insights into gendered work. Virginia Woolf famously conjured the figure of Judith Shakespeare in *A Room of One's Own* to argue that the material conditions and social norms shaping women's lives—especially in relation to sex, childcare, and household labor—made female literary production and creative attainment extremely difficult in the early modern period and continued to exert a significant constraining force in subsequent centuries. Panjwani traces the work performed by Judith Shakespeare as a symbol of the female writer whose potential is thwarted, and who continues to travel through time, fascinating, provoking, and being reinvented by subsequent writers, including Marilyn French, Emma Whipday, and Jo Hamya. Panjwani asks what the ongoing interest in Judith Shakespeare says about the contemporary conditions in which women attempt creative and intellectual work.

Given the restricted career opportunities historically available for women and, as Woolf vividly illustrates in the figure of Judith Shakespeare, the conventional feminization of childcare and domestic labor, it is no surprise that work has long been a central issue for feminists. As we have noted in our discussion of paid versus unpaid housework and in our analysis of Maya Angelou's poetry, the topic of work immediately highlights the implausibility of any universalized female subject. In her 1851 speech, later given the title 'Ain't I Woman,' Sojourner Truth uses her experiences of enslaved labor to point out how little prevailing ideas about womanhood, within as well as without the feminist movement, had attended to African-American experience: 'I have ploughed and planted, and gathered into barns, and no man could head me!,' she says, 'And ain't I a woman? I could work as much and eat as much as a man—when I could get it—and bear the lash as well! And ain't I a woman?' (42). In Britain, as Laura Schwartz has shown in *Feminism and the Servant Problem*, domestic servants and feminists involved in the early twentieth century suffrage movement were 'sometimes united—when servants became feminists—and sometimes at odds with one another—when feminists employed servants,' as they all 'grappled with the question of what it meant to employ another woman to do a form of work that you yourself would rather not' (1).

In the second half of the twentieth century, the figure of the housewife and assumption that female fulfilment was to be found in keeping house were widely critiqued, from Friedan's identification of the 'problem that has no name' in 1963 to the Wages for Housework movement's challenge to the invisibility and apparent naturalness of women's domestic work through the demand for a wage (Federici). Angela Davis pointed out, however, that the experiences of women of color, especially Black women, in the US, as well as the experiences of working-class women in general—who have frequently been paid for doing housework—suggest that the focus on the wage as a means to greater equality is misguided, obscuring the central importance of the socialization of housework tasks. In the same period, the strikes at Grunwick (1976) and Dagenham (1968) in the UK showed that, if women's domestic work was often invisible, then their paid work was often undervalued and unequally paid. In the twenty-first century, normative femininity is embodied not in the older figure of the housewife, but rather in the career woman (see McRobbie) who 'has it all' and effortlessly balances paid work and private life. In this context, Nancy Fraser argues, the labor women have traditionally been responsible for—the work of care, of maintaining supportive bonds, of looking after the very young, the very old, and the ill—is increasingly under severe time pressure. In the UK context recent books such as Emma Dowling's *The Care Crisis* and the Care Collective's *The Care Manifesto* express the need for urgent political action to address the gaps in care provision produced by changing norms about gender and work, as well as by years of austerity and cuts to the welfare state.

The second section of the book, 'The Work of Change,' therefore considers the ways that feminist activism concerning working conditions, as well as the labor involved in feminist activism itself, are mediated by literature. Given the long history of feminist protest in relation to work, and the forms of typically unpaid work involved in protest itself, we consider how literature has sought to express activist ideas, and how it becomes significant in the pursuit of social and political change. This section of the book focuses on twenty-first century anglophone texts, all of which have been published very recently, and thus offers analysis of texts that have not yet been the focus of sustained scholarly inquiry. These chapters contribute to a transhistorical approach by showing how the long history of women's activism regarding work is informed and furthered by today's writers, artists, and protestors.

In Chapter 4, 'Comics in the RESISTance: A Model for Feminist Scholarly Praxis,' Leah Misemer reflects on her own experiences with *Resist!*, a comics anthology newsletter produced in response to the election of Donald Trump as US President in 2016 and distributed to protestors at the 2017 Women's March. Misemer examines the role played by *Resist!* as a physical object, in the protest, and the way it facilitated the connection of new networks of solidarity. She also reflects on her own labor as both an academic and an activist, and how these two forms of labor are related.

In her own academic work, Roberta Garrett (author of Chapter 5) has long been concerned with the literature of motherhood. Where her 2020 book *Writing the Modern Family: Contemporary Literature, Motherhood and Neoliberal Culture* outlined the key tropes of contemporary motherhood literature, her chapter for this volume considers what has changed in the genre since the COVID-19 pandemic and the 2022 reversal of the *Roe v. Wade* decision in the US Supreme Court. In particular, she detects a new radicalism in the literature—a stronger focus on critiquing the social and economic conditions under which mothering takes place.

Finally in this section, Leighan Renaud focuses on contemporary literature from the Caribbean and draws attention to two experiences that are often characterized as mundane and ordinary in this literature: the experience of violence, both interpersonal and institutional, and the undertaking of domestic work. In Chapter 6, Renaud examines the narrative strategies used by Cherie Jones' novel *How the One-Armed Sister Sweeps Her House* (2021) to explore these topics and their interrelation in the context of colonial legacies and the neo-colonial impact of the tourist industry. Taking campaigns against gender-based violence in the Caribbean as a starting point, Renaud considers how the novel uses representations of routine work and routine violence to inform one another, illuminating both of these topics and their political significances.

The book's third section, 'The Employment of Form', focuses primarily on literature's aesthetic qualities. What, it asks, are the formal strategies through which writers have sought to register and respond to feminized work? What are the aesthetic features through which the literary work comes to examine work in its broader sense? In this Introduction, we have already pointed out some of the forms through which literature engages with feminized work: the circular, for example. The third section of the book extends this focus, exploring other formal strategies through which literary texts seek to grapple with the gendering of work. 'The Employment of Form' takes as a starting point writers from the 1960s and 1970s, focusing on Adrienne Rich, Nell Dunn, and Buchi Emecheta. While Rich is closely associated with the feminist politics of the period, Emecheta and Dunn have been less frequently discussed in this context and have both recently received more critical interest after a period of some neglect. The chapters show how the aesthetic strategies used by these writers travel across time, either through the way their formal structures invite intertextual dialogue with earlier writers, or by the way they illuminate contemporary questions of gender and work.

In Chapter 7, Lindsay Turner examines twentieth-century US poet Adrienne Rich's use of fragments, arguing that the fragmentary quality of the poetry Rich wrote when she had three small children is not only a reflection of the discontinuous and interrupted time of care work, but neither is it simply produced by—a formal consequence of—this broken-up time. Rather, Turner shows how Rich's fragments reveal another, radically different form of temporal experience, which stands in stark contrast to the endlessly broken time of domestic work.

In Chapter 8, Helen Charman ranges transhistorically across George Eliot's *Daniel Deronda* (1876), Penelope Mortimer's *The Pumpkin Eater* (1962), Doris Lessing's *The Golden Notebook* (1962), and Nell Dunn's *Talking to Women* (1964) to consider the formal strategies through which literary texts from the UK have represented and examined women's speech. Feminized, often denigrated, forms of speech, labeled 'chat' or 'gossip,' have been highly significant for both psychoanalysis and the UK Women's Liberation Movement. Tracing this connection, Charman examines the formal devices through which speech enters literary texts and argues that it serves a crucial function for the exploration of women's working conditions.

In the final chapter in the collection, Ida Aaskov Dolmer and Emily J. Hogg consider Buchi Emecheta's *Second-Class Citizen* (1974), a novel in which the main character, Adah, experiences quite starkly different working conditions in Nigeria and London. As an employee at a library and as an abused wife and mother, Adah is required not only to bring in a wage but to do all the family's domestic tasks. Dolmer and Hogg consider the temporal structures and reflections on time in Emecheta's novel and situate them in relation to the narratives of progress which suggest that an increase in the proportion of women undertaking paid employment over the past fifty years can be read as a straightforward index of societal progress for women. Although teleological progress narratives have long been critiqued from queer, postcolonial, and feminist perspectives they also have, as Carolyn Dinshaw has pointed out, a tremendous cultural force and staying power. This chapter shows how the plot of *Second-Class Citizen* can be read as a rejection of straightforward progress narratives about women and work, and instead implies a more nuanced and complex understanding of the changing roles of women over time and between geographical contexts.

The book concludes with an afterword by Christina Lupton. As the chapters range across contexts, so too does Lupton's identification of the themes and connections brought to light by the contributions. Reading across the analyses provided in the collection, Lupton draws out a central paradox of feminized labor: the place of creative work, especially writing, within a feminized existence. Lupton builds on the conclusions and questions offered by the collection, imagining what a feminization of *life* might offer as a solution to the bind of feminized work.

Notes

1. Notably, Bracke et al. open their piece with a reading of the poster 'A woman's work is never done' (See Red Women's Workshop, 1974), highlighting the efficacy of this type of work in condensing political issues and their usefulness to us as scholars.
2. A notable exception in the related realm of media studies is the collection *Gendering the Recession*, edited by Diane Negra and Yvonne Tasker, which, while focusing primarily on economic precarity, acknowledges feminization as a key force in the post-recession cultural landscape (7).

Works Cited

Adkins, Lisa. "Cultural Feminization: 'Money, Sex and Power' for Women." *Signs: Journal of Women in Culture and Society*, vol. 26, no. 3, 2001, pp. 669–95. *Summon 2 (syddansk.summon.serialssolutions.com)*, https://doi.org/10.1086/495625.

Adkins, Lisa, and Eeva Jokinen. "Introduction: Gender, Living and Labour in the Fourth Shift." *NORA—Nordic Journal of Feminist and Gender Research*, vol. 16, no. 3, Sept 2008, pp. 138–49. *Taylor and Francis+NEJM*, https://doi.org/10.1080/08038740802300947.

Angelou, Maya. "Woman Work." *And Still I Rise*. Random House, 1978, pp. 31–32.

Armstrong, Paul B. "In Defense of Reading: Or, Why Reading Still Matters in a Contextualist Age." *New Literary History*, vol. 42, no. 1, 2011, pp. 87–113. *Project MUSE*, https://doi.org/10.1353/nlh.2011.0001.

Bhattacharya, Tithi, editor. *Social Reproduction Theory: Remapping Class, Recentering Oppression*. Pluto Press, 2017.

Bracke, Maud, et al. "Women, Work and Value in Post-War Europe: Introduction." *Contemporary European History*, vol. 28, no. 4, Nov. 2019, pp. 449–53. *Cambridge University Press*, https://doi.org/10.1017/S0960777319000225.

Bronstein, Michaela. *Out of Context: The Uses of Modernist Fiction*. Oxford University Press, 2018. *University Press Scholarship*, https://doi.org/10.1093/oso/9780190655396.001.0001.

Brouillette, Sarah. *Literature and the Creative Economy*. Stanford University Press, 2014.

Coombs, David Sweeney, and Danielle Coriale. "Introduction." *Victorian Studies*, vol. 59, no. 1, 2016, pp. 87–89. *DOI.org (Crossref)*, https://doi.org/10.2979/victorianstudies.59.1.04.

Cvetkovich, Ann. *Mixed Feelings: Feminism, Mass Culture, and Victorian Sensationalism*. Rutgers University Press, 1992.

Davis, Angela Y. *Women, Race and Class*. Vintage, 1983.

Dinshaw, Carolyn. *How Soon is Now? Medieval Texts, Amateur Readers, and the Queerness of Time*. Duke University Press, 2012.

Douglas, Ann. *The Feminization of American Culture*. Anchor Press/Doubleday, 1988.

Dowd, Michelle M. *Women's Work in Early Modern English Literature and Culture*. Palgrave Macmillan US, 2009.

Dowling, Emma. *The Care Crisis: What Caused it and How Can We End It?* Verso Books, 2021.

Dresvina, Juliana. *Thanks for Typing: Remembering Forgotten Women in History*. Bloomsbury Academic, 2021.

Fabricius, Charlotte J., and Emily J. Hogg. "Past forms, present concerns. Reading transhistorically for feminized labour." *Textual Practice*, vol. 38, no. 12, 2024, pp. 1799–1819. https://doi.org/10.1080/0950236X.2023.2281701.

Felski, Rita. "Context Stinks!" *New Literary History*, vol. 42, no. 4, 2011, pp. 573–91. *Project MUSE*, https://doi.org/10.1353/nlh.2011.0045.

Federici, Silvia, "Wages Against Housework." *Revolution at Point Zero: Housework, Reproduction, and Feminist Struggle*. PM Press, 2020, pp.15–22.

Ferguson, Susan J. *Women and Work: Feminism, Labour, and Social Reproduction*. Pluto Press, 2020.

Finck, Liana. "Write to distract yourself from life, make cartoons to distract yourself from writing, take on freelance to distract yourself from cartoons, teach to distract yourself from freelance, and focus on life a bit to distract yourself from anxiety over not having enough work." *Instagram*, 14 December 2021, https://www.instagram.com/p/CXecYRZF1yx/. Accessed 14 April 2023.

Fraser, Nancy. "Contradictions of Capital and Care." *New Left Review*, no. 100, Aug. 2016, pp. 99–117.

Friedan, Betty. *The Feminine Mystique*. 1963. Penguin, 2010.

Gago, Verónica. *Feminist International: How to Change Everything*. Translated by Liz Mason-Deese. Verso Books, 2020.

Gallagher, Tess. "I Stop Writing the Poem." *Moon Crossing Bridge*. Graywolf Press, 1992, p. 64.

Gotby, Alva. *They Call It Love: The Politics of Emotional Life*. Verso Books, 2023.

Haraway, Donna. "A Cyborg Manifesto: Science, Technology, and Socialist-Feminism in the Late Twentieth Century." *Simians, Cyborgs, and Women: The Reinvention of Nature*. Routledge, 1991, pp.149–81.

Hayot, Eric. "Against Periodization." *On Literary Worlds*. Oxford University Press, 2012. *University Press Scholarship*, https://doi.org/10.1093/acprof:oso/9780199926695.003.0011.

Hochschild, Arlie Russell. *The Time Bind: When Work Becomes Home and Home Becomes Work*. Metropolitan Books, 1997.

Hochschild, Arlie Russell, and Anne Machung. *The Second Shift: Working Parents and the Revolution at Home*. Viking, 1989.

Hogg, Emily J., and Peter Simonsen, editors. *Precarity in Contemporary Literature and Culture*. Bloomsbury Academic, 2021.

Jenson, Jane, et al., editors. *Feminization of the Labor Force: Paradoxes and Promises*. Oxford University Press, 1988.

Korte, Barbara, and Frédéric Regard. *Narrating Poverty and Precarity in Britain*. De Gruyter, 2014.

Levine, Caroline. "Model Thinking: Generalization, Political Form, and the Common Good." *New Literary History*, vol. 48, no. 4, 2017, pp. 633–53. *DOI.org (Crossref)*, https://doi.org/10.1353/nlh.2017.0033.

Lorde, Audre. *Sister Outsider: Essays and Speeches*. Crossing Press, 2007.

Massey, Doreen. *Spatial Divisions of Labour: Social Structures and the Geography of Production*. Macmillan Education UK, 1995. *DOI.org (Crossref)*, https://doi.org/10.1007/978-1-349-24059-3.

McRobbie, Angela. "Top Girls?: Young Women and the Post-Feminist Sexual Contract." *Cultural Studies,* vol. 21, no. 4–5, 2007, pp. 718–37.

Morini, Cristina. "The Feminization of Labour in Cognitive Capitalism." *Feminist Review*, no. 87, 2007, pp. 40–59.

Negra, Diane, and Yvonne Tasker, editors. *Gendering the Recession: Media and Culture in an Age of Austerity*. Duke University Press, 2014.

Oakley, Ann. *The Sociology of Housework*. 1974. Bristol University Press, 2018.

Pollard, Clare. "Circuit." *Incarnation*. Bloodaxe Books, 2017, p. 23.

Rys, Michiel, and Bart Philipsen, editors. *Literary Representations of Precarious Work: 1840 to the Present*. Palgrave Macmillan, 2021.

Schwartz, Laura. *Feminism and the Servant Problem: Class and Domestic Labour in the Women's Suffrage Movement*. Cambridge University Press, 2019.

Smith, Helen. *"Grossly Material Things": Women and Book Production in Early Modern England*. Oxford University Press, 2012.

Standing, Guy. "Global Feminization through Flexible Labor." *World Development*, vol. 17, no. 7, July 1989, pp. 1077–95. *ScienceDirect*, https://doi.org/10.1016/0305-750X(89)90170-8.

Stevenson, Prue, et al. *See Red Women's Workshop*. Four Corners Books, 2016.

Sykes, Roberta. "The Treadmill of Life." *Eclipse*. University of Queensland Press, 1996, pp. 31–32.

The Care Collective. *The Care Manifesto: A Politics of Interdependence*. Verso Books, 2020.

Trettien, Whitney. *Cut/Copy/Paste: Fragments from the History of Bookwork*. University of Minnesota Press, 2022.

Truth, Sojourner. "Ain't I a Woman." *The Penguin Book of Feminist Writing,* ed. Hannah Dawson. Penguin, 2021, pp. 42–43.

Watts, Carol. "Time and the Working Mother: Kristeva's 'Women's Time' Revisited." *Radical Philosophy*, no. 091, 1998. *www.radicalphilosophy.com*, https://www.radicalphilosophy.com/article/time-and-the-working-mother.

Wayne, Valerie. *Women's Labour and the History of the Book in Early Modern England*. The Arden Shakespeare, 2020.

Weeks, Kathi. "Down with Love: Feminist Critique and the New Ideologies of Work." *WSQ: Women's Studies Quarterly*, vol. 45, no. 3–4, 2017, pp. 37–58. *DOI.org (Crossref)*, https://doi.org/10.1353/wsq.2017.0043.

PART I

THE LABOR OF LITERATURE

1

Feminist Bibliography: Aki Hayashi, Literary Assistant

Nicola Wilson

Feminist Methods: Tools to Think With

Feminist bibliography is philosophy and method. It promotes continuing work on women's lives and labor by providing tools for feminist scholars to use in their work, while simultaneously building a framework that allows such work to flourish.

(Kate Ozment, 'Rationale for Feminist Bibliography', 2020, 151)

Regardless of the gender identity of those who perform unpaid or underpaid labor in the culture industries of art, literature and the academy, there is a historic association between women and the economic and social undervaluing of their work. Those who type, organize conferences and review or edit books perform the necessary tasks without which the academy would not flourish, but are often not guaranteed the safe harbour of tenure or a stable multi-year employment contract. The contemporary job crisis in academia makes scholarship on the historic and cultural contexts for the devaluing of women's work all the more relevant.

(Catherine Hollis, 'M.E. Fitzgerald: Office Manager to Modernism', 2021, 11)

Feminism exists in a perpetual identity crisis – with a vexed past, an unstable present, and an uncertain future. The task for a scholar interested in this charged identity is how to manage such existential conditions in order to enable their transformative ambitions.

(Lisa Mendelman, 'Who Are We? Feminist Ambivalence in Contemporary Literary Criticism', 2019, 190)

I would like to begin by situating this chapter—and the collaborative workshop that developed it—in relation to a multi-author volume, *The Edinburgh Companion to Women in Publishing, 1900–2020*, that I have recently co-edited. The aim of that book is explicitly feminist (in all that term's ambivalence) in its attempt to uncover women's long-running, diverse and deeply embedded work in modern publishing across a range of functions: from the high profile—publishing directors, editors, and literary agents—to behind-the-scenes office staff and type designers, through illustrators, translators, and the publishing-adjacent: booksellers, lecturers, librarians. The process of editing collaboratively was frantic work in its final stages, but fulfilling and rewarding—involving both the care work that several of our contributors theorized in their own contributions on editorial labor, and the fact that (as Lauren Klein points out concerning the work of abolitionist editors, Mary Ann Shadd and Lydia Maria Child):

> editorial work exemplifies what is often called invisible labor, a term that has come to encompass the various forms of labor that are literally invisible because they take place out of sight, or economically invisible because they take place away from the marketplace. (24)

Our names—there is a team of eight editors, all women—are on the title of the book, and the chapters and interviews with contemporary 'women in publishing' bear the traces of our thoughts and contributions. Along the way, we have certainly 'employed editing as a method of community formation' (Klein 24). For while the value of edited collections over the traditional monograph is uncertain in assessment exercises like the UKRI's 'Research Excellence Framework', we have valued collaborating and 'thinking together': work that is not to be underestimated, as the authors of the radicalizing *The Slow Professor* remind us, when 'collaboration can allow us to challenge neoliberal models of higher education and the remasculinization of the academy' (Berg and Seeber 89).

I open with this privileged (I have a permanent post and can make choices about what I work on) personal reflection on editing and the value of certain types of (individual) work in contemporary academia because recuperation—or rather 'the project of infusing value and credit into invisible labor' (Klein 24)—is at the heart of contemporary feminist bibliography. This adjacent field to literary history, which has much to offer material histories of women's work, provides the methodology of this chapter. Feminist bibliography and book history is a thriving and recently galvanized area—notably ignited by Kate Ozment's 'Rationale for Feminist Bibliography'—which engages 'women's studies and studies of the book on a theoretical level' (Ozment 149). Adding to earlier foundational work by Leslie Howsam, Simone Murray, Michelle Levy, Sarah Werner among others (this is a richly citational field, as we traced in our General Introduction to the new volume, 'Making Fields: Women in Publishing'), feminist bibliography uses 'bibliographic methodologies to revise how book history and related fields categorize and analyze women's texts and labor' (Ozment 151). It posits different—female—origin stories in terms of the canonical scholarship, and values different types of literary work: turning especially away from categories often historically gendered male—'booksellers, printers, and public authors'—and instead towards evidence of women's bibliographic labor in other, often 'feminized', professions, such as librarianship or collection-building (Ozment 167).[1] In Digital Humanities-informed textual scholarship, meanwhile, Lauren Klein draws on Sarah Blackwood (2014 n.p.) to theorize 'editing as another form of reproductive labor: care work', in turn calling on Arlene Kaplan Daniels's theory of 'invisible work' (1987), which builds on the idea of reproductive labor articulated by Silvia Federici (1975). The premise of feminist bibliography and book history, as traced by the contributors in our new volume (published spring 2024), is to show the manifold ways in which women's work has contributed to literature and the making of literary history more generally. This is something which I have been interested in unpicking in my own scholarship: from thinking about female authors' contributions to working-class writing—Ethel Carnie Holdsworth (1886–1962), Ellen Wilkinson (1891–1947), Shelagh Delaney (1938–2011), and Buchi Emecheta (1944–2017); to the impact of women secretaries, managers, and editors behind-the-scenes in publishing houses like the Hogarth Press. Or how a critic like Sylvia Lynd (1888–1952), on the judging committee for the Book Society (Britain's first celebrity book-of-the-month club), contributed as a 'middle-woman' to the making and distribution of interwar literary culture.

One tension our contributors grappled with in *The Edinburgh Companion to Women in Publishing* was the rhetoric and practice—indeed, the celebration—of invisibility as par for the course in publishing. To quote from our collaborative introduction:

> The idea that not only the typographers and book designers, but also the editors, marketers, book travellers, press staff, managers, typists, book-keepers, and printers should be aiming for their work to vanish in the service of the book itself is common across the publishing industry. True professionalism often equates directly to invisibility: as Ellah Wakatama points out in her interview with Shercliff, one shouldn't see the editor's

> work lest it distract from the illusion of unmediated communication between author and reader: 'no mention of me means that I've done a really good job'. This discourse of and indeed ideal of invisibility creates a particularly complex set of considerations for historians engaged in recovery work, especially when this rhetoric is socially and historically tied up with particular understandings of gender, class, and race. (Battershill et al. 8)

Contributor Anna Mukamal tussled with this dynamic, especially in an essay on *transition* magazine editor Maria Jolas (1893–1987), who was 'not only co-founder, secretary and translator, but also financial patron and catalytic intellectual force behind much labour attributed to [her husband] E. Jolas' (289). 'What should contemporary feminist modernist scholars do', Mukamal asks:

> when the subjects of their historical analyses themselves abscond, downplay, or minimise their own labour? When they see and/or present their labour in terms that resist the arguments we might wish to fashion about their contributions? When their ambivalence inevitably becomes our own? (289)

Rhetorical self-effacement is often found in historical accounts of editing, book work, and wider literary labor (Sylvia Beach's 'midwife' metaphor for *Ulysses*, which she published and distributed via her own business, is hard to dislodge).[2] I turn now to a story of intersecting structures of oppression about an immigrant worker to address some of these questions about feminization and the value of women's work as creative, literary, and intellectual labor. The rest of this chapter centers Aki Hayashi (1889–1962), literary assistant for thirty-five years to poet Edmund Blunden (1896–1974), to explore some of these questions.

Aki Hayashi

> I am wondering if you are coming up to town this Saturday. If you do, don't let me know, it will save your Trouble. I'll be at Wallis at 1.40 or so. If not, *I'll be glad to have a card.*
>
> (AH to EB, Thurs, n.d., emphasis added)

Aki Hayashi's dedicated, near lifelong, work for Edmund Blunden has previously been documented in a detailed biographical/critical study by

Sumie Okada, *Edmund Blunden and Japan: The History of a Relationship* (1988).[3] Aki Hayashi features on the cover of this book but is occluded in the title, despite Okada's stated aim being 'to publish a selection of Edmund Blunden's letters to Aki Hayashi together with a chronological narrative of their friendship and notes' (1). Hayashi's letters to Blunden are not included in the volume. Okada notes initially that about 200 survive as part of the Edmund Blunden papers in the Harry Ransom Center (HRC) at the University of Texas at Austin, along with seven pages torn out from her diary. In the bibliography, Okada revises this number down, counting Hayashi's surviving correspondence to Blunden at 139 items.[4] I have examined these in situ during research for a group biography on the Book Society (1929–69), Britain's equivalent to the American Book-of-the-Month Club, where Edmund Blunden was a judge on the selection committee between 1932 and the end of the Second World War. The letters from Hayashi selectively reproduced and quoted in this chapter are my transcriptions of her handwritten correspondence held at the HRC. This comprises a variety of material documents (postcards, memos, letters) handwritten in English, most simply signed 'A', and not previously published that I am aware of.

Okada's study, *Edmund Blunden and Japan*, is a sensitive portrait of what writer John Bayley describes in a foreword (coming from a white male academic, clearly meant to lend Okada's work prestige) as:

> a strange and touching [story], throwing a lot of light on both English and Japanese behaviour at the time in relation to one another's culture and customs. It was far from being a Madam Butterfly situation, because Aki Hayashi was a remarkable and determined woman who might herself have become a writer . . . (xi)

Okada outlines the biographical contours of Hayashi and Blunden's relationship: from their meeting at a summer school for Japanese teachers of English in Karuizawa[5] in 1925 (Hayashi aged thirty-six; Blunden twenty-eight, and married); through the early days of their romance and plan for Hayashi to join Blunden as his permanent secretary, returning to England with him in 1927; through her difficulties living in London as an 'enemy alien' during the Second World War; and her professional commitment to Blunden's literary oeuvre, despite him marrying two other women (in 1932, and then again in 1944), after once assuring her that if 'I should ever marry a second time I should in all likelihood marry Aki' (EB, Jan 17, 1927; Okada: 21). The international, intercultural affair between Hayashi and Blunden, as outlined by Okada, is a fascinating love story, unusual for its time, though not my prime concern here. Okada's book does the close work traditionally expected of literary study, parsing Blunden's poetry to explore the influence of Japan, 'and more particularly his emotional relationship with Aki', on his outlook and poetry (32). Okada reminds her readers of the under-appreciated, time-consuming editorial work involved in making previously unpublished letters, 'all in disarray' (1), available in book form. For Okada, this involved the preparatory work of putting more than 1,400 letters written between 1925 and 1962 in chronological order, before the tasks of transcription, typing, editing, and annotation.[6]

The most interesting part of Okada's book for my purposes in this chapter (and another labor-intensive aspect of her own research), is the twelve-page appendix Okada includes, detailing the 'Chronology of Aki Hayashi's Work for Edmund Blunden'. This is a fascinating example of feminist bibliography and the kind of scholarship of ambiguous status (it is not part of a critical argument but presented as an appendix) that is nevertheless crucial scaffolding for future feminist labor and research.

In 1925, when Blunden first proposed that Hayashi join him and work as his secretary, he described the oppressive 'list of Works' weighing upon him and how she might assist his creative writing and literary and biographical scholarship:

> The Proofs of my forthcoming book called 'English Poems' were on my table and I spent a great deal of the night in correcting them – they are to be published in November, so my list of Works is growing all the time . . . I have had many letters of all kinds, and need a Secretary. Well, and I shall have one . . . yours unfailingly O sweet companion! (29 August 1925; Okada 11)

Two days later they had begun 'the secretaryship' (EB to AG, 31 August 1925; Okada 12), with Hayashi spending time sorting Blunden's letters and putting his First World War poems in order, which would later form the last part of his influential memoir, *Undertones of War* (1928). In its beginnings, the arrangement was tied up in a desire to keep Aki close, but respectably, without causing gossip: 'you must be my refuge if ever my friends forsake me', Blunden wrote in August 1925, worried that his friend Siegfried Sassoon might not support him financially when he returned to England if he knew of the affair. 'But it will help us, if we can keep a secret', Blunden wrote (EB to AH, 31 August 1925; Okada 97).[7] 'Blunden ingeniously contrived a place for Aki to occupy in his work and life – she could not be his wife but could be his permanent secretary or copyist', Okada notes (11). Entangled in a romantic sexual relationship, we do not know what Hayashi made of her early work (her letters from this period have not survived) but plans moved fast and six months into the relationship the couple were saving up money for Aki to travel with Edmund when he returned to England. Clearly, she was sufficiently invested in both the work and relationship to transform her life circumstances: quitting the teaching career she found unsatisfying, applying for a passport then a visa to stay and work in Britain as Blunden's permanent secretary. Risking her relationship with her family, Hayashi set herself up in a flat in Hampstead with good access to the British Museum and the Colindale newspaper library. Late August 1939, she heard from her sister that her mother had passed away that June (the initial letter had gone astray) and Hayashi wrote to Blunden: 'Now I feel as if I were entirely cut off from Japan. The other relatives never care for me' (25 August 1939). Hayashi spent a great deal of her working life in the British Museum reading room and developed close relationships with the staff there (suffering racist persecution from her neighbors during the Second World War, she had her mail redirected c/o the British Museum). In 1949, she would be naturalized as a British subject, meaning giving up her Japanese nationality.

While Hayashi's romance with Blunden did not progress in the way that she might have desired, she nevertheless nurtured and developed an intimate working relationship with him that lasted for over thirty-five

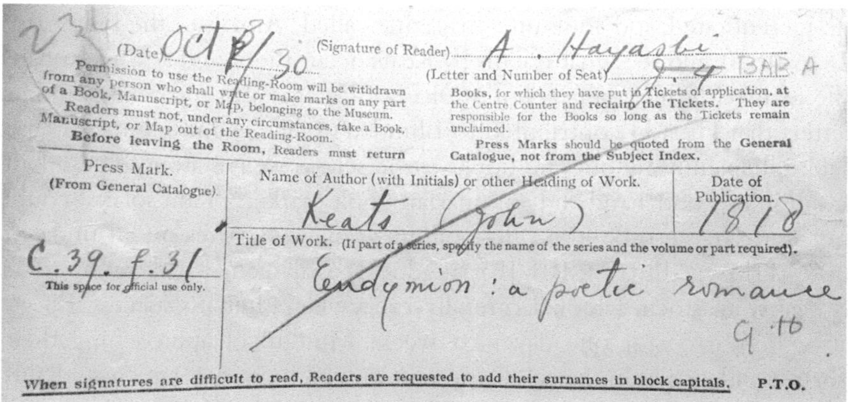

2 3 4

(Date) Oct 2/3/30 (Signature of Reader) A. Hayashi

(Letter and Number of Seat) J. 4 BABA

Permission to use the Reading-Room will be withdrawn from any person who shall write or make marks on any part of a Book, Manuscript, or Map, belonging to the Museum.

Readers must not, under any circumstances, take a Book, Manuscript, or Map out of the Reading-Room.

Before leaving the Room, Readers must return **Books,** for which they have put in Tickets of application, **at** the Centre Counter and **reclaim the Tickets.** They **are** responsible for the Books so long as the Tickets **remain** unclaimed.

Press Marks should be quoted from the **General Catalogue, not from the Subject Index.**

Press Mark. (From General Catalogue).	Name of Author (with Initials) or other Heading of Work.	Date of Publication.
C. 39. f. 31	Keats (John)	1818
This space for official use only.	Title of Work. (If part of a series, specify the name of the series and the volume or part required). Endymion: a poetic romance 9.10	

When signatures are difficult to read, Readers are requested to add their surnames in block capitals. P.T.O.

Figure 1.1 Aki Hayashi's British reading room request for Keats's *Endymion: a poetic romance*. Dated 2/3 Oct 1930. Harry Ransom Center, Edmund Blunden papers, Manuscript Collection MS-0426, Box 89.7

years. We know from their correspondence that Hayashi checked dates for Blunden's many publications, as well as copyediting, indexing, and proofreading his manuscripts, but her work for him went well beyond the secretarial (requesting the extension of her visa in 1927, Blunden had described Hayashi as 'my amanuensis [. . .] my assistant in the preparation and transcription of my literary works' (Okada 129)). Working for Blunden in the British Museum and other libraries from 1927 (aged thirty-eight) to 1961 (aged seventy-two), Hayashi pursued various academic subjects and became a specialist bibliographer on the Romantics, sorting letters and copying poems, often engaged in the detailed, scholarly work of collation, transcription, and textual editing. As Okada notes, 'Aki did a considerable amount of work for Blunden in the British Museum, which included some discoveries of previously unknown literary material' (212). Conducting primary research for Blunden's hundreds of publications and major works (these included *Leigh Hunt: A Biography* (1930); *The Poems of Wilfred Owen* (1931); *Charles Lamb and his Contemporaries* (1933); *Keats's Publisher: A Memoir of John Taylor* (1936); *Thomas Hardy* (1941)), Hayashi transcribed Owen and Keats, worked on Coleridge manuscripts, and identified unknown letters to John Clare and a previously unknown Shelley article.

This was detailed, highly skilled bibliographical research and editorial labor. In October 1930 for instance, Blunden sent Hayashi a copy of Keats's poetry edited by Victorian bibliographer H. B. Forman and asked her to enumerate any differences from the original editions: 'No matter how small the difference between it & the original, please make a note of it', he requested, and 'look up a magazine called "Annals of the Fine Arts" 1816–1820, and see what poems by Keats occur there, and again compare the texts with those here given?' (Okada 145). It is also apparent from her letters that Hayashi contributed to Blunden's practice and reputation as a bibliophile, hunting out rare books by herself, as well as alongside him, in London's second-hand and antiquarian book market.[8] 'I am sorry I could not find Grandison's book, any volume at all' she writes on an undated note (Friday). 'Today F. Rd. [Farringdon Road] seem'd to be very poor & scanty in stock. I look'd carefully everywhere, but no success. I'll go again tomorrow or one day next week.' Mindful of approaching their correspondence as historical documents in which *personae* are created, this note conveys a typically complex mix in Hayashi's letters of apology, self-justification, devotion, and determination.

Hayashi and Blunden had a formal employment relationship. Hayashi was paid regular amounts by Blunden for her work, and the economics of her labor, alongside the material reality of her living conditions, frequently arise. 'May I remind you of my okane?' [money], she writes on 5 May 1928,'My gas goes so quickly! I wish I had a coal stove'.[9] Labor and her difficult working conditions are a key theme in the surviving letters, with Hayashi's descriptions of her research coded to signal dedication and perseverance against the odds (resonating with a deeply moralistic aspect of Japanese culture that values dedication and hard work over, or as much as, the outcome), while reminding Blunden of the intersecting issues she faced in accessing rare books and manuscripts, finding obituaries, looking at authors' correspondence, and hunting down sales catalogs in this period. 'This week I was unlucky in every way' she writes after the temporary closure of the British Museum's Manuscript room for redecoration:'Hearing a small room is opened for small number of people I got in there, but many want to take a place & the light is very poorly fixed – very high. I simply struggled to copy only a few pages' (Friday, n.d., c. 1933). 'Another unlucky matter is that I wanted an obituary notice from *Gentleman's Magazine*. Just 1864 numbers (2) are in the hand of a bookbinder's! Next week everything will be all right I hope.'

In the same letter, describing her work on the library of Keats's publisher John Taylor, Hayashi clearly stresses the material, cultural, and interpersonal challenges impeding the kind of detailed archival research she was engaged in:

> Now you will wonder what I did with the Sale Catalogue. I got it only Today! I thought I could get any sale catalogue as easily as the reading room books, but not so. I had to wait until today – as it is treated as an important book I have to go to North Library. It was not by Christie as you see by this ticket. Oh. I am surprised at the immense amount of books Taylor had. I thought I could finish in one day, but I don't think I can though I do all day tomorrow, & after this trouble to the staff in order to get this catalogue I think I must finish without break. If I miss a day or so any books will go back to their place, & I must go on until I finish. I wonder if you want all the copy of Taylor books & MSS. (Friday, n.d., c. 1933)

Here we see Hayashi conscious about not putting others out to do her work—not troubling the staff excessively—as well as feeling under pressure, compounded by ill health, probing Blunden's instructions by pushing back on the scale of appraisal and copying he has asked for. Hayashi's articulation of her sometimes-difficult encounters with the institutional archive anticipates a recent body of postcolonial, feminist, and decolonial criticism that interrogates categories of power and silence in the historical archive, underlining the intersectional nature of the researcher's personal encounter (see Bryant-Davies and Johnson-Williams; Hartman). For Hayashi and Blunden, the specifics of their personal relationship were intersected by the cultural dynamics of the time as well as the broader gendered, sexist, and racialized structures of the working environment Hayashi was occupying as a single, unmarried Japanese woman; a paid migrant researcher tasked with accessing rare materials in the scholarly spaces of nationally prestigious libraries.

The relationship between Aki Hayashi and Edmund Blunden is not especially unusual in terms of the broader history of writing. Many authors have employed researchers to assist them, whether in research and preparation, or in the presentation of their material (many of course still do), while a much greater number have relied upon the unpaid labor of family members or friends to contribute to or help produce their work. The ubiquity of this form of recognition in acknowledgment pages led to the social media phenomenon *#Thanks for Typing* in 2017, followed by a volume of essays in 2021, *#Thanks for Typing: Remembering Forgotten Women in History*. Once publishers started to expect to receive typescripts rather than manuscripts in the early twentieth century, many authors were compelled to hire a professional typist to do the work.[10]

The co-dependent relationship I have traced in this chapter between famous author and unknown assistant has echoes of other research relationships, such as that discussed by Carolyn Steedman in *History and the Law: A Love Story* between two male historians: professional historian E. P. Thompson and Edward Dodd, a local historian, who Thompson paid to do some of his primary archival research for him. Analyzing their fifteen-year correspondence, Steedman sets out the men's uneven relationship in terms of 'the eighteenth-century service relationship', where 'the employer told much more of his personal life than did the employee' (33). But pleasure and shared investment in the work clearly animated the correspondence that grew out of it.

It is difficult to know what motivated Hayashi in pursuing her and Blunden's literary work over such a long period of time (twice that of Dodd and Thompson). Once she had taken the leap and moved to London, what other choices did she have? Surviving records cannot answer this question, but they do suggest that for Hayashi, the personal and professional aligned in a 'passion project' that was also contractual, paid research.[11] As an educated, professional working woman living in Japan in the 1920s, Hayashi can be viewed as a 'New Woman' [*atarashii onna*], challenging traditional social and gender boundaries by participating actively in society (Sato 13).[12] Born in Tokushima into a well-to-do family, she was part of the new 'intellectual class' [*chishiki kaikyu*], educated at a Protestant missionary school and taking up teaching after training at the prestigious women's college, Tsuda College, in English language and literature (Sato 116).[13] According to employment office data, well-educated women of this class in the 1930s typically worked as salesclerks, office workers, telephone operators, nurses, teachers, sometimes domestics (Sato 116). We know from Sassoon and Blunden's letters that Hayashi faced prejudice from at least parts of literary society when she was first introduced to Blunden's friends in London in 1927.[14] But she was welcomed by others and socialized alongside Blunden with some, such as his friend and publisher, Rupert Hart-Davis, in addition to working for other writers (including Siegfried Sassoon, George Orwell, Graham Greene, and Edith Sitwell). Clearly, Hayashi's relationship with, and work for, Edmund Blunden altered fundamentally the life choices and opportunities available to her.

Okada argues that Aki Hayashi's story is defined by cultural attitudes of *giri*, a sense of obligation and duty to a person which is a lifelong commitment in Japanese society, binding people tightly (210). Certainly, in her letters, devotion to Blunden and his family is uppermost, as well a rhetorical tendency (at least) to put Blunden first, before her own needs. Struggling with her own health issues, Hayashi often worried about Blunden (he suffered badly from asthma), and regularly told him not to reply to her letters: 'Do <u>not</u> specially write to me. I know how busy you are. [. . .] you are doing such a lot for others. You must think of your own health first.' (Nov 1, no year). Aware of his anxiety around public speaking, she offered care and affirmation, 'Your fine face delivering the lecture still delights me. It was a fine lecture. It was a pity you had to cut the latter part off' (Nov 1, no year). These are the letters that Blunden and his later executors (including his third wife, Claire Blunden) chose to keep. But as the correspondence is underpinned by precarity and uncertainty (Hayashi was often forced to chase on late payments) alongside a more general anxiety about whether they would meet in person when Blunden was next up in town, an undertone of stress and resentment remains.

Blunden's part in this story does not come off well. Throughout his life, Blunden was constantly entangled—emotionally and financially—in what he called some 'long-sustained loyalties' (EB to Sylva Norman, 6 Feb 1932; Webb 199). Aki Hayashi was one of these. It is clear from Blunden's published correspondence that he forcibly broke off the romantic relationship in early 1932, after his divorce from his first wife, Mary, when he started courting writer Sylva Norman (Norman would become his second wife in July 1933). In a long, animated letter on 9 March 1932, which, as Okada points out, 'shows clearly how strained their relations were at this time' (150), Blunden sets out the new terms of his relationship with Hayashi:

> I may ask you to be absolutely content with working for me, and with having my friendship and continued care and trust: to avoid all attempt at a love affair with me; to behave quietly and respectfully towards me, as a secretary should; to expect that I shall not visit you alone as much as I have done. (Webb 202)[15]

Hayashi's correspondence from this period has not been preserved.

During the Second World War, Hayashi suffered racist persecution and her material and working conditions worsened with the frequent closure of the British Museum. When Japan entered the war in December 1941, she asked Blunden for help, and he and Rupert Hart-Davis leveraged their contacts to write her a character letter that reached the Home Office, ensuring she would not be interned (she had to hand over all the maps in her possession and register as an 'enemy alien' with the police). A year earlier, she wrote to Blunden at the start of the Blitz. I want to end with Hayashi's own words here to signal the complex effect of anger, frustration, and protectiveness informing her relationship with Blunden, as her former lover and continued employer:

> I rang up to Colindale & found out your card dated last Thursday arrived there only this morning! Even telegrams, I am told, take a long time!
>
> Oh! What a time I'm having!! Thank God, I am alive. I never spend nights in my house, I've to go to a public underground shelter, full up: no sleep for 7 nights except a few hours in the morning after coming back here.
>
> Please do not come to London nothing is going on during raids which last nearly all day & all night. I think you do not realise how dreadful it is in London. Please wait until it is better. I may have to go to Oxford, I'll write again or send a telegram. A
>
> (17 September 1940)

Coda

> When I watched him having a glass of beer at The Croner, he looked so quiet and so modest: nobody can believe that he is a great poet. I saw him off at Waterloo station at 9.24. (AH, excerpts from diary)

In the mid-1960s, bibliographer Brownlee Jean Kirkpatrick (1919–2007)—apparently known to the men she worked amongst as 'Miss K.', and already a renowned bibliographer of Virginia Woolf and E. M. Forster—was persuaded by publisher Rupert Hart-Davis, by then retired, to undertake Blunden's official bibliography. As Hart-Davis writes, and Kirkpatrick confirms, she spent many 'hundreds of hours [. . .] in newspaper offices and the British Museum Library at Colindale' uncovering Blunden's 'over 3000 contributions to periodicals and newspapers' (Kirkpatrick: xii–xiii). In a not untypical example of historical forgetting or omission, Hayashi appears nowhere in Kirkpatrick's extensive 725-pp *Bibliography of Edmund Blunden* (1979). But it was only thanks to Hayashi's daily labor behind the scenes—as uncovered and itemized by Okada—that Blunden could be quite so prolific or, as Kirkpatrick puts it, 'a man of much generosity, [who] invariably responded to appeals from editors and others for poems or prose' (xiii).

This chapter has sought to acknowledge the extent of Aki Hayashi's literary research and bibliographic labor by way of her complex relationship with Edmund Blunden and what can be parsed from the fragments of her material correspondence, selectively preserved. It represents one case study, but I hope it forms part of the feminist scaffolding that helps undergird the literary and bibliographic history of women's work as deeply embedded, intersectional, often knowledgeable, labor. For we need to 'get alternative archives', as Lisa Mendelman writes in a powerful survey of contemporary feminism, 'and, hopefully, better practices' (191).

I would like to thank colleagues who read and commented on an early version of this piece—Nicola Abram, Claire Battershill, Alice Staveley, Helen Southworth, Katsura Sako—as well as the editors and attendees of the 'Feminized' workshop at the University of Southern Denmark, Odense, May 2023, for such a collegial and generative workshop. I also thank the Harry Ransom Center for a Research Fellowship (2022), which enabled me to pursue some of the primary research for this chapter.

Notes

1. On women's long historical work as booksellers, printers, and authors see, for instance, Cait Coker and Kate Ozment, eds, *Women in Book History. A Bibliography* htpps://www.womensbookhistory.org/ [accessed 1 March 2023].
2. Beach described her work as first publisher of *Ulysses* by way of the biological, role-defined metaphor in her 1959 memoir, *Shakespeare and Company*. 'And after all, the books were Joyce's. A baby belongs to its mother, not to the midwife, doesn't it?' (205). For an excellent early critique see Benstock (20–42).

3. This is published in Japanese as ブランデンの愛の手紙—ひとつの日英文化交流史 (20 世紀メモリアル [*Blunden's Love Letters: A History of Japan-UK Cultural Exchange*]. Note: transliterations in this essay are given as in the sources cited.
4. Hayashi's surviving correspondence to Blunden is held within his papers (Manuscript Collection MS-0426) at the HRC, University of Texas at Austin, across three containers (undated, 1926–46; 1948–50; 1953–62). This consists of 87 ALS (autograph letters signed); 30 ALI (autograph letters initialled), 2 ANS (autograph notes signed), 1 ANI (autograph note initialled), 4 APCS (autograph postcards signed), 15 ACPI (autograph cards initialled) (17 no date, 17 including date). Within Blunden's papers, the HRC also holds two autograph letters signed from Hayashi to Claire Blunden (Blunden's third wife); Hayashi's autograph manuscript/draft of an article 'A visit to Elia's grave'; her 'Catalogues of books of Coleridges and Pitman', and an autograph/handwritten manuscript by Hayashi of *The poems of Wilfred Owen* with handwritten notes by Blunden, '205 pages, approximately 1930'. See Sibley and Wokeman 2018.
5. Karuizawa is a famous summer retreat in Japan, popular among expats and Japanese society before the Second World War (part of Hayao Miyazaki's 2013 film, *The Wind Rises*, about engineer Jiro Horikoshi (1903–1982), is set here). Thanks to Katsura Sako for this information.
6. Okada had access to Blunden's letters to Hayashi via the personal archive of Blunden's surviving wife, Claire Blunden.
7. Blunden's correspondence with Sassoon has been published in three volumes, edited by Carol Z. Rothkopf. Hayashi first appears in the correspondence of the two men as 'my Japanese secretary' (9 May 1927; 1: 149) then 'my Japanese amanuensis' (31 August 1927; 1: 158).
8. Blunden's library (of about 10,000 volumes) was bought intact and is now housed in Ohio University Archives and Special Collections. Aki Hayashi's contribution is not noted. https://www.ohio.edu/library/collections/archives-special-collections/rare-books/edmund-blunden-collection. [Accessed 15 October 2023.]
9. It is notable that Hayashi uses the Japanese word for money rather than the English.
10. Fascinatingly, social attitudes to typists changed over the first half of the twentieth century, as clerical and secretarial labour moved away from being seen as a relatively elevated male profession, to being viewed as lower grade, feminized women's work. See Price and Thurschwell (3–7); and on the male clerk, Wild.
11. This is Melanie Micir's term to describe how biographical acts were used by queer feminist writers 'to resist the marginalization and exclusion of their friends, colleagues, lovers, companions, and wives from dominant narratives of literary history' (3).

12. The New Woman's Society [新婦人協会, *Shin-fujin kyōkai*], was founded by Hiratsuka Raichō (1886–1971) and Ichikawa Fusae (1893–1981) in 1919 to enhance women's rights in education, employment and suffrage, as well as protecting women from venereal disease.
13. Tsuda Umeko (1864–1929) was a champion for women's education in Japan, sent to the US at the age of six as part of the Iwakura Mission of Japanese diplomacy (1871–3), later educated at Bryn Mawr College, Philadelphia, and St. Hilda's College, Oxford.
14. According to the correspondence between the two men, influential society hostess Lady Ottoline Morrell advised Sassoon to try and persuade Blunden to ask 'Miss Hayashi to return to Japan' (31 October 1927; 1: 168), to try and avoid a scandal (Blunden was still married to his first wife, Mary). Sassoon supported Blunden's right to privacy, advising 'candour' between all those concerned.
15. Okada chooses not to reproduce this letter in full, unlike Blunden's biographer, Webb.

Works Cited

Battershill, Claire, Alice Staveley, and Nicola Wilson. "Making Fields: Women in Publishing." *The Edinburgh Companion to Women in Publishing, 1900–2000*, edited by Nicola Wilson et al. Edinburgh University Press, 2024, pp. 1–17.

Beach, Sylvia. *Shakespeare and Company*. Harcourt, Brace, 1959.

Benthall, Jonathan. "Obituary. Brownlee J. Kirkpatrick, 1919–2007," *Anthropology Today*, 23.4, 2007, <https://www.deepdyve.com/lp/wiley/brownlee-j-kirkpatrick-1919-2007-7aqQE0cqou>. Accessed 14 February 2024.

Benstock, Shari. *Women of the Left Bank. Paris, 1900–1940*. University of Texas Press, 1986.

Berg, Maggie, and Barbara K. Seeber. *The Slow Professor: Challenging the Culture of Speed in the Academy*. University of Toronto Press, 2016.

Blackwood, Sarah. "Editing as Carework: The Gendered Labor of Public Intellectuals." *Avidly*, 6 June 2014, <https://avidly.lareviewofbooks.org/2014/06/06/editing-as-carework-the-gendered-labor-of-public-intellectuals/>. Accessed 14 February 2024.

Bryant-Davies, Rachel, and Erin Johnson-Williams, editors. *Intersectional Encounters in the Nineteenth-Century Archive: New Essays on Power and Discourse*. Bloomsbury Academic, 2022.

Daniels, Arlene Kaplan. "Invisible Work." *Social Problems*, vol. 35, no. 5, Dec. 1987, pp. 403–15.

Dresvina, Juliana, editor. *#Thanks for Typing: Remembering Forgotten Women in History*. Bloomsbury Academic, 2021.

Federici, Silvia. *Wages against Housework*. Power of Women Collective and Falling Water Press, 1975.

Hartman, Saidiya. *Wayward Lives, Beautiful Experiments*. Serpent's Tail, 2019.

Hollis, Catherine. "M.E. Fitzgerald: Office Manager to Modernism." *#Thanks for Typing: Remembering Forgotten Women in History*, edited by Juliana Dresvina. Bloomsbury Academic, 2021, pp. 11–21.

Howsam, Leslie. "In My View: Women and Book History." *SHARP News* vol 7, no. 4, 1998, pp. 1–2.

Kirkpatrick, Brownlee J. *A Bibliography of Edmund Blunden*. Clarendon Press, 1979.

Klein, Lauren. "Dimensions of Scale: Invisible Labor, Editorial Work, and the Future of Quantitative Literary Studies." *PMLA*, vol. 135, no. 1, 2020, pp. 23–39.

Levy, Michelle. "Do Women Have a Book History?" *Studies in Romanticism*, vol. 53, no. 3, 2014, pp. 297–317.

Mendelman, Lisa. "Who Are We? Feminist Ambivalence in Contemporary Literary Criticism." *American Literary History*, vol. 32, 2019, pp. 190–200.

Micir, Melanie. *The Passion Projects: Modernist Women, Intimate Archives, Unfinished Lives*. Princeton UP, 2019.

Mukamal, Anna. "'Unnamed but ever-present consulting editor': A feminist problem." *The Edinburgh Companion to Women in Publishing, 1900–2020*, edited by Wilson et al. Edinburgh UP, 2024, pp. 288–308.

Murray, Simone. *Mixed Media: Feminist Presses and Publishing Politics*. Pluto, 2004.

Okada, Sumie. *Edmund Blunden and Japan: The History of a Relationship*. Macmillan, 1988.

Ozment, Kate. "Rationale for Feminist Bibliography." *Textual Cultures*, vol. 13, no. 1, 2020, pp. 149–78.

Price, Leah, and Pamela Thurschwell, editors. *Literary Secretaries/Secretarial Cultures*. Ashgate, 2005.

Rothkopf, Carol Z., editor. *Selected Letters of Siegfried Sassoon and Edmund Blunden, 1919–67*. Pickering & Chatto, 2012. 3 vols.

Sato, Barbara. *The New Japanese Woman: Modernity, Media, and Women in Interwar Japan*. Duke UP, 2013.

Sibley, Joan, and Richard Wokeman. "Edmund Blunden: An Inventory of his Papers at the Harry Ransom Center." 2018. <https://.norman.hrc.utexas.edu/fasearch/findingAid.cfm?eadid=01247. Accessed 13 October 2023.

Steedman, Carolyn. *History and The Law: A Love Story*. Cambridge UP, 2020.

Webb, Barry. *Edmund Blunden: A Biography*. Yale UP, 1990.

Werner, Sarah. "Working toward a Feminist Printing History." *American Printing History Association New Series*, 2018; Combined Issue 2020, pp. 27–28.

Wild, Jonathan. *The Rise of the Office Clerk in Literary Culture, 1880–1939*. Palgrave Macmillan, 206.

2

Reading Women's Work in the Karen Brahe Library

Lucie Duggan

The household account books (*regnskabsbøger*) of early modern Danish noblewomen offer a fascinating glimpse into the running of noble households in the Kingdom of Denmark in a period spanning the seventeenth and early eighteenth centuries. In the account book of Sophie Brahe (1578–1646) for example, we find records of purchase and sale of land, property, livestock, as well as an array of expenses ranging from charitable donations to dental work, to the procurement of items such as oranges and lemons, silk, spices, and zither strings. Among the items that appear throughout these accounts are books. In 1634, Sophie Brahe recorded the payments made for books to: 'bookseller Ellsseuir [Elzevir] in Holland'; 'Jahann Johannsen bookseller in Amsterdam'; 'Jørgenn Holst, bookseller'; and 'Johann Hollender bookbinder in Copenhagen' (Paulsen 108). In 1635, an entry records payment for '2 books for Sophie Sandbierg's children,' 1 psalm book for 5 mk,' '1 psalm book for 3 mk,' '5 Danish books in Copenhagen, 3 ½ dlr.' (Paulsen 124). In 1637 she paid for '1 medical handbook and 1 colour book' (Paulsen 158). At Viborg market in 1639 a purchase was made of '2 books with landscapes for the children' (Paulsen 198).[1]

Such records tell us something of the vibrant book industry and its networks spread across seventeenth-century Northern Europe (from the publishing houses of Amsterdam to bookbinders in Copenhagen, to booksellers at regional marketplaces), but also of how this industry intersects with the lives and duties of Danish women of the upper nobility. They tell us something of how books functioned as tools of women's work within the domestic sphere—responsible for maintaining overviews of estate administration and household finances (the account book), as well as the spiritual and moral education of those within their households (the psalm-book), and indeed the provision of medical care (the medical handbook).

Sophie Brahe's *regnskabsbog* provides useful evidence of women's book acquisition and ownership but the insights it offers into how such books were used is fleeting. As the matriarch of the household of Holger ('the Learned') Rosenkrantz, we can assume that many of the books recorded in Sophie's account book found their way into the internationally renowned household library at the Rosenkrantz estate at Rosenholm; little of that library survives, with most of its contents sold, appropriated, or destroyed during a period marked by military invasion of Denmark by Swedish forces (Andersen; Lauritz Nielsen).

However, a number of Sophie Brahe's books have survived in another private library, that of noblewoman Karen Brahe (1657–1736). Among the books in Brahe's collection is a copy of the funeral sermon of Dorte Lange by the priest Jens Giødesen, printed in 1613. The following inscription is found in the book: 'this book belongs to me Anna giøe and was given to me by my dear aunt this year 1619' ('denne bog hør mig Anna giøe thil med rete och gaff min hierte kiere moster mig den. Anno 1619'). The name 'Sophie Brahe' has been added in Karen Brahe's hand as the aunt in question. Related through the Brahe family line, Karen came into the possession of Sophie's books by way of her great aunt, Anne Gøye (1609–1681) who had spent part of her childhood under the care of her maternal aunt Sophie at the Rosenholm estate. Anne Gøye was an avid book collector and bequeathed her substantial collection of books to her niece, who continued to expand its contents until her death. The Karen Brahe library survives intact today, and its contents provide an important insight into the diverse uses of books among women of the Danish nobility, both as practical tools that testify to their responsibilities in managing the estates, households, and assets of prominent families in early modern Denmark and also as objects symbolic of the intellectual, literary culture in which these women actively participated as readers, writers, and translators.

In this chapter I trace the connections and networks of book transmission among these women and examine how their books bear witness to diverse forms of work, in the form of the practical work of estate administration and household management but also the literary and scholarly work of reading, authoring, and translating of texts. I also consider how women book owners inscribed themselves on their books, and how their inscriptions and annotations (what Lori Humphrey Newcomb has called 'deliberate readerly labors') function as forms of family history writing where the act of safekeeping is accompanied by various inscriptional practices that aim to commemorate as well as record (Humphrey Newcomb 245). Pertinent to my analysis is the concept of *bookwork* developed by Whitney Trettien, for whom the term encompasses on the one hand 'the actual labor of making a codex ... the book's tangible presence as the product of a specific class of labor' and on the other 'all the conceptual labor that springs out of books . . . and especially the ways these bookish pursuits propel readers back into the world' (20). I draw on Trettien's description of the book as both 'an assembled product of knowledge' and also 'an engine of knowledge production' to consider how women used their books to shape and fashion readerly identities, thus asserting their claim to a place within a male-dominated intellectual and scholarly milieu.

I begin by describing the Karen Brahe library itself, how it came to be (and the role of its compilers in ensuring its survival across the centuries) and an overview of its contents. I then discuss a selection of items that bear witness in various ways to women's work, and that illuminate the interconnected nature of women's reading and women's work in early modern Denmark. The analysis of the Karen Brahe library presented in this chapter is made possible by digital analysis of the collection's catalogs, in their iteration as digital datasets. In the second half of the chapter, I consider how these catalogs lay bare further traces of bibliographic labor, and how practices of feminist digital bibliography offer an opportunity to identify, in the historical record, the readerly labors of the past alongside those of the present.

The Karen Brahe Library

The Karen Brahe Library is known today by the name of its last owner, but its story begins with the noblewoman Anne Gøye, who lived from 1609 until 1681. Anne was one of ten children of the nobleman Henrik Eskildsen Gøye and his wife Birgitte Axelsdatter Brahe. The sister of the aforementioned Sophie Brahe, Anne's mother Birgitte (1576–1619) was also an owner of books, a number of which survive in the Karen Brahe library. In one of her books we find this inscription: 'this book belongs to me berrete brade hendrekk giøes [Birgitte Brahe] and was given me by my dear sister [Sophie Brahe] God give us mercy, Copenhagen 5 April 1610' ('denne bog hør mig berrete brade hendrekk giøes tell medt Rete og gaff mig den min hiete kierre søster soffie [Brahe] gudt gieffue os bode aff sin naade datom Kiøbenhanff den 5 aprilis 1610').[2] The book in question is a funeral sermon, printed on the death of Sophie's two-year old daughter Ide in 1609, the year that Birgitte's own daughter Anne was born. The author's dedication—addressed to Sophie—tells us that the sermon was written on 22 March, three years to the day of Ide's birth. Birgitte's inscription, along with the paratextual details of the sermon, represent a possibility for enlarging our understanding of bookwork here, where inscriptions, brief though they may be, bear witness to bonds of sisterhood and kinship, and work as records of these familial ties for the next owners and readers.

Birgitte died in 1619, and ten-year-old Anne was sent to live with her aunt Sophie at the Rosenkrantz estate at Rosenholm, where she was surely encouraged and supported in the formation of her own library; among her books are those authored by the learned men of the day with whom Holger Rosenkrantz (a prominent theologian as well as an influential patron of scholarship) was connected (Madsen 174). By the time of her death in 1681, Anne had amassed a substantial collection of around 1,000 items. A number of weeks before her death in early 1681, Gøye wrote to her old acquaintance, the Danish professor Jacob Bircherod, informing him of her decision to leave her book collection to her grand-niece, Karen Brahe, who was then 23 years old. Of her collection she wrote:

> Then I must let you know this, as a friend of mine and my books, that I have taken care of them after my death that they, which I have collected with such great diligence and joy, must not be scattered, and therefore given my brother's daughter Karen Brahe them all, who shall not love, esteem and benefit from them less than I have done . . .
>
> (Saa maa jeg og lade Eder viide dette, som en Ven af mig og mine bøger, at jeg haver taget omsorg for dem efter min død, at de, som jeg med saa stor fliid og glæde haver samlet, maatte icke blive spredt, og derfor givet min Broder-Datter Karen Brahe dem allesammen, som icke skal mindre elske, agte og føre sig nytte af dem, end jeg haver giort . . .)[3]

She asked Bircherod to keep her books in mind, and she requested that he compile a printed catalog of her collection, for which she set aside funds for Bircherod to access.

Following Anne Gøye's death, the collection passed to her grand-niece. Born in Næsbyholm in 1657 to one of the leading families of the Danish nobility, Karen Brahe was brought up surrounded by educated women, among them her aunt Anne, who had spent part of her last years with the Brahe family at their estate in Hvedholm. The writings of Karen's mother Susanne Gøye are found among the manuscript items of the collection, including translations, psalm verses, and letters in which she wrote of her education in French. Following the death of their mother, Karen and sister Birgitte were appointed administrators of one of their father's estates—Østrupgaard on the island of Funen, which had fallen into disrepair (Madsen 177). The sisters successfully revived the estate so that it was economically viable, and the handwritten records contained in Brahe's library give some insights into what her duties as an administrator of the estate may have entailed—contracts detailing the sale of cattle, extracts from royal ordinances on various taxes in Denmark in different years, account book records of timber yields.

The library of Anne Gøye was clearly known among the leading intellectual figures of late-seventeenth century Denmark; among those who consulted her collection was the philologist Peder Syv, who thanked Anne Gøye for access to her library in his seminal work on Danish language and literature (Bjerring-Hansen 99). A number of years following the inheritance of her aunt's library, Karen Brahe found herself having to defend her position as a book collector in her own right. In 1686, the Danish legal scholar Peder Hansen Resen wrote to Jens Bircherod (son of the aforementioned Jacob Bircherod) that he had become aware of ninety-five manuscripts in the collection that he felt should form part of his own collection of Danish books. He urged Bircherod to persuade the 'noblewoman owner of the library' to transfer the books to Resen for a fee; he offered assurances that he would include her name in his printed catalog (Madsen 179).

Brahe's response—via Bircherod—reads as a firm dismissal of Resen's offer:

> They are certainly not for sale. I am also a bibliophile, and would rather add to my collection than be parted from those books that my dear aunt so long and carefully gathered and left in my care. But if among my Manuscripts there are some which Herr. Justitsraaden requests, I shall gladly, when given a list, have them copied and sent to him.
>
> ('thi for Penge er de ingenlunde fall – Jeg er selv liebhaber heri og heller forbedrer tallet paa min danske Bøger, end skiller mig ved dem, som af min sal. Søster længe og med Umage er samlet og mig foræret for at holde vedlige. Men hvis iblandt mine Manuscripter findes nogle, som Hr. Justitsraaden kan være begjærendes, skal jeg gjerne, naaar mig derpaa gives Fortegnelse, dennem lade copiere og hannem tilsende.') (Madsen 179)

Brahe thus made clear that she intended to be generous in allowing interested parties to access her collection, but that the contents of her library were not for sale.

As their surviving letters attest, book ownership was an important part of Gøye and Brahe's noble status and identity (indeed, in a surviving portrait of Anne Gøye, she is depicted holding a richly bound book in her left hand). Moreover, these women understood that their role as book owners had particular responsibilities attached to it, including to preserve and safeguard the collection for future generations. Concerned that her collection could potentially be broken up and scattered (the fate of so many private libraries of the period), Anne Gøye clearly based her decision to leave her books to her niece on family ties and kinship, but also on a recognition of a shared appreciation of (and emotional investment in) her books (as one who would 'love, esteem, and benefit from them'). As her response to Resen's request shows, Karen Brahe determined to honour her aunt's wishes.

Having inherited her aunt's collection, Brahe assumed her responsibility as a careful custodian but also as an active collector, expanding the contents of the library substantially throughout her lifetime. The catalogs of the collection reveal that she made major purchases in the early 1700s, including from the auction of the well-known library of the Danish collector Frederik Rostgaard in 1726, including thirty-six manuscript items (Larsen 64). In 1716, Brahe founded the Odense Adelige Jomfrukloster (a secular convent intended for the accommodation and upkeep of unmarried noblewomen); a similar institution had been established in Roskilde in 1699 by noblewomen Margrethe Ulfeldt and Berte Skeel. In the official document recording the establishment of the Jomfrukloster, Brahe made clear her intention to leave her collection to the Convent, where it was to remain for posterity.[4] Brahe made detailed stipulations about the care of the library, as well as making financial provisions for the hire of a librarian tasked with overseeing the collection (Susanne Lykke Vølzgen Nielsen 'Bøger Maler Billeder—Karen Brahe Set Gennem Sin Bogsamling' 26). The reading room—still preserved today—with its custom-built bookshelves is a reminder of the material circumstances necessary for a library to exist; not only did the books require a room of their own, but also adequate funds for their cataloging and maintenance, including, presumably, the labors of domestic servants tasked with dusting bookshelves and cleaning rooms.

Literary Labors: Women's Literary Work as Writers, Readers, Translators, Annotators

The contents of the collection have been recorded most recently in two catalogs: Anne Riising completed her catalog of the manuscript items in 1956, and Susanne Lykke Nielsen compiled an online catalog of the printed works in the early 1990s. These remain the definitive catalogs of the Brahe library, offering a detailed overview of the contents of the collection. These catalogs provide us with access to a collection which makes visible diverse forms of early modern work. Among the items in the collection are works that can be categorized as household texts or practical manuals. One such item is an anthology of 'household books,' published in 1649 under the title *Oeconomia Nova eller En Ny Husholdingsbog* (New Economy or A New Household book) by the Copenhagen bookseller Jørgen Holst. Similar to other household compilations popular across Europe, Holst's *Oeconomia* served as a practical handbook or manual with advice on various aspects of household and land management. The household genre of early modern literature was understood to have a broad remit; the *Oeconomia* included a household and agriculture book; a color book (how to make various dyes); an illumination book (on the preparation, mixing, and application of various colors); a horticultural manual; a culinary handbook; a manual on food preservation, vinegar production, and beer brewing; a guide to fishing; and a handbook on beekeeping. The contents page announced as its target audience both the 'fathers' and 'mothers' of the house ('alle husfæder og huus-Mødre') and included original Danish publications as well as translations from German-language texts.

Numerous examples of women's authorship in the Karen Brahe library draw our attention to how women writers engaged in and shaped early modern literary and intellectual culture. Many of the women whose writings are preserved in the collection were known and celebrated during their lifetime as being among a select number of learned women.[5] The Danish intellectual Birgitte Thott (sister-in-law to Anne Gøye) was a renowned translator of Seneca, whose major published work—a translation of the Stoic philosopher's moral works into Danish in 1658—earned her the accolade 'the tenth muse' from the Dutch scholar Anna Maria van Schurman (Ebbersmeyer 4). Like van Schurman, Thott was a powerful advocate for women's education and, in what the scholar Marianne Alenius has called 'the earliest example of Danish feminism in print,' Thott explicitly dedicated her translation to learned women, arguing eloquently in favor of women's access to learning through reading (Alenius 'Birgitte Thott (1610–1662)'). Thott's Seneca translation is a monumental volume, its appearance in print ensuring a widespread readership and consolidating Thott's status as an intellectual figure. It is among the very few published translations attributed to a named female translator found in the printed items of the collection.[6]

Among the *manuscript* items in the collection, however, there are numerous examples of translations authored by women, many of them members of the Gøye and Brahe families. These include a translation from French to Danish of the first book of Juan Luis Vives's popular conduct manual *De institutione feminae Christianae* (The Education of a Christian Woman) from 1524. The first book of Vives's manual—dedicated to Queen Catherine of Aragon, mother of the future Mary I of England—was concerned with the education of girls and unmarried women, and addressed the role of mothers in instructing their daughters in their native language, so that they might read works of devotional literature in translation (Vives and Fantazzi). The manuscript translation in Karen Brahe's library was made by her mother, Susanne Gøye, during the early years of her daughter Karen's life, and Anne Gøye's accompanying inscription reads: 'My dear brother's daughter Susanne Gøie (wife of Preben Brahe) has translated this work from French into Danish and with her own hand written 1659' (Riising 171). The manuscript—and the context of its production that Anne Gøye's inscription provides—affords the possibility of imagining spaces of female literary agency, discussion, and critical engagement with the major texts of European intellectual thought; like Thott's published translation of Seneca, Gøye's translation assumes—and exhorts—an audience of learned women, encouraged in their literary endeavors from a young age.

Other translations by women include a psalm written in Danish, which is accompanied by Anne Gøye's note: 'this psalm has been translated by my sister Karen Bille from French' (Riising 38). Elsewhere, a translation from German to Danish of Johann Arndt's *Four Books on True Christianity* is attributed again to Karen Bille (Karen Brahe's maternal grandmother) in 1657 (in a note in Karen Brahe's hand) (Riising 41). Many of the texts translated by women are devotional in nature, but other genres are represented too; among the manuscripts identified as works with historical subject matter is the Danish translation from Latin of the first three books of Julius Caesar's *Commentarii de Bello Gallico* by the writer Anna Margrethe Qvitzow, regarded as a female scholar and literary figure of renown in her own time, though little-known today (Alenius 'Otto Sperlings 1.399 Lærde Kvinder Og Hans Kilder'). Several translations by Birgitte Thott are also found among the manuscript items (Riising 42–43). The inscriptions that accompany these manuscripts reveal the authorial agency that women achieved through their translations, where the literary labor of undertaking a translation is underscored in the formula 'this book has been written by me in my own hand,' variations of which are found throughout the manuscript items.[7]

Attending to women's literary work in the manuscript items of the Karen Brahe library highlights the importance of genres that are often overlooked in studies of early modern book culture, but that were central to women's literary activities, including private prayer books and genealogy books.[8] The latter played a role in documenting the lineage of the families of the Danish landowning aristocracy, providing evidence of a noble family's unbroken lineage over four generations and thereby substantiating a family's claim to the privileges of noble status. The family history book (*slægtebog*) and armorial book (*våbenbog*) were often compiled by the women of noble families and contained detailed information on the ancestry of individual families, as well as intricate, hand-colored illustrations of armorial bearings (William Christensen 'Nogle Slægtebogs-OgVåbenbogs-Undersøgelser'). Among the genealogy books found in the Karen Brahe library are those of Lisbet Bryske, Sophie Below, Mette Giøe, and Anna Eilersdatter Rønnow (Riising 105–06). The first woman listed, Lisbet Bryske (1585–1674), was a prolific author of genealogical literature, as well as a translator. Two of her genealogy books are preserved in the library, containing records of noble families with accompanying illustrations of coats-of-arms. Lisbet Bryske's inscriptions on the first page of her book can be read as emphatic assertions of her ownership and authorship. The first reads: 'this book belongs to me Lisbet Bryske by right, and I have painted and written it, so it can plainly be seen, that it is my own work and the work of my hands, written at Thirsbech, 17 July 1651, when I was 66 years old. Lisbet Bryske her own hand.' ('Dene Bog hør mig Lisbet Bryske till med Rette, oc haver ieg den sell mallitt oc skreven, som det er gott att see, att det er mitt egitt Arbed oc Henders Gierninger, skreffuit paa Thirsbech den 17 Julli 1651, da var ieg 66 Aar gamell. Lisbett Bryske egen Hand.'). Another inscription follows directly below: 'This armorial book has been given by me to my dear daughter's daughter Ellen Bille, so that she may have as a reminder, that it is my own work. 20 August 1674. Lisbet Bryske her own hand.' ('Dene Våbenbog haver ieg givet min kiere Datter-Datter Ellen Bille, att hun den skall have till en Hukomelse, at det er mit eget Arbed. Af Weill [Vejle] den 20 August 1674. Lisbett Bryske egen Hand.'). Bound within the book is Lisbet Bryske's own autobiography, written in 1665. This fascinating document, written by Bryske in the later years of her life, begins with an account of her early years with her parents; she writes that she received an education in her catechism until the age of six, after which she was taught to read and write along with her sister and brother by a tutor at the family estate. Bryske's charitable work is emphasized (establishing a charity hospital and lodgings for the poor—and organizing the rebuilding of the same lodgings after their destruction during the 'last Swedish war 1657') but so too are her literary labors: her translation of a German text every Sunday and other holy days during the war and a book that she translated from German and attempted to have published.[9] The document—likely intended for a wider public audience—emphasized a life in which reading and writing were central throughout; she remarked that despite her considerable age, the many sorrows over which she had shed tears (Bryske outlived most of her thirteen children), and much time spent engaged in literary pursuits, she could still read and write without glasses.[10]

Numerous examples of prayer books written and owned by women are also found among both the manuscript items of the collection and the printed texts.[11] The prayer book—a collection of texts including prayers and psalms—functioned as a manual for private devotion within the home (and an aid in the religious instruction of household members), but in their translation, compilation, and publication they were also a means by which pious and devout women could achieve influence in a wider public sphere, as the published examples of women's prayer books demonstrate, some of them (such as the books of Sidsel Høg, Kirsten Munk, and Sophie Bille) remaining popular after their original publication with multiple reprints throughout the seventeenth and eighteenth centuries (Appel 554). As the manuscript prayer books in Karen Brahe's library also show, the devotional labors they implied (daily prayer exercises to be carried out at different times of the day) were shared collectively, often over multiple generations—as many as twenty-four hands can be identified in one of Karen Brahe's manuscript prayer books, and the inscriptions found in many are a reminder that prayer books were objects that were often given as gifts.

Readerly Labors

The inscriptions found throughout the collection reflect the extent to which Karen Brahe and the women in her family shaped their intellectual identity around their bookish pursuits and reading practices. From the 1690s until her death in 1736, Karen Brahe made records of her own reading on the pages of her books. On multiple dates in October of 1690, she recorded her reading of devotional texts in German, including three of Martin Luther's writings. Some of her records note how she returned to a book in different years: a devotional text in German was marked as 'read [16]90 . . . read again 8 July 97'.[12] A psalter of 1571 bears signs of sustained reading and engagement, including multiple notes and underlined passages in the text, as well as the following record: 'begun 1722 23 February. Also read through in 1723'.[13] A copy of Johann Arndt's *Paradisgartlein* was marked as read multiple times from 1723 to 1734. Thomas a Kempis' *De Imitatione Christi* was an acquisition by Karen Brahe, bearing her inscription 'bought 1732. Read the same year and in 1734'. Another purchase, made in 1736, was 'read immediately'.[14]

Brahe's inscriptional practices make visible the various forms of readerly labors associated with book ownership. Her records of her reading allow us to glimpse a reader *working* at her text, and they appear to signal a private and personal reading practice that may also have been intended to have a more public audience—her notes might function as reminders to herself, informing her own future reading of the same work, but she surely anticipated that her readerly records would be visible to other readers, in her own time and after. Her records thus serve for future readers as important evidence of her readerly labors, but they also offer examples of texts working for their reader, providing comfort in difficult times. For example, in her copy of Sigismund Scherertz's *Fuga Melancholiæ* (1682), Brahe made a record of her reading in 1736, following the death of her young nephew Jørgen during a hunting accident, 'and found comfort and guidance to bear with patience the sorrow that God let pass over our house on the 14th of July the same year' ('og funden trøst og Raad til tolmodig at bere, den Hjerte sorrig Gud lod gaa ofver voris Huss d.14.jullj en lofver dag same Aar').

The work that a devotional text might perform for its reader can thus be read alongside the commemorative work that inscriptional practices enable. Among the devotional texts in the collection is a 1613 edition of Martin Moller's *Manuale de Praeparatione ad Mortem* (A Manual for the Rightful Art of Dying), which bears multiple inscriptions. Anne Gøye has written her name on the title page; on the preceding page is the inscription of her mother Birgitte Brahe, who records that she has given the book to her young daughter, Anne Gøye, on 11 February 1619, at Turebygaard, just a few months before her death. Birgitte's words are repeated on the inscription on the inner leaf of the binding, where Anne Gøye has confirmed herself as the owner of her mother's book: 'this book belongs to me Jomfru Ane Giøe by right and was given to me by my dear mother God give us both of his mercy Turebygaar 11 Feb. 1619.' Inscribing her name in her mother's book, Anne Gøye left her mark as the new owner of an old book that was to be used, but also safeguarded for future generations. Marks of ownership and inscriptions thus serve to remind us that books were cherished items, valued both for their intellectual and spiritual content (as aids to devotion, as well as practical advice on illness and household management) and their uses as sentimental items (bearing inscriptions that evoke memories of loved ones).

Bibliographic Labor in the Digital Age

My analysis of the Karen Brahe collection—and the ways in which it bears witness to diverse forms of literary labors in centuries past—is made possible by the presence of the catalogs of the library's contents. These catalogs represent an important mediation of the collection and are themselves an example of the kind of painstaking bibliographic labor involved in ensuring that knowledge of the contents of a library is accessible.[15] The first steps of my own research have been to transform the information within these catalogs into digital bibliographic data that can then be analyzed computationally. This process has involved building on the work of the individuals who cataloged the collection in the second half of the twentieth century—Anne Riising (1926–2017), who compiled the catalog of the manuscript items, and Susanne Lykke Vølzgen Nielsen, whose electronic registration of the printed items in the collection forms part of the library at the University of Southern Denmark. Riising was a historian and archivist at the Regional Archives in Funen (where she later become the first woman appointed as director of a national archive in Denmark) where the Brahe collection was housed from 1907 until 2010.[16] In her introduction to the catalog, published in 1956, she acknowledged the enormous undertaking of the task, but expressed a satisfaction that the overall aim had been achieved: a working catalog that could provide access to and knowledge of the contents of the manuscript items in the Karen Brahe collection (Riising 10). Over thirty years later, Susanne Nielsen carried out the electronic registration of the printed works in the University of Southern Denmark's database.[17]

Both Riising and Nielsen acknowledged the fact that their work built on the efforts of previous attempts to catalog the collection (the most comprehensive of which was that of Victor Madsen in the 1930s), as well as the weight of responsibility that the library—still intact—represented.[18] As the only private library from the seventeenth century to have survived intact in Denmark, the continued presence of the books in the Adelige Jomfrukloster in Odense (in shelves flanking a seventeenth-century fireplace) was deemed, by the turn of the nineteenth century, at such risk of hazards (not least fire) to warrant removal to a more secure location under the care of the national archive authority (from where it was also evacuated during the Second World War). The necessity of a comprehensive cataloging of the collection—a key concern in both Anne Gøye and Karen Brahe's testaments—was surely felt to be acute by the second half of the twentieth century.

The ontological nature of these catalogs—and the wealth of bibliographic metadata encoded within them—bears consideration. In their digital form, they are a mediation of the collection itself, conveying the information deemed most necessary by archival and library professionals for future readers and users of the catalogs. Information is categorized according to certain bibliographic standards and systems in the field.[19] The catalogs are thus crucial access points to the collection, but use of them necessarily involves retracing the steps of the individuals in the past who have categorized and registered the bibliographic data. These bibliographic labors often go unnoticed in an academic context where end results (published in peer-reviewed articles, monographs) often eclipse the processes of knowledge retrieval that precede them.[20] Yet these labors are fundamental to the access that researchers have to data—whether it involves consulting the index of a scholarly compendium or typing a query into an online search tool.

The recent computational turn in humanities scholarship has brought a renewed focus on the mediated nature of our datasets and the ways in which data is constructed, organized, and arranged for computational and machine-learning purposes, and the significant amount of precarious labor (often carried out by teams of research assistants) involved in the preparation and processing of these data (Boyles et al.; Graban et al.; Nyhan; Pilsch and Ross). Feminist practitioners of digital methodologies in the humanities have emphasized the embodied practice that underpins and supports digital and computational work. In their account of work carried out as part of *Women's Print History Project*, a digital database of comprehensive bibliographic information on women's contributions to print during the eighteenth century, Sharren, Ozment, and Levy describe their praxis as feminist digital bibliography, in which the 'reconstructive powers of bibliography join forces with the recuperative energies of feminist recovery' where the former 'provides the essential knowledge needed to formulate large-scale understandings of women's contributions to literary culture and labor' (Ozment; Sharren et al. 892). Key to this praxis is an understanding that digital bibliography—like traditional bibliography—is always an embodied endeavor and depends upon the collective labors and critical decision-making of a range of human actors, from catalogers to student researchers to IT professionals to humanities scholars.

Elsewhere, Bonnie Mak's work on modern information practices draws attention to the often-overlooked practices around the production of knowledge, including the work of cataloging library collections. As Mak reminds us, the digital cataloging systems that are now the standard practice of most libraries have their genealogy in the pre-digital, tangible, material form of the card catalog, which in turn relied on the printed or manuscript inventories of previous centuries. The encoding of bibliographic information—which library users now access online at the click of a link—has a history rooted in earlier technologies (manuscript, typewriter) and the embodied practices of the human beings who registered this information over time (Mak).

The registration of entire bibliographic collections is a process that is also fundamentally concerned with selection criteria, and inevitably involves making decisions about what information should be included (often at the expense of information that is not) (Lahti et al. 7). The cataloging of provenance information, and the specialized skills it may require—such as the deciphering of historic handwriting—have a key role to play in identifying women owners of early modern books (Ziegler). This is evident in the case of the Brahe library, where the transcription and systematic registration of handwritten inscriptions and other marginalia for the individual contents allow for a remarkably rich overview of the networks of transmission that underpin the collection. For example, it is precisely the bibliographic labors of the catalogers (Riising and Nielsen) that have allowed me to identify relationships between books and people across time in the Karen Brahe collection. In particular, the registration of information on annotations and inscriptions in the contents of the collection allows for an individual book's role within a network of readers to be reconstructed, as in the case of Sophie Brahe's book mentioned at the outset of the chapter. The bibliographic metadata thus facilitate the identification of connections and affinities across time and space. They remind us that the information available to us is the result of the labor of many individuals, often over many centuries. It is vital that we acknowledge these many layers of labor upon which the survival of a cultural heritage entity such as an early modern private library depends, and the various commitments (including time and financial resources) it requires from various individuals and institutions.

Conclusion

Attending to the various forms of bookwork found within the Karen Brahe library allows us to perceive the myriad ways in which early modern women engaged with and participated in the intellectual culture of the day as writers and translators, but also as readers, inscribers, and annotators, whose literary labors—in the margins of the printed book or manuscript—have historically been overlooked. The material traces that long-ago readers and owners left on their books in the form of ownership marks and inscriptions are themselves an important form of bookwork, constituting a record of how books were used and valued *beyond* their texts, often as cherished objects passed down or gifted from family members and friends.

By inscribing themselves upon the pages of their books, Anne Gøye, Karen Brahe, and the women of their families performed vital work in ensuring that a record remained of their literary labors long after their own time. This in turn reminds us that the survival of fragile cultural heritage objects (such as books) is largely dependent on the attachments that people have historically formed to their possessions, and the commitments they make to safeguarding and preserving such items for posterity, without knowing if, how, or by whom they will be used in the future. But as their surviving letters show, Gøye and Brahe also keenly perceived the challenges of safeguarding and maintaining their collection, the survival of which (intact) was far from guaranteed. They recognized that the caretaking, safeguarding, and maintenance of their collection was an ongoing task that required recourse to legal structures of inheritance, financial provision for upkeep, adequate physical space for housing such a library, and crucially, the right person or institution to carry on these tasks in the future. As new evidence of early modern women's books and libraries comes to light (Coolahan; Knight et al.; Malay), the catalog—a valuable point of entry to book collections then and now—affords new possibilities in the digital age for making visible the many forms of women's literary labor in earlier times. Its sustained value hinges on the efforts of libraries, research institutions, and individuals to preserve and maintain its functionality over time.

Notes

I am grateful to the Augustinus Foundation for a research grant that enabled this work to be carried out as part of the project Reading Women: Karen Brahe and Female Book Ownership (1609–1736).

1. Transcription reads: 'to bøger med posserit lanndschaffter til børnen' (Paulsen 198).
2. Shelf-mark U.21-556.
3. Translations throughout are my own. The text of the entire letter is reproduced in Madsen. Anne Gøye's brother's daughter was in fact Susanne Gøye (mother of Karen Brahe). For further discussion of the Brahe library see Duggan.

4. The library remained in the Odense Adelige Jomfrukloster until 1907, when it was moved to the Provincial State Archives of Funen. It was moved to Roskilde in 2010, where it remains under the guardianship of Roskilde Cloister.
5. The 'lærde Fruentimmer' (learned women) genre is discussed in Alenius.
6. There are, however, published translations written by women but who remained anonymous. Mette Giøe's translation of Lewis Bayly's *Praxis Pietatis* is an example (shelf mark A.9-24); See also Gjøe and Reitzel-Nielsen.
7. The inscriptional formula is discussed in Appel.
8. As David Pearson writes, quoting Andrew Cambers: 'the history of devotional reading has been one area in the history of reading which has suffered relative neglect' (5). For the role of translation as a significant genre in early modern women's literary culture, see Belle; Brown.
9. The document is transcribed in William Christensen, 'Lisbeth-Bryske-Tekster.' The attempt to have the book (referred to only as 'det gyldne klenodie') published was ultimately unsuccessful, despite apparently receiving the approval of official censorship authority; it appears that someone else had translated the same work and had reached the printers before Bryske (Møller Christensen 5).
10. Marie Møller Christensen suggests that Bryske's autobiography, written in the third person, may have been intended for her funeral sermon.
11. There are approximately thirty-six prayer book manuscripts in the library. In her seminal study on women's manuscript prayer books, Marie Møller-Christensen provides an overview of twenty-three handwritten prayer books of women owners in the Karen Brahe library. The published prayer books attributable to the following female authors are found among the printed items: Sidsel Høg (1582–1648), Anna Catharina Krag (1616–1687), Kirsten Munk (1598–1658), Anne Jensdatter, and Sophie Andersdatter Bille.
12. Shelf-mark A.4-55.
13. Shelf-mark A.1-52.
14. Shelf-mark A.10-158. Works of a secular nature were also recorded as read; in her copy of Caspar Bartholin the Elder's major textbook on anatomy, *Institutiones Anatomicae* (1648), Brahe made a note that she had completed her reading of the book in July of 1702, and in Birgitte Thott's handbook on the ancient philosopher (Epectiti) she also recorded her reading in 1699.
15. The recent growth in data-driven book historical studies that work to reconstruct collections that no longer survive by way of their catalogs has highlighted the value of descriptive bibliographic works such as library sales catalogs and inventories as historical sources. See, for example, Jagersma and Rozendaal; Montoya.
16. Lars Bisgaard has described Riising's pioneering work as a historian.
17. See Nielsen 1998, 1996, and 1992.
18. See Riising's discussion of the catalog history of the Karen Brahe library. Victor Madsen's card catalogs are preserved in the Royal Library, Copenhagen; see also Madsen.

19. The electronic records of the printed works adhere to the Danish version of the international automated library system MARC (Machine Readable Cataloging Record).
20. See Pollack and Mak. On the intersections of humanities and information science (and the impact of new technologies of information creation, storage, and retrieval) see Blouin and Rosenberg.

Works Cited

Alenius, Marianne. "Birgitte Thott (1610–1662)." *Danish Writers from the Reformation to Decadence, 1550–1900, Dictionary of Literary Biography vol. 300,* Thomson Gale, 2004.

—. "Otto Sperlings 1.399 Lærde Kvinder Og Hans Kilder." *Fund og Forskning i Det Kongelige Biblioteks Samlinger* vol. 51, no. 187, 2015, pp. 187–212.

Andersen, J. Oskar. *Holger Rosenkrantz Den Lærde: En Biografisk Skildring Med Bidrag Til Belysning Af Danske Kirke-Og Studieforhold I Det Syttende Aarhundredes Første Halvdel*. Bang, 1896.

Appel, Charlotte. *Læsning Og Bogmarked I 1600-Tallets Danmark*. Det Kongelige bibliotek, Museum Tusculanums forlag, 2001.

Belle, Marie-Alice. "Locating Early Modern Women's Translations: Critical and Historiographical Issues." *Renaissance and Reformation*, vol. 35, no. 4, 2012, pp. 5–23.

Bisgaard, Lars. "Anne Riising (19. Februar 1926 – 26. Januar 2017)." *Historisk Tidsskrift*, vol. 118, no. 1, 2018, pp. 180–85.

Bjerring-Hansen, Jens. "Kulturformidling I Det Lærde Tidsrum: Peder Syvs Betenkninger . . . ." *Danske Studier*, 2013, pp. 97–115.

Blouin, F.X. and W.G. Rosenberg. *Processing the Past: Contesting Authority in History and the Archives.* Oxford University Press, 2011.

Boyles, Christina et al. "Precarious Labor and the Digital Humanities." *American Quarterly*, vol. 70, no. 3, 2018, pp. 693–700.

Brown, Hilary. "Introduction." *Women and Early Modern Cultures of Translation: Beyond the Female Tradition*, Oxford University Press, 2022, pp. 1–18.

Christensen, Marie Møller. "Adelskvinders Bønnebøger Som Andagtskultur Og Bogmedium: Fra Reformationstiden Til Midten Af 1600-Tallet." Unpublished PhD dissertation, Københavns Universitet, 2020.

Christensen, William. "Lisbeth-Bryske-Tekster." *Personalhistorisk Tidsskrift*, vol. 52, no. 9-4-1, 1931, pp. 1–56.

—. "Nogle Slægtebogs- Og Våbenbogs-Undersøgelser." *Personalhistorisk Tidsskrift* vol. 50, no. 2, 1929, pp. 1–37.

Coolahan, Marie-Louise. "My Lady's Books: Devising a Tool Kit for Quantitative Research; or, What Is a Book and How Do We Count It?" *The Huntington Library quarterly*, vol. 84, no. 1, 2021, pp. 125–37.

Duggan, Lucie. "Karen Brahe and Female Book Ownership in Denmark (1609–1736): Inheritance and Transmission." *Corpus Feminae: Auctorialité et Matérialités des Écritures Féminines dans l'Europe Moderne 16e–18e siècles*), Presses universitaires Blaise-Pascal (forthcoming).

Ebbersmeyer, Sabrina. "Establishing a Female Intellectual Identity in Early Modern Denmark: Birgitte Thott's Seneca Translation (1658) in a European Perspective." *Orbis litterarum*, vol.79, no. 1, 2023, pp. 14–29.

Gjøe, Mette and Erik Reitzel-Nielsen. "Mette Giøes Biografi". *Personalhistorisk Tidsskrift* vol. 78, 1958, pp. 57–80.

Graban, Tarez Samra et al. "Introduction: Questioning Collaboration, Labor, and Visibility in Digital Humanities Research." *DHQ: Digital Humanities Quarterly*, vol. 13, no. 2, 2019.

Humphrey Newcomb, Lori. "Frances Wolfreston's Annotations as Labours of Love." *Women's Labour and the History of the Book in Early Modern England*, The Arden Shakespeare, 2020, pp. 243–66.

Jagersma, R. and J. C. Rozendaal. "Female Book Ownership in the Eighteenth-Century Dutch Republic. The Book Collection of Paper-Cutting Artist Joanna Koerten (1650–1715)." *Quaerendo*, vol. 50, no. 1–2, 2020, pp. 109–40.

Knight, Leah et al., editors. *Women's Bookscapes in Early Modern Britain: Reading, Ownership, Circulation*. University of Michigan Press, 2018.

Lahti, Leo et al. "Bibliographic Data Science and the History of the Book (C. 1500–1800)." *Cataloging & Classification Quarterly*, vol. 57, 2019, pp. 5–23.

Larsen, Knud. *Frederik Rostgaard Og Bøgerne*. Vol. 3, Gad, 1970.

Madsen, Victor. "Karen Brahes Bibliotek I Odense." *Nordisk tidskrift för bok-och biblioteksväsen*, vol. 6, 1919, pp. 171–185.

Mak, Bonnie. "Cataloguing." *Transmissions: Critical Tactics for Making and Communicating Research*, 2020, pp. 229–238.

Malay, Jessica. "Reassessing Anne Clifford's Books: The Discovery of a New Manuscript Inventory." *The Papers of the Bibliographical Society of America*, vol. 115, no. 1, 2021, pp. 1–41.

Montoya, A. C. "Enlightenment? What Enlightenment? Reflections on Half a Million Books (British, French, and Dutch Private Libraries, 1665–1830)." *Eighteenth-century studies*, vol. 54, no. 4, 2021, pp. 909–34.

Nielsen, Lauritz. *Danske Privatbiblioteker Gennem Tiderne*. Nordisk Forlag, 1946.

Nielsen, Susanne Lykke Vølzgen. "Bøger Maler Billeder—Karen Brahe Set Gennem Sin Bogsamling." *Fynske årbøger*, 1998, pp. 16–39.

—. "Hiellp Gudt: Birgitte Brahe (1576–1619)—En Biografisk Skitse Og En Bogreol." *Personalhistorisk Tidsskrift*, 1996, pp. 95–155.

—. "Om Katalogiseringen Af Karen Brahes Bibliotek." *DF-Revy*, 1992, pp. 235–37.

Nyhan, Julianne. *Hidden and Devalued Feminized Labour in the Digital Humanities: On the Index Thomisticus Project 1954–67*. Taylor & Francis, 2022.

Ozment, Kate. "Rationale for Feminist Bibliography." *Textual Cultures*, vol. 13, no. 1, 2020, pp. 149–78.

Paulsen, Henning. *Sophie Brahes Regnskabsbog 1627–40.* Jysk Selskab for Historie, Sprog og Litteratur, 1955.

Pearson, David. *Book Ownership in Stuart England.* Oxford University Press, 2021.

Pilsch, Andrew and Shawna Ross. "Labour, Alienation, and the Digital Humanities." *The Bloomsbury Handbook to the Digital Humanities.* Bloomsbury, 2022, pp. 335–345.

Pollack, Julia and Bonnie Mak. "The Performance and Practice of Research in a Cabinet of Curiosity: The Library's Dead Time." *Art Documentation: Journal of the Art Libraries Society of North America*, vol. 32, 2013, pp. 202–21.

Riising, Anne. *Katalog over Karen Brahes Bibliotek I Landsarkivet for Fyn.* Håndskriftsamlingen, 1956.

Sharren, Kandice et al. "Gendering Digital Bibliography with the Women's Print History Project." *Eighteenth-Century Studies*, vol. 54, no. 4, 2021, pp. 887–908.

Trettien, Whitney. *Cut/Copy/Paste.* University of Minnesota Press, 2021.

Vives, J.L. and C. Fantazzi. *The Education of a Christian Woman: A Sixteenth-Century Manual.* University of Chicago Press, 2007.

Ziegler, Georgianna. "Patterns in Women's Book Ownership, 1500–1700." *Women's Labour and the History of the Book in Early Modern England*, The Arden Shakespeare, 2020, pp. 207–24.

3

The Labors of Shakespeare's Sisters

Varsha Panjwani

Adam Smith is widely regarded the father of political economy but, in 2016, journalist Katrine Marçal was interested in finding out who cooked his dinners as he penned *The Wealth of Nations*. Turns out that it might have been his mother (see Marçal). William Shakespeare is widely considered the world's foremost playwright, and it is worth wondering who cooked his dinners when he nurtured his craft. In her germinal essay, *A Room of One's Own*, first published in 1929, Virginia Woolf thought that it might have been his sister, Judith Shakespeare; as a woman, she would have been expected to 'mind the stew' rather than read like her brother (70).

Woolf's scenario is fictional because Shakespeare did not have a sister named Judith and Woolf is writing an imaginary story.[1] However, the reason that we can see strong parallels between Shakespeare's fictional sister and Smith's factual mother is because Woolf anchored Judith's tale in the economic reality that Marçal wrote about later: women, through the ages, have been expected to perform a large proportion of unpaid or underpaid labor which has tangible detrimental effects on their careers. On the one hand, it leaves them physically and emotionally drained and, on the other, it perpetually traps them in financial vulnerability and dependency.[2] According to the Office of National Statistics in the UK, over forty percent of female workers are part-time (Cox 113). Social historian Pamela Cox asserts that this is due to the 'fact that many are still combining paid work with unpaid work' and 'many feel that they have no option but to sacrifice their dreams of higher pay or promotion to their need for flexibility' (113). In her ground-breaking study, Caroline Criado Perez cites the data collected by both the McKinsey Global Institute and the Organization for Economic Co-operation and Development (OECD), which proves a 'strong negative correlation' between time spent in unpaid care work and women's participation rates in paid labor force (246). Even this data collection is rare because most of this work remains hidden or unacknowledged to the extent that it is not even counted in the Gross Domestic Product (GDP), which measures the monetary value of goods and services produced in a country. Feminist journalists such as Marçal and Perez have assembled research and data from various disciplines to demonstrate that women's labor is often invisible or rendered invisible by sociopolitical culture and economic infrastructure. It is my contention in this chapter that authors such as Woolf, and subsequently Marilyn French in *The Women's Room*, Emma Whipday in *Shakespeare's Sister*, and Jo Hamya in *Three Rooms*, have written companion pieces to such research work by sociologists and journalists. I further argue that by filling the gaps in official records, Woolf's essay, French and Hamya's novels, and Whipday's play are sometimes able to go beyond facts and data to tap into lived experiences of women's labor. They have used the trope of Shakespeare's imaginary sister, Judith, to always keep women's labor within our sight. They have made sure that women's labor is represented and accounted for in fiction and remains part of our literary and cultural imaginary.

Virginia Woolf, *A Room of One's Own*

In *A Room of One's Own*, Woolf famously conjures a fictional sister for Shakespeare with these words: 'Let me imagine, since facts are so hard to come by, what would have happened had Shakespeare had a wonderfully gifted sister, called Judith, let us say' (69). The clause that breaks her sentence draws attention to the idea that she is resorting to imagination because 'facts are hard to come by'. Woolf demonstrates how women's histories can sometimes only be recounted through imagination due to the facts of women's lives not being recorded as they were not deemed important enough to archive. She goes on to envision that even if this sister was 'extraordinarily gifted', she would have 'remained at home' and be expected to contribute to household tasks while Shakespeare went to grammar school to read and learn 'Latin—Ovid, Virgil, Horace—and the elements of grammar and logic' (70). If she 'picked up a book now and then, one of her brother's perhaps, and read a few pages', her parents would tell her to 'mend the stockings or mind the stew and not moon about with books and papers' (70). Woolf is aware that they would admonish her not because they were unkind but because they 'knew the conditions of life for a woman' (70).

Although Woolf's account is not factual, it does reflect the instruction manuals of Shakespeare's time. Even Humanist scholars, who supported women's education, had strict ideas about what reading was allowed and, crucially, when. In his popular and influential treatise, *The Instruction of a Christian Woman*, Juan Luis Vives, tutor to Mary Tudor, advises women to 'read and hear such [books] as shall lift up the mind to god, and set it in a Christian quietness, and make the living better' (12v). But so insistent is he that this should not be at the expense of housework that he mentions it twice. He writes that women should read on holy days when they return from mass but not before they have 'over looked thy house, as much as pertainith unto thy charge' (12v). Then, a few sentences later, he writes that women should read on some working days, too, but only if they are not required for performing 'some necessary business in thy house'(12v). The message is clear: even reading holy books is secondary to domestic chores that are the primary duty of a Christian woman. Besides a reputation for being an excellent Christian woman, however, this domestic labor would not buy the woman any financial independence because it was uncompensated. For money, she would be dependent on her father and then her husband who would, in turn, expect more unpaid domestic labor, thereby further curtailing both her time and energy as well as any financial freedom to access her passions.

Given such a culture, Woolf is right to imagine that if 'Judith scribbled some pages up in an apple loft on the sly', she would 'hide them or set fire to them' lest her parents discover it and chide her for slacking in her duties (70). Thus, Woolf concludes that 'it would have been impossible, completely and entirely, for any woman to have written the plays of Shakespeare in the age of Shakespeare' (69) because she argues that genius has to be cultivated and imaginative work that goes into writing not only requires talent or felicity but also needs 'grossly material things, like health and money and the houses we live in'—things not easily available to most women (64). In Woolf's story, Judith is trapped in a society that prescribes housework as education, and instead of enabling her to earn a living by writing for the theater, coerces her to devote her energy to good housewifery and childcare. Unable to reconcile her social situation with her desire to write plays, Judith dies by suicide without having written a word.

By writing a potential woman Shakespeare into Shakespeare's world, Woolf outlines how women Shakespeares were wiped out of that world in two ways. First, the uncompensated labor (which is based on real details) would make it impossible for women to achieve the things that they wanted. Secondly, if there were such women who were struggling to write, their lives have not been recorded for us to study because they are perhaps in unmarked graves. Woolf's Judith 'killed herself one winter's night and lies buried at some crossroads where the omnibuses now stop outside the Elephant and Castle' (72). Woolf hopes that such rewriting of history through fiction would be generative and the figure of Judith would help women to understand, articulate, and fight the social factors in the way of their creative freedom. She thought that, by this process, Judith would be resurrected because, as she explains to her readers, Judith is latent 'in you and me, and in many other women who are not here tonight, for they are washing up the dishes and putting the children to bed' (150). If given an opportunity, Woolf believes that 'Shakespeare's sister will put on the body which she has often laid down' (151). In other words, Judith might live and thrive and write if we created a society in which she could think, read, and create while someone else took responsibility for doing the dishes and putting children to bed.

Marilyn French, *The Women's Room*

French, who, coincidentally, was born the year that Woolf's essay was published, revived Judith Shakespeare in her novel, *The Women's Room*, which clearly recalls Woolf's essay in the title itself. The novel was published in 1977 but is set in the US in the 1940s–60s. Around this time, feminists were, once more, drawing attention to women's unpaid or poorly-paid domestic labor. Betty Friedan's non-fiction book, *The Feminine Mystique*, often credited with kick-starting the Western second-wave feminist movement, collected qualitative and quantitative data to debunk the notion that women were fulfilled in their roles as wives and mothers—roles that kept them both dissatisfied and extremely busy. Susan Faludi sees French's *The Women's Room* as the 'fiction equivalent' to Friedan's work (520). In this novel, the narrator invokes Woolf's Judith but offers a rewrite: '[Woolf] imagined a violent, an apocalyptic end for Shakespeare's sister, whereas I know that isn't what happened' (French 45–46). The narrator revises the ending of Woolf's story not because the conditions for women have improved so much that they do not have to take recourse in suicide. Rather, she explains that women usually die slowly or live a half-life as underpaid office help on a low wage or as suburban housewives doing unpaid work. According to her, Judith of the mid-twentieth century does not write but probably types in an 'office for thirty-five dollars a week' (45). Alternatively, she 'handles her husband with language: she carps, cajoles, teases, seduces, calculates, and controls this creature' (46).

Thus, she lives but she uses 'her genius, the genius she might have used to make plays and poems with' in making her marriage work (46). Sometimes, the two are combined so that, instead of imagining plays, Judith has to live out her life 'scraping the shit out of diapers with a kitchen knife, finding places where string beans are two cents less a pound, learning to wake at the sound of a cough, spending one's intelligence in figuring the most efficient, least time-consuming way to iron men's white shirts or to wash and wax the kitchen floor or take care of the house and kids' as well as 'work at the same time and save money' (46). This is why the narrator asserts that women cannot write because 'when your body has to deal all day with shit and string beans, your mind does too' (47).

French updates Judith's plight and uses her to relate the barriers that women face in the mid-twentieth century just as Woolf had used Judith to talk about the obstacles that a sixteenth- or seventeenth-century woman might have faced if she wanted to write. However, French's novel does more than just introduce Judith in this short passage. Instead, as I shall demonstrate, the novel's protagonist, Mira, is modeled on Woolf's Judith and this helps French to expand Judith's story and stretch the trope further.

In *A Room of One's Own*, Woolf tells us that Judith is 'wonderfully gifted' (69). Although she is not sent to school, she tries to read her brother's books. Mira, too, is a 'bright child' (French 10). French depicts her as someone who 'finished all the textbooks on the first day of school and, bored, spent the rest of the term enlivening her classmates. The solution decided upon was to move her ahead, into a class "more on her level", as the teacher put it. She was moved ahead several times, but never found such a class' (10). It is interesting to notice how French creates a parallel between Mira and Judith but also registers the difference between their situations in that Judith 'was not sent to school' (Woolf 70) whereas Mira is able to go to school and feed her hunger for reading.

The spatial coordinates of Judith's fictional biography, too, are paralleled with Mira's spatial journey. Woolf sets up a contrast between Shakespeare and his imaginary sister. As he grows older, Shakespeare goes to grammar school whereas Judith 'remained at home' even though she was 'as adventurous, as imaginative, as agog to see the world as he was' (Woolf 70). Whereas Shakespeare reads extensively and has access to literature and philosophy books, Judith's space is intruded upon and we learn that her 'parents came in' as she was attempting to read (70). Then, as Shakespeare, who was well known to be a 'wild boy' poached rabbits and shot deer, Judith 'scribbled some pages up in an apple loft on the sly' (70). Thus, while Shakespeare's world expands at every turn,

Judith's space gets cramped. Her most freeing moment comes when she lets herself 'down by a rope one summer's night and [takes] the road to London' (Woolf 71). However, she soon discovers that the world is not shaped for a woman, and she travels from cramped rooms to hostile spaces in which she is sexually harassed. French delineates Mira's experience similarly. We read that 'Mira was an independent baby, fond of removing her clothes and taking a stroll on a summer's day to the local candy store' (French 10). Although she knows her way home, her mother, 'Mrs Ward began to tie her up' (10). Just like Judith's parents, she did not 'mean to be unkind' (10). Her justification for tying her up is that she had been 'crossing a busy boulevard' (10). Mrs Ward uses 'a long rope, so Mira could still move around, and tied it to the handle of the front door' (10). Therefore Mira gets trained into occupying less space. In time, the leash gets removed and 'Mira showed herself to be a docile and even timid child, only somewhat given to sullenness' (10). Even though, unlike Judith, Mira goes to school and excels, her mother is chiefly interested in making her a desirable marriage partner, so she receives lessons geared towards that goal in elocution, dancing, piano, and watercolor painting (10). This upbringing is gendered; she cannot choose to be 'wild' like the boys because she is taught 'not to climb trees with boys, not to play tag in the alley, and not to speak in a raised voice' (10). Her most liberating moment is when she dances in a pub and is enjoying herself but, like Judith, she is immediately threatened with sexual violence and has to retreat to a locked bedroom for safety (33–36).

Both Judith and Mira seek a man not because they are desirous to marry or settle down but to protect themselves from further unwanted sexual advances. Woolf writes how 'at last Nick Greene the actor-manager took pity' on Judith (71) and Mira feels that 'her dream of choosing and living a life of her own had vanished . . . she had no choice but to protect herself against a savage world she did not understand and by her gender alone was made unfit to deal with' (French 38). So, she marries Norm who treats her kindly. After her marriage, Mira leaves her studies and takes up a job as a 'clerk-typist for $35 a week' so that Norm can continue his medical education (39). Despite the difference in circumstances, however, just like Judith, Mira finds herself pregnant. But her fate differs from Judith. While Judith dies by suicide, Mira survives.

However, instead of being able to realize her ambitions, Mira gets pregnant again. When her kids are young, she is shown juggling housework and caring duties. When they grow older and her material circumstances improve, they move to a bigger house. However, here, too, her organizing skills are employed in domestic duties:

> She bought herself a small file box and some packages of 2x3 cards. On each card she wrote one task that had to be performed, and filed them in sections. The section headed WINDOW WASHING would contain cards for each room in the house. Whenever she washed the windows in one room, she would mark the date down on the card, and place it at the end of the section. The same was true for FURNITURE POLISHING, RUG SHAMPOOING, and CHINA . . . She did not make cards for ordinary, daily cleaning, only for the large, special tasks. So each day, after the small chores of cleaning kitchen, making beds, and cleaning the two main bathrooms, she would also perform a thorough cleaning of one room, washing mirrors and windows, waxing any visible wooden floors, cleaning the small ornaments, dusting ceilings and walls and furniture surfaces, and vacuuming. She would then mark on the appropriate card the large task accomplished. That way, she reasoned, she would always keep up. It took her two weeks to go through the whole house – ten working days. (168–169)

Like the rewrite of Judith in French's novel, Mira too uses her intelligence in 'good housewifery' (169). French, therefore, is urging her readers to see Mira as a mid-twentieth-century Judith. With this depiction, she reveals how, despite Woolf's optimism and expanded opportunities for women, the material circumstances that would lead to creative freedom were still not accessible to women by this point.

Emma Whipday, *Shakespeare's Sister*

In 2016, Whipday revived Judith yet again in her play, *Shakespeare's Sister*. This time, Judith is back in Shakespeare's London as Whipday sets the work in the late sixteenth century. Whipday traces the lineage of her play directly to Woolf. In an episode of the *Women & Shakespeare* podcast, she recalls how up until that point, the literary canon that she had encountered as an undergraduate student at the University of Oxford was very male. Then, she happened to read *A Room of One's Own*:

> I can still really vividly remember sitting in the big circular library, the Radcliffe Camera at Oxford, and reading this idea of these lost female voices from history, these lost female geniuses, and Woolf's vision of a

> kind of literary lineage for herself. And it really did change my mind, changed my life, changed the way I thought about myself as a writer and a scholar ... I thought, "Oh, well I love this narrative of Shakespeare's sister that Woolf's created. It's doing such interesting, important work. I could just adapt it." (Interview)

When we meet Judith Shakespeare in Whipday's play, she is busy scribbling and writing and neglecting the pot of stew that hangs over the fireplace. We realize that she would rather choose the labor of writing than the labor of cooking. In Woolf's version, Judith 'was to be betrothed to the son of a neighbouring wool-stapler' even though 'marriage was hateful to her' (71). In Whipday's version, Judith refuses an offer of marriage from a certain William Underhill and incurs the displeasure of her parents, Mary and John. Mary tells her, 'Judith, you have let this stew spoil. I did not bring you up for a slattern' (*Shakespeare's Sister* 10). Then, as the stage direction informs us, 'Mary *pours water from a pitcher into the stew, and busies herself about the room*' (10). John, on the other hand, forces Judith to confess that she was busy writing a play and says, '[s]o it is for this that you neglect your house affairs' (11). It is significant that both her mother and father frame their disapproval in terms of domestic labor. John proceeds to burn and scatter the pages of the play about the floor and declares, 'Here is your work. Here is your place. Minding your family, not staining yourself with ink. I did not raise you to prostitute yourself to the pen' (12). In their mind, so intrinsic is the connection between women and domestic labor that any neglect of domestic chores signals rebellion and must be curbed.

After this incident, Whipday's Judith follows Woolf's Judith in running away to London. It is there, however, that Whipday makes the biggest change in Judith's story. When Woolf's Judith reached London, she could not even get past the stage-door. Whipday's Judith, however, does enter the theater and moreover, she finds employment there. The theater impresario, Philip Henslowe, does not give her the chance to write for the stage but he does hire her to assist with the costumes. This detail is significant because this is not a complete fabrication of what could have happened. This is the way in which a lot of women participated in Shakespeare's theater. We now know a lot more about women's lives in the period and their involvement in the theater than we knew in Woolf's time. For instance, in her book, *Labors Lost: Women's Work and the Early Modern English Stage*, Natasha Korda marshals a broad range of evidence to challenge the view of Shakespeare's theater as an all-male space and details the 'diverse ways in which women participated in the work of theatrical production' (1). One of the important ways in which they contributed was through working on costumes. Korda gives the example of Mary, niece of the owner of the Rose Theatre in Shakespeare's time, Philip Henslowe. She recovers a record dated 1595 where Henslowe paid for an apprenticeship for his niece Mary so she could 'Learne to sowe al maner of workes & to Lerne bonelace' (quoted Korda 27) and speculates that 'Mary's skill as a sempstress and lace maker would have been a valuable asset in Henslowe's theatrical ventures' (Korda 29). Thus, Judith's profession in Whipday's play names and stages a significant labor that was undertaken by women backstage in Shakespeare's time.

Moreover, as a costume assistant, Judith meets three other women in the theater in Whipday's play: Lucy Morgan, Dorothy Clayton, and Joan Henslowe. Although there is no evidence that these women knew each other, each of them did exist in early modern London. Lucy Morgan, a sex worker in Whipday's play, was a brothel-keeper in Shakespeare's time (Kaufmann 30). Lucy is a playful character in Whipday's play but we find that she is scared of being apprehended and confides how she 'hid in rags in a gutter' when she saw the authorities 'drag the girls from the brothels.' Upon hearing this, Dorothy Clayton assures her and says, 'there, there, love. It's not so bad. They took me last year, and I survived it well enough. Sometimes they let you ride on the cart – they bare your breasts and display you through the streets! It's like a parade' (*Shakespeare's Sister* 35, 55, 56). These details, too, are historically accurate as carting and shaming by making a spectacle of such marginalized women were common enough punishments meted out in Shakespeare's time. The historical Dorothy Clayton was certainly arrested and shamed. On 3 July 1575, the Alderman court records note that one Dorothy Clayton, spinster, 'contrary to all honesty and womanhood commonly goes about the City apparelled in man's attire. She has abused her body with sundry persons and lived an incontinent life. On Friday she is to stand on the pillory for two hours in men's apparell and then to be sent to Bridewell until further order' (quoted Howard 420). In Whipday's play, the woman in charge of these sex-workers is Joan Henslowe. The historical Joan was the stepdaughter of Philip Henslowe and married Edward Alleyn, one of the foremost actors of Shakespeare's day. The historical records are sketchy but documents belonging to Henslowe indicate that Joan was advancing loans to actors on Henslowe's behalf and letters between Joan and her actor-husband indicate that she was somehow involved in his business because he asks her to properly store his white waistcoat and dye his tawny woolen stockings a deep black—both these might have been theatrical costumes. Besides, her husband mentions that he heard a rumor that she was carted along with her companions in his absence. Although this could have been a joke, it might present the possibility that she was more involved in all their businesses than has been hitherto acknowledged.[3]

In Whipday's play, these women join Judith to mount a secret performance of the play she has written because they are all determined to prove themselves to be better performers than the boy and men players. They rehearse and enact Judith's play based on the biblical story from The Book of Esther. In Whipday's play, Judith does not die by suicide but rather is executed on a trumped-up charge of sedition. However, due to the community that she creates around herself, her play does receive one secret performance. Thus, Whipday imagines what might have happened to Shakespeare's sister if she had encountered the company of other women in Shakespeare's time who were similarly struggling to express themselves creatively.

By placing these women in the company of Judith, Whipday not only uses Judith to bring working women out of the archives and put them center stage but she also embeds Judith more firmly in historical consciousness. If Woolf had placed Shakespeare's sister in Shakespeare's London, Whipday fleshes out her life there, imagines the subjects she might write about, the company she might keep, the routes she might take to employment, and ultimately what obstacles she might face because, like other women of Shakespeare's time, she remains on the edge of the public stage and does not flourish as a playwright.

Jo Hamya, *Three Rooms*

Jo Hamya's 2021 novel, *Three Rooms*, is set in the aftermath of the financial crisis of 2008 and post-Brexit Britain; it begins by quoting *A Room of One's Own* and refers to it throughout. Hamya does not directly invoke Judith, like Woolf or French or Whipday do. However, the narrator of Hamya's novel is a Judith-like figure. She is a reader and a writer. She is both struggling to find a room to write and trying to earn by writing so she can afford a room. Although we do not know the protagonist's name, we do know that she is young and is a woman of color. As the novel is set in Britain in the twenty-first century, the protagonist has not only been allowed to go to school and college but also has multiple degrees. However, gig economy and feminized conditions of the labor market mean that an access to a room of one's own and financial independence that would lead to creative freedom are ever more inaccessible to young people, especially those at the intersection of marginalizations. Since women of color are at the crossroads of both gender and race marginalization, they end up with poorly paid and unstable jobs at best and unemployment at worst.

This is true for Hamya's protagonist. Part I of the book begins as she secures the position of a postdoctoral assistant at the University of Oxford after 'almost a year of unemployment; had sent out dozens of applications a week, landing just enough fixed-term minimum wage and freelance work to survive' (Hamya 10). At Oxford, her days are not filled with her own writing, but she is working constantly. In the fifth chapter of this part of the novel, almost every paragraph begins with the words, 'I worked' (42–47) and describes things like grading essays, about which she has disputes with her male supervisor. Although she lives in a room at this prestigious university, she is not able to fully inhabit it as her own. For instance, when she accidently spills a cup of tea on the carpet, she starts frantically mopping because she is panicking that she's 'going to have to pay for this stain out of [her] deposit' (39).

After her time at Oxford, she is filled with a desire to write in the 'real world' (11) by which she means outside academia. Part II of the novel is set in London. However, the job she secures is not writing but copyediting at the 'country's last society magazine' (79). While working here, she lives on a couch in London for £80/month. That is all she can afford because her job pays a day rate of £65, and she works in an environment where the management thinks nothing about the fact that her salary is delayed by a couple of weeks. The girl whose couch the narrator rents often forgets to clean the bathroom. One day the narrator decides to bring this up. 'You forgot to clean the bathroom, I said. It's not a big deal but I ended up having to do it after I got home from work stressed' (143). Her flatmate first appeared unmoved, but the narrator describes that '[e]ventually, I heard her blow out a, Sorry, and as she passed on her way out a murmured, It's my bloody bathroom anyway' (143).

Finally, the narrator fails to secure a permanent job at the magazine and must move back to her parents' house. On route, she remembers how it is a house with 'thin walls', where the last time that she had been to stay 'during the night, I had heard my parents turning in their bed; my father's whistling snore and my mother's gentle breathing. In the morning I had woken them up by closing the front door too loudly when I went out for a run at six. I had irritated them by buying impossible quantities of bread which were invariably left in cupboards to mould past the time I left. Now, I did not even have a set of house keys' (188–89).

Just as she finds it hard to find physical room for her in all these rented and borrowed spaces, there is no space for her in society too and she is psychologically hemmed in. At Oxford, she cannot help noticing that the systems of power are still controlled by elite White men. She cannot fully inhabit Oxford because she knows that this is also the place responsible for 'spawning the government that daily diminished [her] ability to afford a mortgage or the cost of rent' (7). At her London office, she knows that she will never be welcomed because she does not belong to a privileged set. When the former copyeditor is inducting the narrator, she gives an account of the kind of people who work at the magazine. Pointing towards the desks of various people, she says:

> You'll want to know that her father is in the house of Lords, *she* used to sleep with every musician that you can think of in the nineties, and *her* sister does PR at Buckingham Palace. This guy here, his wife is the former editor of the magazine upstairs. What else . . .? He went to uni with a bunch of royals. Ah, and she's about to marry into acting royalty. The rest of them are normal, but either they have been there longer than you've been alive or they're working pretty much for free. (89)

Later, she feels her lack of connections and her status as a woman of color keenly when she explains to her flatmate that '[y]ou should see what it's like in the office. One of my colleagues is rich, typically English-looking girl . . . She's terrible at her job. But she's treated like a daughter by everyone because she has perfect skin, and fits sample size . . . I am not looking to be accepted by them, I just think that it's bollocks that she's more rewarded than I am because she was born one of them' (155–56). So, Hamya traces how women of color writers are rare because this precarity of employment is linked to precarity of space to think, is linked to mental precarity. When you are busy worrying about your next paycheck and your next home, there is no space to create and write, physically or mentally.

Judiths: A Literature of One's Own

Women writers keep coming back to this imaginary figure that Woolf has created. It is worth remembering that, as a writer, Woolf was not in Judith's position. Even though Woolf did not have access to a university education or to libraries that were free to men, she still had the means to write. So, she created the figure of Judith to emphasize the pressures of women's labor in the sixteenth and seventeenth centuries and make the reasons for their comparative exclusion from creative success visible. Woolf demonstrates that one of the things women who are free to write can do is create is a sort of imaginative history that takes account of obstacles in the path of women's creative freedom. These histories may not be factual but might be truthful as they reflect the conditions of most women at the time and make us understand what has been unrecorded and thus gets overlooked as an obstacle in the path of creative freedom.

French makes similar use of the Judith figure. She draws out the impediments in Mira's path, but she also makes something visible. In the final pages of the book, we discover that the narrator, who was updating Judith's story and recounting Mira's life, is Mira herself. Consequently, we realize that that it is Mira who has etched out parallels between Judith and herself. We glean that she is now in her forties, is divorced, her two boys have grown up, and she works at a community college. At this moment, she has discharged her duties for the year at the college, and she has decided to write the story of her life and friends. She has vowed to 'write it all down, go back as far as I have to, and try to make some sense out of it' (French 9). The result of all this writing is the book that we have been reading. When *The Women's Room* was published, it broke many literary conventions of its time. One of its biggest departures from the tradition of women's fiction of the time was that it took the subject of women's work seriously and the patterns of this work informed the style and structure of the book. For instance, Section 1 of Chapter 2 begins with Mira arriving home from the hospital after giving birth to her baby and finding 'dirty dishes' at home (63). The following pages describe her schedule from when she would wake up, first from 2:00am–3:00am to feed one of her babies, and then from 6:30am or 7:00am until night. It lists all the things that she would do in the day from changing 'urinous sheets', cleaning the apartment, getting 'bottles in the steriliser', to cooking, shopping, taking children to the park, balancing carriage, purse, baby, and groceries to scrubbing the floors (63–66). Another section in this chapter details her friend Adele's list: 'Eric [her child] to Cub Scouts, pick up a case of soda for Cub Scout meeting; get Paul's [her husband's] grey suit from the cleaners; Billy [also her child] to the DiNapolis to work on project. MILK, she had scrawled in large letters at the bottom of the page' (92).

Reviewing the book for *The New York Times*, Anne Tyler wrote that the book is 'very long and very narrow' (n.p.). However, she admits that this narrowness is, 'I believe (or hope), intentional'(n.p.). I would argue that it is very deliberate—in fact, it is the whole point. Tyler attests that the novel 'strains our patience, argues, wears us down' (n.p.). Thus, what French has essentially done by giving page upon page of thick description of women's lives is that she has made the reader experience the tediousness of these women's schedules and demonstrated the hundreds of day-to-day unpaid demands on time, labor, and emotional energy that keep women from having successful careers. However, what it significant is that her protagonist, Mira, ends up writing precisely about these details. She makes her schedules, lists, frustrations, and thoughts into her content and uses these as raw materials for her writing. If Woolf's Judith was to come alive when someone else did the dishes and put the children to bed, French suggests that one of the things that Judith could do was write about doing the dishes and putting children to bed. Woolf had proposed that Judith needs a room of her own. French agrees and, in fact, her protagonist, Mira, is unable to write until she has a room of her own. But, by paralleling Mira and Judith and showing her writing, French indicates that women should start writing about their experiences and their life because one of the ways in which Judiths would succeed would be by creating such literature.

The records of the women that Whipday writes about have still not appeared in the *Oxford Dictionary of National Biography* even though there are entries for Philip Henslowe and Edward Alleyn. So, the *herstories* of women and their work get obscured by *history* and the way it is presented. This systemic erasure from the records is the reason for Woolf's claim that 'facts are so hard to come by' (69). Her remedy is to model the use of imagination to reconstruct women's lives and their undocumented labors through the figure of Judith. French takes up Woolf's provocation and makes her readers experience the drudgery of women's routines in the late twentieth century through her construction of two Judiths—one placed in Shakespeare's time and another in the twentieth century. Whipday also espouses Woolf's model; although she bases her Judith on archival records of women workers from the period, she asserts that even if such archival records and facts are available, 'imaginative engagement' with these archives is important as well because the records that we have are 'hugely mediated by men' (Interview). To illustrate Whipday's point, the histories of all three women—Joan, Lucy, Dorothy—are only available to us in documents that are written by men and this is why Whipday suggests that combing through the record for women's lives is important 'but at the same time . . . imaginative work can also give us a way into those voices and experiences, because they always come to us in so mediated a form anyway that actually imagining into the history is one way of sort of filling some of those gaps and those spaces where we know those voices and performances were, but which we can't access' or at least we can't access in their own words (Interview).

Hamya is a woman of color herself. So, her Judith-like figure does important work. It adds to the narratives of Woolf, French, and Whipday by making her reader inhabit the interiority of a narrator who is at the intersection of gender and race marginalization. As Shahidha Bari writes in *The Guardian* review of this book, Hamya gives us a heroine who is 'able neither to afford a home nor to feel at home – not in her temporary accommodations, her workplace, her society or even her nation' (n.p). Hamya's Judith works constantly but shows how material things such as money and space remain outside the reach of most women of color.

Judith thus becomes a trope to think and write about both documented and undocumented unpaid domestic labor or poorly-paid supporting jobs in the capitalist economy that are undertaken by women. In each case, feminist writers such as Woolf, Whipday, French, and Hamya employ the imaginary figure of Shakespeare's sister to demonstrate how these labors expected of women are physical and psychological obstacles in the path of their creative and intellectual aspirations. But paradoxically, they also use her to make room for literature that deems the subject of such feminized labor worthy of recording. By studying the multiple texts in which Judith comes alive, this chapter has demonstrated how Woolf's creation has become both a transhistorical literary barometer to measure women's labors and a device with which to create a canon of women's literature that takes women's work seriously as a literary subject. In other words, Judith Shakespeare does not only appear in *A Room of One's Own*. Rather, she is a room, which can be occupied by writers to articulate an overlooked history of women's labor and turn it into literature of one's own.

Notes

1. Henceforth, I am following Woolf's example of referring to William Shakespeare by his last name, 'Shakespeare', and his fictional sister by her first name, 'Judith'.
2. It is interesting that Marçal acknowledges Woolf's essay in the prologue to her book.
3. For the claim that Joan was advancing loans, see S. P. Cerasano. MSS 7, folios 11r, 65v, and 90r (MSS-7/011r MSS-7/065v MSS-7/090r) [online essay], https://henslowe-alleyn.org.uk/essays/henslowes-diary-1591-1609/. For the letters, see MSS 1 Articles 9 and 11, digitized online, https://henslowe-alleyn.org.uk/transcriptions/mss-1-article-9/ and https://henslowe-alleyn.org.uk/transcriptions/mss-1-article-11/.

Works Cited

Bari, Shahidha. "*Three Rooms* by Jo Hamya review – On Belonging and Inequality." *The Guardian*. 8 July 2021, https://www.theguardian.com/books/2021/jul/08/three-rooms-by-jo-hamya-review-on-belonging-and-inequality.

Cox, Pamela. "Working Women." *Unfinished Business: The Fight for Women's Rights*, edited by Polly Russell and Margaretta Jolly, British Library, 2020.

Faludi, Susan. Afterword. *The Women's Room*, by Marilyn French. 1977. Virago Press, 2014.

Friedan, Betty. *The Feminine Mystique*. George J. McLeod Limited, 1963.

French, Marilyn. *The Women's Room*. 1977. Virago Press, 2014.

Hamya, Jo. *Three Rooms*. Penguin, 2021.

Howard, Jean E. "Crossdressing, the Theatre, and Gender Struggle in Early Modern England." *Shakespeare Quarterly*, vol. 39, no.4, 1988, pp. 418–440.

Kaufmann, Miranda. "'Making the Beast with two Backs'– Interracial Relationships in Early Modern England." *Literature Compass*, vol. 12, no. 1, 2015, pp. 22–37.

Korda, Natasha. *Labors Lost: Women's Work and the Early Modern English Stage*. University of Pennsylvania Press, 2011.

Marçal, Katrine. *Who Cooked Adam Smith's Dinner? A Story of Women and Economics*. Translated by Saskia Vogel, Pegasus Books, 2016.

Perez, Caroline Criado. *Invisible Women: Data Bias in a World Designed for Men*. 2019. Vintage, 2020.

Tyler, Anne. "Starting Out Submissive." *New York Times*. October 16, 1977, https://www.nytimes.com/1977/10/16/archives/starting-out-submissive-submissive.html.

Vives, Juan Luis. *The Instruction of a Christian Woman*. Translated by Richard Hyrde, c.1528.

Whipday, Emma. *Shakespeare's Sister*. Samuel French, 2016.

—. Interview with Varsha Panjwani. "Emma Whipday on Shakespeare's Sister, Shakespeare's Domestic Tragedies, and Practice-Based Research." *Women & Shakespeare*, series 3, Ep. 4, 2022 [podcast] http://womenandshakespeare.com/.

Woolf, Virginia. *A Room of One's Own*. 1929. Pan Macmillan, 2017.

PART II

THE WORK OF CHANGE

4

Comics in the RESISTance: Modeling the Feminized Work of Activism

Leah Misemer

Comics have always been a form of and for resistance. Panel and page divisions and juxtapositions allow creators to 'speak back' through simultaneous representations of a variety of viewpoints, while comics anthologies capture further diversity of thought by also representing multiple creators and styles within the same volume. Yet that resistance has the potential to move beyond the page, to occur via circulation and, in doing so, draws on the strengths of the scholar and the activist, the comic and the protest poster, the print and the digital, the local and the national, the historical and the future-looking. Such was the case for *Resist!*, a comics anthology newspaper meant to build solidarity around protest of the 2016 election of Donald Trump as President of the US (Mouly and Spiegelman 'Submissions'). Trump brought with him a right-wing, anti-woman, xenophobic political agenda that emboldened those with sexist and racist viewpoints, and the 2017 Women's March was organized in protest of these perspectives.[1] Edited by women cartoonists Françoise Mouly and Nadja Spiegelman, the iconography, publication details, and public discourse surrounding *Resist!* situated the anthology within a genealogy of protest comics, feminist print culture, and feminized labor. At the same time, the format, circulation methods, and diverse representations of women-affirming words and images built solidarity around protest of election results by allowing participants and readers to envision a different world that shared their values, rather than the world suggested by the election results.

This discussion of *Resist!* within a volume about the feminization of labor foregrounds comics as a historical and contemporary form of feminist resistance at the same time that it highlights the feminized labor of activism performed by the cartoonists, editors, and distributors of *Resist!*.

This is not to say that all comics are culturally resistant, but they all have the potential to be. From the perspective of comics scholarship, my focus on labor makes us consider comics as not just a form to be read and analyzed, but also as physical objects that circulate as people use them to make arguments and further their agendas. I situate myself within a genealogy of women comics scholars who have remarked on comics as a form of social protest, building on their feminist scholarly labor by combining the techniques of textual and visual analysis with a self-study methodology.[2] The goal of making visible the feminized labor of activism, applied through a self-study methodology more often used in social sciences, contributes to the field of comics studies and literary studies by bringing comics analysis off the page and into the world. Paying attention to comics in circulation allows me both to acknowledge the community building potential they possess as physical objects and to position comics within a larger feminist visual culture that includes protest posters and photographs posted on news sites and social media.

The compilation, distribution, and rhetoric surrounding *Resist!* alluded to the feminized labor of activism as much as it drew on the political power of comics. The self-study methodology, grounded in my own roots in education as a feminist practice, helps make visible the feminized labor of feminist activism.[3] In framing the unpaid labor of activism as feminized labor, I align with Maud Bracke et al, who approach the concept of 'work' through the notion of 'value' (449), as well as with Susan J. Ferguson, who encourages feminists to consider work not necessarily outside of capitalist systems, but work that is life giving rather than life taking within those systems, such as the work of community building (114). All these scholars place paid and unpaid labor alongside one another to consider political, ideological, cultural, and emotional value in addition to economic value and insist that feminized labor does not necessarily have to be performed by women or women-identifying individuals. Instead, feminized labor refers to work traditionally associated with women. I argue that the work of protest qualifies because women have been a historically oppressed group and thus have continually organized activism meant to raise the visibility of, and combat, their oppression. While it may not have economic value and is traditionally unpaid, activism can have emotional, intellectual, cultural, and political value for its participants and others who support a movement. The modeling, artmaking, editing, curating, facilitating, organizing, community building, distributing, and protesting involved in *Resist!* constitute the feminized labor of activism and fall under the rubric of 'work' because each action involves time, effort, resources, and skill. My analysis of *Resist!* recognizes the feminized labor of the cartoonists and editors of the publication and my self-study of organizing a distribution network for *Resist!*, using a combination of old-fashioned and digital tools, both describes what the feminized labor of activism can look like and performs the feminized activist labor of skill sharing. By viewing this work as feminized as well as feminist labor, I open up the possibilities for building bridges across identities and movements, considering how these methods have been or might be deployed by other oppressed groups (Ferguson 134–135). In the conclusion, I discuss how the methods and tools of feminized work I used in distributing *Resist!* transferred to the multiple instances of protest that have pervaded the first few decades of the 21st century.

Genealogies of Protest

The story of how *Resist!* came into being as related in the press situates the publication within a genealogy of protest comics. Gabe Fowler of Desert Island Comics publishes *Smoke Signals*, a quarterly tabloid comics anthology that itself references other comics tabloids from the 1970s counterculture, such as *Yellow Dog* and *Yarrow Stalks*. Fowler asked Françoise Mouly, former editor of the *RAW* alternative comics anthology, to edit a special issue of *Smoke Signals* with comics by women created in response to the election (Mouly and Spiegelman, Interview). In collaboration with her daughter, Nadja Spiegelman, Mouly posted a call on social media and received thousands of responses from both published and unpublished cartoonists who were doctors, school teachers, and, in one instance, a 13-year-old girl. To add to this genealogy, Mouly often situated *Resist!* alongside French protest comics like *Charlie Hebdo* and *Hara Kiri Hebdo* in interviews (Landsbaum; Mouly and Spiegelman, Interview). Elsewhere, I suggest that comics gain this potential for protest through what I call 'correspondence zones,' dialogic spaces within comics that mobilize the tension between sequentiality and simultaneity at different scales—the level of speech or thought bubbles, panels, pages, issues, and so on—to model different ways that marginalized groups can speak back to racist, sexist, misogynist, or otherwise discriminatory claims and opinions of mainstream culture.[4] In the case of this newspaper comics anthology, the various cartoonists model different ways to respond to Trump and his supporters. The modeling in the correspondence zone is a form of skill sharing that follows a feminist print culture tradition. As Jess Baines points out, for example, community poster printers in London in the 1960s and 1970s, such as the See Red Women's Workshop posters discussed in the Introduction to this volume, saw teaching women printing methods as a means of empowerment ('The freedom of the press ...' 116–118). Similarly, in their discussion of workshops in the Women's Liberation Movement, D-M Withers highlights the role of skill sharing in developing women's autonomy (221–229). In the contexts both these authors discuss, the discontinuation of the practice of skill sharing points to the fact that skill sharing and skill learning are forms of feminized work in that they take effort, time, and other resources, and are performed by women in the feminist movement (Baines, 'Nurturing Dissent? ...' 188–189). While the skill sharing these two authors discuss refers to physical labor with mechanical tools, recognizing the intellectual labor of modeling that the cartoonists of *Resist!* perform instead brings to the fore the work of a diverse group of women.

Meanwhile, Spiegelman also positions herself and Mouly within the tradition of feminized labor, specifically care work. Spiegelman told *Vice* that she and Mouly 'were more midwives than editors,' as they were 'trying to add in as many voices as possible so there's the full range and diversity of the collective voice' (Masad). By describing them as 'midwives,' Spiegelman suggests that she and Mouly might curate, arrange, edit, and facilitate the cartoonists, aligned in Spiegelman's metaphor to birth givers, in performing the work of artistic production. In essence, Spiegelman positions the creation of *Resist!*, both the cartooning and the editing, as an act of feminized labor. While previous feminist movements have been critiqued for the ways they alienated working-class women, as well as women of color, women with disabilities, and LGBTQ+ women, Spiegelman's quote also highlights how the low barrier to entry results in diversity of not just skill, but race, age, and ability. This diversity is so important to Mouly and Spiegelman that they mention it in the introduction to *Resist!*: 'The quantity, quality, and the diversity of the work we collected are staggering. Artists of all genders, ethnicities, religions, and sexual orientations, Midwestern artists and immigrants, celebrated cartoonists and 13-year-old girls heeded the call and grabbed their pens.' This diverse community of creators allows multiple representations of how the community reading the publication can speak back against the Trump administration and its followers. Mouly and Spiegelman encourage attention to that diversity through captions on each entry in the publication that identify the perspectives of the various creators.

Figure 4.1 'A Matter of Time' excerpt, MariNaomi, 2017. Used with permission

For example, the caption for MariNaomi's 'A Matter of Time' identifies them as Japanese-American and the creator of the Cartoonists of Color and Queer Cartoonists databases. The comic shows how the multiplicity of the comics form—its division into panels, thought bubbles, and speech bubbles for different characters in this case—along with the simultaneous presence of these multiple parts on a single page, creates correspondence zones that represent a method for speaking back against the racism that became so visible after Trump's election. In the first three panels, we see the main character as the only one drawn with some detail in color amongst a crowd of white silhouettes. The main character's thought bubbles are the central focus, drawn large and centered within the three top panels as the character wonders how many of the faceless white silhouettes do not want them there or whether they should get out before the 'point of no return' that the victims of the Holocaust faced. In the second row of panels, the main character gets on the subway and MariNaomi depicts them seated on the other side of the bench from a white man and woman who are the same colour as the white silhouettes in previous panels, only they are shown in the same detail as the main character with faces and clothing. The man wears a red cap evoking the 'Make America Great Again' (MAGA) caps so popular with Trump supporters. In the central panel of the bottom row, where MariNaomi depicts faces for the first time and draws people in more detail, the central positioning of the speech bubble coming from the white woman says, 'Go back to your country.' In the first three panels, the main character wanders in relative anonymity, though drawing attention because of their colour, wondering which of the white people they move amongst might want them to leave. In this bottom central panel, the people who 'don't want me here' make themselves known as symbolized by the fact that they acquire faces. The presence of the red MAGA hat at the moment of recognition seems to reference the way such racism was emboldened and thus became visible after Trump's election. Yet the main character gets to speak back and have the last word, here, as they say 'This is my country' in a speech bubble placed with a similar primacy to the speech bubble from the white woman in the previous panel. The two different speech bubbles within two different panels show MariNaomi taking advantage of the multiplicity of the comics form both to represent what they are speaking out against and to model a response, as the racist comment and the response appear on the page simultaneously, with the same positioning within the panels. Yet if we read the comic sequentially, the main character, the character of colour, has the last word, demonstrating the speaking back that comics enables. Unlike whatever racism might exist amongst the silent, anonymous crowd, the main character can voice their objections in the interpersonal interaction on the subway.

Cartoonist Cece Bell provides a different perspective on using one's voice in protest of Trump's public denigration of, in her case, the deaf community in her comic 'Voice.' Mobilizing the multiplicity of the comics form, Bell both represents Trump's mocking comments about deaf actress Marlee Matlin and responses to those comments from the deaf community, specifically responses from Matlin and Bell. The title of the comic highlights how this kind of printed response allows her to talk back to Trump. Indeed, in the final panel of the comic, she identifies the comic as her voice, even though it is printed, and uses a speech bubble to implore readers to remember that Trump represents only himself and we should love each other no matter what. However, whereas MariNaomi's speech bubble represents a short interpersonal interaction that we might characterize as 'verbal,' Bell's is distinctly printed, long and composed rather than conversational. Also, unlike MariNaomi's main character, Bell's response is non-confrontational, acknowledging her hurt and reminding herself and her readers that Trump does not represent the whole world, a fear that echoes MariNaomi's main character's fear in the first three panels of their comic.

Figure 4.2 Untitled, Quinn Nelson, 2017. Reprinted with permission

While MariNaomi and Bell use verbal and printed words to speak back, 13-year-old Quinn Nelson uses an image of raw emotion: a single panel depicts a young girl screaming with her eyes clenched and neck straining. The image is tense, angry, and confrontational with teeth exposed in the girl's wide-open mouth. The girl is disheveled, hair coming undone, and overalls slipping off her shoulder. Blood drips from the top of the panel behind the figure. The text surrounding the figure references frustration with her suppression as a young girl, implying that her will to scream and fight will fill the deafening silence that suppresses her. This image printed in this publication is how Nelson speaks, or rather, screams, back and contributes to the fight with the other artists whose work is represented here. Rather than one element of the comic coming in dialogue with another element of the comic, as happens with the speech bubbles in both Bell's and MariNaomi's comics, the correspondence zone in Nelson's comic exists between her and the imagined oppressors she responds to.

Taken together, MariNaomi's, Nelson's, and Bell's comics represent the diversity of contributors who bring a variety of responses to the publication. While MariNaomi and Nelson express anger and frustration with a world that silences or wants to erase them, Bell responds by acknowledging her hurt and then reminding herself that Trump does not represent the whole world. Looking at additional contributions only expands the range of responses. Jess Hutchison's distressed psychedelic faces accompanied by the words 'shock,' denial,' and 'anger,' along with Jazmine Boatman's depiction of a black woman pierced by an American flag, are contributions that demonstrate emotional response similar to Nelson's. Julie Wilson's contribution suggests a prescient link between comics and protest posters considering how protestors used *Resist!* at the Women's March: her comic consists of a 3 × 4 grid of squares with each square containing iconography and text that you might find on a protest poster, such as the panel with 'We shall overcomb' surrounded by multi-colored combs, which references Martin Luther King Jr.'s 'We shall overcome' slogan from the Civil Rights era and combines it with mocking Trump's comb-over hairstyle. Through their reference to protest posters, Wilson's panels suggest that another way to speak back is through collective activism, a common response from many contributors. Many contributions depict diverse groups of women standing together in various settings, such as outside Planned Parenthood (Radtke), in front of armed policemen (Zarders), colored by a rainbow flag (Taylor), or coming after Trump (Seitchik). As mentioned in famous cartoonist Alison Bechdel's contribution, these diverse groups are a direct response to the fact that suburban white women mostly voted for Trump over Hillary Clinton. In her comic, Bechdel uses her characters from *Dykes to Watch Out For* to offer a variety of possible responses to Trump's election, from the outrageous—building a fallout shelter and deleting all social media—to the emotional—depression, fear, anger—to the practical—call your representatives and don't get paralyzed with despair. The final panel spans the whole page and gathers all the characters together for a toast to 'One for all and all for one,' suggesting that collective action should be accompanied by support of one another across differences. Such shows of support are particularly important when it comes to violence perpetrated against specific groups, as indicated in the final speech bubble's reference to 'When they came for the trade unionists . . .,' a well-known saying associated with the way Nazis attacked different groups during the Second World War. Regardless of who we might agree with, this diversity of perspectives on how to respond to the post-election world represents an advantage of the way the anthology format can represent a community in a single print space without flattening its differences. All these contributors engage in the feminized labor of modeling responses in the tradition of skill sharing. The next section continues in the tradition of skill sharing as I detail my experience organizing a distribution network for *Resist!*, highlighting the digital and face to face opportunities for community building to move out of the anthology and into the real world.

Organizing Circulation

There was much commercialization of the Women's March that used audience investment in feminist messaging to market products such as t-shirts, pussy hats, buttons, bags, and so on. Yet Mouly, Spiegelman, and Fowler worked against such commercialization and trivialization of activism by providing *Resist!* for free. Instead of tapping into the growing network of women following the Women's March Facebook page in order sell them something, the editors of *Resist!* formed a grassroots distribution network, facilitated online, but with the ultimate goal of getting the tabloid-sized publication into as many hands as possible.[5] Mouly highlights this link between the print and digital in the Introduction when she describes the publication as 'a combination of the old-fashioned—a give-away tabloid newspaper, once ubiquitous and now all but extinct—and the new—the impressive democratic power of the Internet.' While I am sure the process of getting involved was different for all participants, I provide my own experience coordinating a *Resist!* distribution network in Madison, WI as an example of how its circulation helped create a sense of solidarity with online spaces facilitating person-to-person relationships. The collection of artifacts for the self-study includes digital correspondence, social media postings (primarily from Facebook), reflections after the fact, and online documentation, which for me combined with the more traditional public scholarly task of popular media appearances, though I arranged the latter in the service of the organizing process. In describing this process, I am at once performing the feminized labor of activism in the form of skill sharing (much like the cartoonists discussed above) and analyzing that labor to make the feminized work of activism visible.

My scholarly interests in the correspondence zones of comics have shown me that art as activism has power, and, as a result, I wanted to help get *Resist!* out to as many people as possible. I coordinated distribution efforts with national and regional personnel and managed seven local volunteers who reached out to me based on a post that I shared on Facebook. Because of the multiple layers of sharing available for Facebook at the time, I ended up with some people from my direct network, but the majority of my volunteers were friends of friends. The volunteers came from a wide range of professions and included librarians, healthcare workers, and one self-described disability activist. Prior to distribution, I deployed asynchronous digital tools to help my local network feel a sense of community, asking folks to introduce themselves and why they were interested in participating as a way of encouraging discussion. Responses ranged from wanting to overcome a sense of isolation to wanting to break the silences surrounding treatment of women of colour to believing in the power of art to change the way people see the world.

These responses helped us start to build a sense of solidarity and some of the organizing we did to facilitate the distribution of 1500 copies of the publication to coffee shops, comics stores, book stores, and the local library in Madison prepared us for other activism in the long months and years to come. For example, one of my participants and I collaborated on a phone script for people to use when contacting potential distributors, a genre that would become increasingly important for future elections. While much of the contact was facilitated digitally, the fact that we were ultimately tasked with distributing a print publication meant that many of us eventually met in person, if only to pick up the allotted copies people were assigned to distribute. At a time when I was personally walking around wondering who I could trust, these person-to-person interactions, accompanied by the asynchronous digital introductions, provided a much-needed sense of community for me and my fellow distributors. We all felt similarly horrified by recent events and it was comforting to see people turning outrage into action.

As the Women's March approached, I shared articles on *Resist!* from high-profile publications like *New York Magazine*, *Huffington Post*, and *Vogue*, while also doing interviews for local newspapers and a local radio broadcast.[6] In these interviews, my expertise as a comics scholar supported my activist message. For example, in the *Capital Times* I said that I 'believe in the power of word and image to expose and confront people with ideas that might not be visible otherwise,' a statement which draws on my research (Christians 'Drawing Attention'). Getting the word out about *Resist!* raised awareness of how comics could be used to build solidarity—first online and then via person-to-person connections—at a time when people were seeking a community that election results threatened to render invisible. Recognizing local expressions of this community helped build awareness of the national community of resistance, while at the same time highlighting the feminized labor activists engaged in.

The day of the March, we were like newspaper boys on corners, hawking this publication of comics by women to marchers. 'Comics' and 'women' were, in my experience, keywords that encouraged people to grab a copy. My small collection was gone in minutes and other organizers reported similar interest. Some marchers read them while waiting to march, others stuffed them in backpacks to share with friends and family later. But the most interesting use of the publication was as a poster. The *Resist!* website posted photos of people from such places as Louisiana, Maine, Washington, San Francisco, and Paris holding up copies of *Resist!* amongst protest signs (Mouly and Spiegelman 'Add to social media'). As a tabloid-sized publication with eye-catching graphic design, *Resist!* encourages this usage. The front cover depicts the title in a bold, red font that mimics a marker-drawn sign above a watercolor image of a crowd of diverse women that recede into the distance (Kabacker), and the full page back image shows a woman at a protest wearing a red hat that says 'Grab back' in high contrast white font (Levine). When someone picked up *Resist!* at the March, it was easy to just open the newspaper and use either side in place of or alongside a sign. These comics add a new dimension to the idea of comics as protest that moves beyond representation to providing actual tools—in this case protest signs—for activism.

From the perspective of skill sharing, the lessons I take away from examining this experience are numerous. While social media provided a useful tool for initially reaching out to an audience beyond one's direct network, applying more direct applications of digital sharing (email, text, WhatsApp, GroupMe, etc.) to follow up on social media connections helped build a clearer sense of solidarity and community that cut through the 'noise' so ever-present on social media. Beyond building community amongst activist participants, phone or text scripts with clear, concise goals helped each member of that community engage while also growing the size of the community and widening its scope. Scholars whose research is related to a movement can help grow that community even more through well-timed public sharing of their research that connects their expertise to concerns of the current moment. While phone scripts and corner distribution might seem old-fashioned, they add value to contemporary activism through synchronous interpersonal interaction and should not be discounted. Print publications in general can help to facilitate both person-to-person interaction, and comics in particular can help, quite literally, to raise the visibility of a cause, especially when they are printed in large format with a design that reads well from far away. In this latter instance, a publication appropriate for private reading can be used as a poster that is part of a collective cause. All these elements—digital community building, community expansion, public sharing, and protesting—constitute the feminized labor of activism in our current political climate.

Conclusion

Unfortunately, the Women's March was only the beginning of a sustained period where activism and protest followed the global rise of the political right. In the US under Trump, the Muslim travel ban, the outlawing of gender-neutral bathrooms, and pandemic response all warranted an activist response. Globally, 2020 saw the rise of the Black Lives Matter Movement and the first Climate Action Day, followed in 2022 by the Women Life Freedom movement in Iran. Most recently as of 2024, protests in the US have centered around women's reproductive rights and trans rights. Elements of the feminized labor I describe here reappeared in these other moments of protest. For example, the phone script, and its cousin the text script, became ubiquitous during subsequent movements as activists sought to encourage people to express their outrage to representatives at all levels of government. Similarly, the use of digital tools to organize the distribution network described here was deployed during protests that took place during the pandemic, when in-person community was a health risk. All of these movements, no matter the cause, involved the feminized labor of protest with organizers using a combination of in-person interaction (when it was safe) and digital organizing.

The work of distributing *Resist!* in conjunction with the Women's March provides a case study for how academics can move expertise outside the ivory tower to engage in the feminized labor of activism. In her article 'Making Academic Feminism More Public,' Margaret McGladrey urges scholars to go beyond media appearances in their outreach and states that 'the work of public intellectuals comprises the art of mobilizing counter-publics,' a claim that highlights how scholars can be activists who perform the feminized labor of protest (1038). This work involves acknowledging both the labor involved in activism and ourselves as scholars and educators with knowledge of historical precedents and pedagogical methods that can be valuable for growing activist communities. Of course, we must not be too quick to take charge when non-academics show leadership potential and should always endeavor to also learn from those around us in activist contexts, but we should acknowledge that we can lend a hand when it is needed, and we should find ways to value the emotional, intellectual, and physical labor of protest.

Comics scholars, who study a form of popular culture that reaches broad audiences through its combination of image and text germane to protest, may position themselves as academic ambassadors. As such, we benefit from moving beyond just visual and textual analysis to consider how people use comics in the world to make things happen. We might benefit from additional research using feminist or other social science-oriented methodologies like self-study that view comics as circulating objects. We might also consider spearheading additional initiatives like *Resist!* that encourage solidarity building through the comics anthology format in conjunction with other forms of activism and other protests.

The lesser-known second issue of *Resist!* demonstrates how important the feminized labor of activism involved in establishing distribution networks was to the spread of the publication and the growth of the activist community. The size of a comic book rather than a newspaper, and mostly distributed through comics shops on a volunteer basis, starting in July 2017 (the publication was available in Diamond Comics Distributors, where most comics shops purchase stock), the publication loses some of its urgency and power. In issue 1, the March was on the horizon, a possibility that had not yet occurred. In that context, the publication served as a vehicle for solidarity building, providing an opportunity to make connections through person-to-person sharing. Issue 2 required no grassroots organizing, and limiting distribution to comics shops meant its audience was mainly comics fans. It was still free but failed to mobilize the feminized labor of activism. However, for issue 2, the March was in the past, and, as a result, became part of the visual iconography that people used to envision the kind of world they wanted to live in, a world where art has power, a world where diversity is valued, a world where protest is a form of community.

Notes

1. For additional scholarship on the Women's March, see Gantt-Shafer et al. 221–240 and Felmlee et al., as well as Presley and Presswood (61–71), who use a self-study methodology similar to my own.
2. See Tilley 161–179; Whitted *EC Comics*; and Galvan 68–85 for examples of women comics scholars discussing comics as a form of social protest.
3. See Hamilton and Pinnegar 234–240 and Feldman 'Validity and Quality' in response for discussions of self-study methodology in education research.
4. See Misemer, 'Subverting Stigma' 135–152 and Misemer, 'Serial Critique' 6–26.
5. Originally, they planned to distribute individual copies online where anyone who wanted could email and ask for a copy. When they were overwhelmed with requests, they started a distribution network where the printer shipped boxes to key sites in larger cities and those larger cities distributed bundles to nearby smaller cities. My bundle came from Chicago. Anyone who didn't

have distribution nearby was able to submit a form and receive an individual copy while supplies lasted.

6. For examples of articles I posted see Landsbaum, 'Here's How Women Artists . . .;' Frank, 'The Radical, Feminist Comic Book We Need,' and Felsenthal, 'Going to the Women's March.'

Works Cited

Baines, Jess. "'The freedom of the press belongs to those who control the press': The Emergence of Radical and Community Printshops in 1970s London." *Communicative Approaches to Politics and Ethics in Europe*, edited by Nico Carpentier, Tartu Press, 2009, 113–127.

—. "Nurturing Dissent?: Community Printshops in 1970s London." *Civic Engagement and Social Media: Political Participation Beyond Protest,* edited by Julie Uldam and Anne Vestergaard, Palgrave Macmillan, 2015, pp. 174–193.

Bechdel, Alison. "Pièce de Résistance." *Resist!*, edited by Françoise Mouly and Nadja Spiegelman, Desert Island, 2017, n.p.

Bell, Cece. "Voice." *Resist!*, edited by Françoise Mouly and Nadja Spiegelman, Desert Island, 2017, n.p.

Boatman, Jazmine. Untitled. *Resist!*, edited by Françoise Mouly and Nadja Spiegelman, Desert Island, 2017, n.p.

Bracke, Maud, et al. "Women, Work and Value in Post-War Europe: Introduction." *Contemporary European History*, vol. 28, no. 4, 2019, pp. 449–53, https://doi.org/10.1017/S0960777319000225.

Christians, Lindsay. "Drawing Attention: As Trumps Inauguration Looms, Madison Artists Respond and Organize." *The Capital Times*, 18 January 2017, https://captimes.com/entertainment/arts-and-theatre/drawing-attention-as-trumps-inauguration-looms-madison-artists-respond-and-organize/article_6cdf5068-1e70-56a2-bbc7-d39d7c31c188.html.

Feldman, Allan. "Validity and Quality in Self Study." *Educational Researcher,* vol. 32, no. 3, 2016, doi: 10.3102/0013189X032003026.

Felmlee, Diane H., et al. "The Geography of Sentiment Towards the Women's March of 2017." *PLoS ONE*, vol. 15, no. 6, 2020, doi:10.1371/journal.pone.0233994.

Felsenthal, Julia. "Going to the Women's March?: You're Going to Want to Get Your Hands on *Resist!*" *Vogue,* 19 January 2017, https://www.vogue.com/article/resist-francoise-mouly-nadja-spiegelman.

Ferguson, Susan. *Women and Work: Feminism, Labor, and Social Reproduction.* Pluto Press, 2020.

Frank, Priscilla. "The Radical, Feminist Comic Book We Need to Survive the Trump Presidency." *Huffington Post,* 26 December 2016, https://www.huffpost.com/entry/women-comic-resist-trump_n_586146a7e4b0d9a59458d0aa.

Galvan, Margaret. "On Anthologies and Activism: Building an LGBTQ+ Comics Community." *The LGBTQ+ Comics Studies Reader*, edited by Alison Halsall and Jonathan Warren, University of Mississippi Press, 2022, pp. 68–85.

Gantt-Shafer, Jessica, et al. "Intersectionality, (Dis)unity, and Processes of Becoming at the 2017 Women's March." *Women's Studies in Communication*, vol. 42, no. 2, 2019, pp. 221–240, doi:10.1080/07491409.2019.1616021.

Hamilton, Mary Lynn and Stefinee Pinnegar. "On the Threshold of a New Century: Trustworthiness, Integrity, and Self-Study in Teacher Education." *Journal of Teacher Education,* vol. 51, no. 3, 2002, pp. 234–240, doi: 10.1177/0022487100051003012.

Hutchison, Jess. Untitled. *Resist!*, edited by Françoise Mouly and Nadja Spiegelman, Desert Island, 2017, n.p.

Kabacker, Gayle. Untitled. *Resist!*, edited by Françoise Mouly and Nadja Spiegelman, Desert Island, 2017, n.p.

Landsbaum, Claire. "Here's How Women Artists Are Reacting to Donald Trump's Presidency." *The Cut*, 21 December 2016, https://www.thecut.com/2016/12/heres-how-women-artists-are-reacting-to-a-trump-presidency.html.

Levine, Gillian. Untitled. *Resist!,* edited by Françoise Mouly and Nadja Spiegelman, Desert Island, 2017, n.p.

MariNaomi. "Matter of Time." *Resist!*, edited by Françoise Mouly and Nadja Spiegelman, Desert Island, 2017, n.p.

Masad, Ilana. "Inside the Anti-Trump Comics Collection *Resist!*" *Vice*, 19 January 2017, https://www.vice.com/en/article/kbbawn/inside-the-anti-trump-comics-collection-resist.

McGladrey, Margaret. "On Making Academic Feminism More Public." *Signs: Journal of Women, Culture, and Society,* vol. 45, no. 4, 2020, pp. 1035–1057.

Misemer, Leah. "Subverting Stigma: Community Building in Serial Comics." *Pathographics: Narrative, Aesthetics, Contention, Community*, edited by Susan Merrill Squier and Irmela Marei Krüger-Fürhoff, Penn State University Press, 2020, pp. 135–152.

—. "Serial Critique: The Counterpublic of *Wimmen's Comix*." *Inks: The Journal of the Comics Studies Society,* vol. 3, no. 1, 2019, pp. 6–26, doi:10.1353/ink.2019.0001.

Mouly, Françoise and Nadja Spiegelman. "Add to social media with #ResistSubmission." *Resist!*, accessed via the Wayback Machine, https://web.archive.org/web/20170802101749/http://www.resistsubmission.com/resistsubmission.html. Accessed 1 March 2023.

—. Interview with Betsy Gomez. *Comic Book Legal Defense Fund,* 13 January 2017, https://cbldf.org/2017/01/exclusive-interview-francoise-mouly-and-nadja-spiegelman-resist/?fbclid=IwAR0ZCfwnXjFx28NpoeeUQ5Yhta-jSQsvWc9T1iiDV7qeJ-Z0HNlWeVo0oqM.

—. "Submissions." *Resist!*, via the Wayback Machine, https://web.archive.org/web/20170723013847/http://www.resistsubmission.com/. Accessed 1 March 2023.

Nelson, Quinn. Untitled. *Resist!*, edited by Françoise Mouly and Nadja Spiegelman, Desert Island, 2017, n.p.

Presley, Rachel E and Alane L. Presswood. "Pink, Brown, and Read All Over: Representation at the 2017 Women's March on Washington." *Cultural Studies, Critical Methodologies*, vol. 18, no. 1, 2018, pp. 61–71, https://doi.org/10.1177/1532708617735134.

Radtke, Kristin. Untitled. *Resist!*, edited by Françoise Mouly and Nadja Spiegelman, Desert Island, 2017, n.p.

Seitchik, Daryl. Untitled. *Resist!*, edited by Françoise Mouly and Nadja Spiegelman, Desert Island, 2017, n.p.

Taylor, Rio Aubry. "The Spirit Will Never Die." *Resist!*, edited by Françoise Mouly and Nadja Spiegelman, Desert Island, 2017, n.p.

Tilley, Carol. "Children and the Comics: Young Readers Take on the Critics." *Protest on the Page: Essays on Print and the Culture of Dissent*, edited by James L. Baughman, et al., University of Wisconsin Press, 2015, pp. 161–179.

Whitted, Qiana. *EC Comics: Race, Shock, and Social Protest*. Rutgers University Press, 2019.

Wilson, Julie. "Build a wall around Trump." *Resist!*, edited by Françoise Mouly and Nadja Spiegelman, Desert Island, 2017, n.p.

Withers, D-M. "The Politics of the Workshop: Craft, Autonomy and Women's Liberation." *Feminist Theory*, vol. 21, no. 2, 2020, pp. 217–34.

Zarders, Sophia. Untitled. *Resist!*, edited by Françoise Mouly and Nadja Spiegelman, Desert Island, 2017, n.p.

5

Mothers of Invention: New Maternal Writings, Women, and Precarious Work Culture

Roberta Garrett

In October 2022, the protest group 'Pregnant Then Screwed', founded by Joeli Brearly, organized marches across the UK to protest the soaring cost of childcare and the continuing workplace discrimination against pregnant women and mothers. Although there has undoubtedly been a resurgence of feminist activism in the last decade, much of this has been focused on sexuality, sexual assault, and gender-based violence.[1] This chapter will argue that other recent events, specifically the attack on women's bodily autonomy in the US (Abrams and Popli), the persistent gender inequalities in domestic labor revealed in lockdown (Casey and Huq), and the gendered effects of casualization and the gig economy (Argawala and Chun; James), have also resulted in a new radicalism in maternal writing and a thematic concern with the precarious and exploitative nature of maternal employment. It uses a combination of feminist sociology and cultural theory and close textual readings to extend the existing critical work on new cycles of maternal writing in the late 1990s and twenty-first century[2] to explore and analyze Rachel Yoder's use of the surreal and the Todorovian fantastic[3] in *Nightbitch* (2021), Anne Whitehouse's searing critique of digital mothering culture in *Underbelly* (2021), and Jessamine Chan's dystopian fantasy of maternal incarceration in *The School for Good Mothers* (2022).

To appreciate the more radical outlook of these texts, it is useful to consider the emergence and evolution of maternal writing in the twenty-first century. In 2001 Rachel Cusk began her landmark maternal memoir, *A Life's Work: On Becoming a Mother* by stating that 'It was my impression, when I became a mother, that nothing had been written about it at all' (3). Cusk is emphasizing what she describes as the 'tone deafness' that younger, childless women often adopt towards the many forms of discrimination that mothers face prior to becoming mothers themselves. Yet in hindsight, it is evident that Cusk was also drawing attention to the absence of feminist work on motherhood following influential second-wave texts such as Adrienne Rich's *Of Woman Born*, Alice Walker's *In Search of our Mother's Gardens*, and Carolyn Steedman's *Landscape for a Good Woman*. Cusk's text was part of the resurgence of autobiographical and fictional texts that brought the exploration of motherhood to the forefront of female-orientated literary culture again (Garrett *Writing* 1–20). Indeed, there have now been much greater numbers of texts on this issue produced in the latter decade of the twentieth and first decades of the twenty-first century than during the peak years of the second-wave feminist writing.[4]

The re-emergence of writing on the maternal coincided with a marked expansion of sociopolitical discourse on parenthood in the 1990s and noughties, much of which cast an unforgiving eye over maternal behavior. As many sociologists and cultural critics have demonstrated[5] the government-led regulation of parenting practices framed neoliberal attacks on social welfare provision and reduced funding for health and education as a child-centered concern with raising parenting standards. State and media discourses (such as parenting-based reality television shows) placed the blame for social problems, such as rising youth crime rates, poor infant health, and educational failure, on 'failing' families and inadequate or lazy mothers (Jensen and Tyler). This punitive discourse emerged in tangent with a highly idealized, greatly expanded, and semi-professionalized maternal role, famously described by Sharon Hays as 'intensive mothering' and Douglas and Michaels as 'new momism.' In the UK and US, the culture of parent-blame emerged with the rise of the new right in the 1980s, but continued under center-left governments.[6] It formed a key part of a longer sociopolitical shift away from consensus politics and social democracy towards the ideological and cultural endorsement of privatization, overt competition, and self-governance that enveloped and came to define 'common sense' attitudes towards child welfare, education, and parenting practices. These attitudes were firmly established prior to the increasing digitalization of much parenting culture with—as we will see in *Underbelly*—predictable consequences in terms of the often competitive, Manichean view of mothering perpetuated by the culture of *Mumsnet* (Jensen 'Mumsnettiquette'), the drift towards the increasing commercialization of mommy blogging (Cummings; Hunter; Meyer and Milestone; Morrison), and more recently, the rise of mother-influencers (Wegener et al.).[7]

The cycles of creative fiction and non-fiction that responded to the punitive sociocultural approach to mothering ranged from those that either covertly or directly endorsed the new orthodoxy of intensive mothering, such as the mother-blaming misery memoir (Garrett *Writing* 21–43) or the comic mom or dad's lit novel (Garrett 'Novels and Children'; *Writing* 97–119) and those that challenged it—such as the maternal memoir or domestic crime novel.[8] The latter tended to focus on conflicts and tensions produced by the enhanced mothering role for married white, middle-class women who had hitherto lived relatively independent lives (Quiney; Garrett *Writing* 71–95). Issues of real economic hardship therefore only surfaced in the most conservative of these cycles, the child-centered/mother-blaming misery memoir, i.e. texts such as Dave Pelzer's *A Child Called It* or Constance Briscoe's *Ugly*, in which the triumphant survivor of childhood abuse castigates the feckless, lower class and/or ethnic-minority maternal figure for their aversion to 'honest' work and the resulting economic deprivation that they experienced (Garrett *Writing* 21–43).

Nevertheless, the issue of whether women could combine professional careers with intensive mothering loomed large in many of the cycles. Maternal memoirs by novelists and academics such as Cusk (2001), Anne Enright (2004), and, more recently, Anna Prushinskaya (2017) and Pragya Agarwal (2021) explore the conflict between artistic and intellectual endeavors and the powerful cultural imposition of socially validated ways of thinking and feeling about motherhood. Coming from a very different sociopolitical perspective, comic mom's lit novels, such as *I Don't Know How She Does It,* written by right-wing columnist Allison Pearson, focused on the challenges faced by mothers in the corporate world.

One of the figures that emerged in the comic mom's lit cycle that has continued to appear in cultural representations of modern working mothers is the 'mompreneur': the mother who leaves full-time employment to establish a successful home-based business using skills that are closely related to her mothering and domestic role. The heroine of Pearson's novel, Kate Reddy, is typical of the late 1990s' fictionalization of this stereotype. Reddy leaves her highly paid job as hedge-fund manager in a blue-chip company to spend more time with her children but also achieves 'work-life balance' by devoting any additional time to acting as a consultant for a small business making traditional dolls houses. The figure of the mompreneur chimes well with the neoliberal endorsement of all forms of individual entrepreneurism while still potentially allowing the mother to succeed at the 'intensive' mothering role. As feminist scholars have demonstrated, the figure of the business-savvy, thriving, financially independent but also unthreateningly feminine mompreneur is a neo-traditionalist fantasy.[9] Ella Harris also points out that this figure was particularly visible after the financial crash of 2008, constituting one amongst many 'compensatory cultures' that attempted to repackage the financial stress and instability that accompanies workplace precarity as flexibility and entrepreneurial opportunity (75–78).

The popularization of the mompreneur in comic mom's lit and multiple press stories glosses over the fact that, far from choosing to become entrepreneurs, many mothers are edged out of professional roles that they strived for many years to obtain due to taking maternity leave (Garrett 'Austerity Culture' 99–114). Many others return to work but struggle to maintain their careers as they are weighed down by the considerable burden of intensive mothering, while their male colleagues are free to focus wholly on their careers whether they have children or not. The intensive mothering role comes with the expectation of high involvement in time-consuming school and extra-curricular activities, sole responsibility for their child's healthcare and the rarely questioned assumption that they will manage all childcare related issues (Glaser; Lockman 19–36; Orgad 26–74). Perhaps more significantly, in addition to ignoring the reasons mothers are either covertly or overtly ejected from their prior careers after becoming mothers, the mompreneur fantasy also conceals the inconvenient fact that most small UK/US business start-ups fail within the first few years (Eisenmann).

Responding to the ubiquity of this figure in female-orientated print and online media platforms, the mompreneur trope was recently parodied in Sharon Hogan's popular BBC comedy, *Motherland* (season 2). Amanda, the most competitive and ideologically compliant of *Motherland*'s affluent mothers, brags of her mompreneur status after opening a lifestyle 'store' which aims to sell luxury items (such as scatter cushions and scented candles) to other wealthy mothers. Amanda struggles to combine work with performative intensive motherhood and succeeds only in alienating even her most loyal mom-friends by demanding their unpaid support. The shop, which has been financed entirely by her high-earning ex-husband, flounders within months. Not wanting to admit defeat, Amanda launches an online selling site which also fails to generate any income. Hogan's sharp-eyed satire of contemporary mothering culture illustrates how far 'mompreneurship' is from providing the perfect solution to what is wrongly described in gender-neutral terms as 'work/life' balance, even for privileged women. The mompreneur fantasy derives from an unequal labor market in which becoming a mother may result in being pushed out of a relatively secure job and towards home-based, small-scale selling ventures that rarely reproduce the mother's previous income or conditions (Garrett 'Novels and Children'; Harris).

It's a Dog's Life: Rachel Yoder's *Nightbitch* and the Failed Mompreneur

Bearing this in mind, I want to turn to the first of the recent novels under consideration, Rachel Yoder's *Nightbitch*. As a novel that focuses on the lives of affluent white, middle-class mothers of young children, *Nightbitch* shares many of the preoccupations of the noughties 'mom's lit' comic novel, with one significant difference. The humor in mom's lit novels came at the expense of other mothers (who, unlike the protagonist, were generally presented as competitive control freaks). In contrast, the gallows humor in *Nightbitch* satirizes the contradictory logic of the neoliberal parenting model and specifically draws attention to the absurdity of the mompreneur trope. The protagonist, who is referred to at the start of the novel only as 'the mother' and later as 'Nightbitch', has been forced to give up a treasured job as a director of a community art gallery. As the novel makes clear, as jobs in the arts and humanities are already 'feminized' in terms of pay—though often demand considerable commitment—they are particularly difficult to justify in terms of the childcare costs. Reflecting on her and her husband's respective roles, the mother bitterly states that,

> He had a job. He made money. He was off on his work trips. *Goodbye*! And *I love you!* . . . She stood with the babe in arms and watched him back the car from the driveway. Her undergraduate degree was from a prestigious university, better than the one he has attended. She held two masters degrees, whereas he held none (she also held a baby) . . . What a nut she had been, this mother! She was just a lady who liked art. She was just a lady who liked art, and that was no way to make a career or money' . . .
>
> She pushed to the very back of her mind that she'd had a job, before the baby, which she actively referred to as 'her dream job'. Of course, the breadth of work required by such as job was not commensurate with the pay, but she was grateful, you know? Grateful that she even got to work in the art world, despite the amount of work. Her classmates from grad school would kill for such a job, and she did it happily.
>
> But then came the baby . . .[10]

Yoder's tale takes a turn towards the Todorovian fantastic as the frustrated, angry, and isolated mother is certain she is turning into a dog. Referring to herself as 'Nightbitch', she sprouts unexpected hair, eats huge quantities of meat, howls and roams around the neighborhood at night killing smaller animals and destroying gardens, engages in rough play with her child and encourages him to bark and sleep in a kennel. Yoder's surreal tale keeps the reader guessing as to whether we should read this transformation as real or psychological. However, like Gregor's transformation into a dung-beetle in Kafka's *Metamorphosis*, it symbolizes both the low status of the mother's socially validated role and her repressed, angry rejection of it.

Through the human to animal transformation, *Nightbitch* also cleverly satirizes the current tendency to justify painful, labor-intensive and restrictive forms of mothering, such as natural childbirth, extended breastfeeding, baby-wearing and co-sleeping, on pseudo-scientific notions of the natural and animal behaviors. As Elisabeth Badinter has argued, this idealization of the natural is rarely applied so forcefully to prescribed behaviors that would involve men eschewing the luxuries of modern existence or willingly sublimating their needs and desires for others. Nightbitch's canine revels suggests that the 'natural' maternal behavior expected of contemporary mothers has more in common with the religious idealization of maternal purity and self-sacrifice than Tennyson's 'red in tooth and claw' view. It is nature shorn of bestial traits, where 'mumma bears' must be available for constant fun, play, and keeping a watchful and protective eye over their offspring, while maintaining high standards of cleanliness, domestic order, and personal attractiveness. Nightbitch's transformation liberates her from the frustrations of her life as a suburban mother and brings her into loving harmony with her young child, but it hardly conforms to sanitized notions of natural or 'attachment' parenting promoted by contemporary childcare experts, such as William and Martha Sears (Sears and Sears).

More significantly, *Nightbitch* uses the animal transformation motif to emphasize the way in which the combination of maternal disadvantages in the workplace and the seductive but disingenuous ideology of maternal entrepreneurism makes mothers of young children vulnerable to unscrupulous companies. One of the more outlandish plotlines—even in a novel in which the central theme is the protagonist's human-to-dog transformation—is that Nightbitch believes that the suburban moms she meets at small-town mother and baby groups are also secretly undergoing the same transformation and that she has spotted three of them in the park in canine form. The plotline moves back towards its initial focus on maternal work patterns as the alpha mother of this group, Jen, the tall blonde mother that Nightbitch believes enjoys a double life as a border collie, invites her to a gathering. Nightbitch assumes Jen wants to reveal her secret canine existence, only to find herself pressured to join a 'mompreneur' pyramid-selling scheme involving herbs. Jen is fully cognizant of the appeal of mompreneur empowerment speak and attempts to motivate the mothers with the following promises:

> These tried-and-true products, when combined with our work at home opportunity and supportive marketing strategies, create a winning situation for all of us in which we can realise our dreams and live our best lives . . .
>
> Next, the projection of an elaborate flow chart that demonstrated the *earning potential* of each mother and how they were weaving *a powerful web of financial support for each other.* They all needed to *project success.* They all needed to *use the products so they could better speak to their restorative qualities when selling.*
>
> Who's ready to join the team? Jen asked, raising her hands in the air and closing her eyes in evangelical ecstasy. (193)

The mothers are persuaded to part with 600 dollars to purchase the herb starter kit but Jen later confesses to Nightbitch that she has wasted $10,000 of her husband's money buying herbs, cannot convince enough mothers to buy them, and is aware that they, like her, will never be able to regain their initial investment: '[E]verybody thinks I'm so successful, but really it's just me buying my own products. The local market is saturated. We all have herbs! We are just trying to sell them to each other' (215). The protagonist rescues Jen—an ex-PR executive—by employing her to market her new performative arts show, *Nightbitch*, in which she invites other mothers to join her in exploring their wilder 'animal' side.

The novel therefore resolves the problem of maternal disadvantage in the employment market through a more successful, woman-led entrepreneurial venture that incorporates feminist themes and requires little external investment as it is staged in the protagonist's own home. The key difference between the comic mom's lit tendency to invoke the mompreneur as an easy solution to the 'motherhood penalty' and the mother's avant-garde performance in *Nightbitch* is that, in the former, this is presented as a smart, plausible choice in which real world financial know-how and project management skills are redirected towards home-based businesses that often produce domestic items. In contrast, in Yoder's surreal novel the upbeat ending amplifies the fantastical, Kafkaesque elements of the text and evokes the carnivalesque and—specifically—Angela Carter's feminist gothic surrealism, as the mother publicly transforms into 'Nightbitch': running amok and terrorizing small animals on stage. Yoder's description of the women-led show constitutes the apotheosis of the novel's gallows humor and fantastical elements while the mother's resentment and Jen's humiliating failure to live up to the mompreneur role are wholly grounded in astute social observation.

Beware of the Trolls: *Underbelly* and the Perils of Mommy-Blogging

Anna Whitehouse's *Underbelly* (co-written by female and male writing duo Anna Whitehouse and Matt Farquharson) also doubles down on maternal exploitation of different kinds but with a specific focus on the online 'mommysphere'. Using many contemporary references and written in a sparse, realist mode, *Underbelly* charts the lives of two very different London mothers who are brought into each other's orbits when their children become friends in reception class. One is a prosperous, married 'mommy' blogger (Lois) who owns a stylish 'Instagrammable' home. Her Instagram account, 'The Lo-Down,' champions feminist issues such as access to breastfeeding spaces and unequal treatment at work, with powerful statements such as:

> I was made redundant. I walked out of the glass revolving door and didn't know what to do . . . I was discarded for trying to feed my child. But why am I still banging on about this? For all the women who can't say anything for fear of losing their job. For all of us who want to work and earn and have a role alongside being a mother, because that is a job, too. It's not a hobby or a side-hustle, it's a privileged position and anyone pushing a mother out of the workforce for trying to feed one has simply forgotten where they came from #raisingthenextgeneration #maternitydiscrimination. (72)

But as the story unfolds, we see the more problematic aspects of the culture of mommy-blogging and 'momfluencers' both in terms of its costs for the blogger herself and its wider effects on the culture of motherhood and family life. As Anneke Meyer and Katie Milestone argue in their analysis of motherhood on social media ('the lonely cloud'), platforms such as Instagram have become prime conduits for reinforcing the normalization of intensive motherhood, the gendered nature of parenting, and individualistic rather than communal attitudes towards family life. They state that:

> Mother-focused social media embody, reinforce and reveal that on the one hand, their affective fabric encourages expressions of emotionality, and on the other hand the exchange of information and knowledge invites individuals to maximize their competitiveness to achieve goals. While social media facilitates interactions and communications between parents, the relations fostered online remain individualist ... Social responsibility and concern for others are limited, as the dimension of warmth love and care is restricted to parents and their own children. (Meyer and Milestone 193)

More recently, Claudia Wegener, Frederike Jage-D'Aprile and Lisa Plumeier suggest that although there are benefits in terms of sharing maternal knowledge and experience, 'mumfluencers' continue to promote unrealistic ideals, stating that, 'The increasing self-professionalization of active "mumfluencers" promotes an image of motherhood that is geared towards complaisance and supports standardized role expectations' (3232).

These issues are explored in *Underbelly* as affluent mommy-blogger / influencer Lo's income relies on sponsorship deals that are only possible if she retains followers. This must be sustained by constantly uploading pictures of her house and family and projecting an image of wholesomeness and family contentment. She is told bluntly by her agent:

> 'you need to post more. Feed the beast. The algorithm rewards volume. The more you post, the more new people it will serve your content to'
>
> 'But I post *every* day'
>
> 'Try twice a day. Do more stories. Get more personal, show them who you really are, what your life is like. People love peeking through the keyhole, so why not fling open the door?' (132)

The initial conflict between the central protagonists occurs as Lo persuades struggling single mom, Dylan, to allow her to post pictures of both their children wearing clothes given to Lo as part of a sponsorship deal with an aspirational children's clothing company. Dylan also aspires to have a public voice. She has written an unpublished novel on her experience of domestic abuse, *The Women Who Watch On*, and has her own obscure blog, 'One Day Soon'. Dylan's blog aims to counter the online profiles developed by more affluent mothers, such as Lo, by offering a gritty account of her life as an impoverished single parent who provides for her young son by making telesales calls from her run-down flat. Although Lo—who is well-meaning but patronizing—assists Dylan by promoting her blog, she only pays her a small sum for the children's photo. Dylan becomes furious when trolls on a site dedicated to attacking mommy-influencers ('influenza') accuse Lo of virtue signaling and hypocrisy as they speculate on the huge sums she is receiving in sponsorship deals. Aided and encouraged by the anonymous trolls, the two women engage in an online war which results in Dylan, the more vulnerable of the two, reopening wounds gained from an earlier period of self-cutting and nearly bleeding to death.

The cover of *Underbelly* strongly resembles comic 'mom's lit' of the noughties in its use of infant school colours (bright yellow and pink) with a cartoon female image at the center. Yet as this brief plot outline suggests, unlike mom's lit, *Underbelly* does not shy away from the darker aspects of maternal experience. In this sense, *Underbelly* has more in common with the still hugely popular genre of the female-orientated, domestic noir crime novel—a form that specializes in exposing the trauma and violence that can lay behind the veneer of bourgeois family life—than the anodyne, conformist mom's lit comedy. While Lo is clearly the more privileged character, she has suffered a series of miscarriages and a period of post-natal depression after the birth of her child. Dylan has a difficult background and lost her father at a young age. She lives in fear of her child's abusive father and is limited to home-based employment as she is frightened to let others collect her child from school. Dylan's home telesales job is tedious, demeaning and badly paid, but as the novel demonstrates, Lo's outwardly 'cushy' role as an influencer is no family picnic either, as it requires her to monetize her private life and attracts vicious personal criticism as well as adulation. Both are isolating, insecure, non-unionized modes of employment that alienate them from other mothers. The only moments of joy in the novel occur when Dylan and Lo are 'bonding' prior to the intervention of the trolls, suggesting the need for a more communitarian vision of motherhood.

Mothering On The Inside: Jessamine Chan's *The School For Good Mothers*

The last of the more radical maternal novels examined here is so relentlessly bleak that it has more in common with Margaret Atwood's classic feminist dystopia, *The Handmaid's Tale*, than any of the mom's lit or even dysfunctional domestic novels of the noughties. Jessamine Chan's futuristic dystopian maternal horror story, *The School for Good Mothers*, in which mothers deemed inadequate by the state are separated from their children and incarcerated in government-run maternal training camps, has largely been discussed in terms of its articulation of fears regarding the state's increasing preoccupation with parental behavior.[11] Chan herself also stated that she was inspired to write it after reading of cases in the US in which generally poor and ethnic-minority mothers were prosecuted and imprisoned for leaving children unattended for even small amounts of time while they performed other tasks—such as household shopping (Eng). However, there are also two important ways in which the novel specifically addresses the problem of maternal work and exploitation.

Firstly, the inciting incident in *The School for Good Mothers*, what the protagonist—a second-generation Chinese-American woman (Frieda) — refers to as her 'very bad day', occurs as she is desperately trying to combine a demanding, skilled but low-paid and low-status job with caring for a sick child. This takes place in the months after Frieda's husband has abandoned her and her young daughter for a younger white woman from a wealthy family. The courts have awarded joint custody, but when Harriet is with her father, his younger girlfriend performs the lion's share of the childcare, allowing him to pursue his chosen career without restraints. In contrast, Frieda—who has a history of depression and has become considerably poorer through the divorce—is juggling her full-time job 'rewriting academic papers as short articles for the business community' (4). She works for tenured, elderly male professors who have grudgingly allowed her to work at home but refuse to communicate by email, necessitating multiple trips into the university for Frieda. As she is paid little and only sees her daughter for half the week, she has no paid childcare assistance and cares for Harriet while also working on the papers.

After a run of sleepless nights and having left important documents at work, she leaves Harriet strapped in a baby chair to collect the documents and ends up buying coffee and leaving the toddler alone for two hours. The neighbors report her and the police swiftly remove her child and inform her that her only chance of regaining custody of her daughter is to enter a state-run residential program to correct her poor parenting skills. When incarcerated in the state program, Frieda meets many other struggling women who have been targeted by the state as 'bad mothers.' Unlike the *faux*-bad mother trope that emerged in comic mom's lit and is now common in mainstream film and television (in films such as *Bad Moms*, or television programs such as the aforementioned *Motherland*), in which the 'bad moms' behavior is generally confined to occasional partying, sloppy housekeeping and cynical comments, the incarcerated mothers have taken real risks in terms of their child's welfare. However, as the book makes very clear, the generally poor, young, single, and/or ethnic-minority mothers receive little state or community support, and are struggling to balance the demands of childcare and work. This results in behavior such as occasionally leaving their kids alone for too long or asking unsuitable babysitters to mind their kids while they perform work tasks. Although they initially judge one another according to the state's assessment of their maternal crimes, the gradually bond over their mutual experience of hardship.

In addition to critiquing the lack of affordable childcare and workplace support for mothers in the US through the punitive maternal correctional program, Chan emphasizes the sociopolitical tendency to regard motherhood in the terms described by Ruth Quiney (Cain): 'the tasks of birthing and raising future workers and consumers are increasingly presented to women as a curious and urgent mixture of career (with its own regimes of training, information and on-the-job surveillance) and sacrificial moral vocation' (20). It is therefore strongly associated with a host of other neo-traditionalist, class, and racially biased attitudes and assumptions about family life in terms of maternal employment. As it emphasizes the sacred and unique bond between mother and child, the belief that 'intensive' mothering is 'good mothering' is therefore implicitly biased towards women who are married to high-earning men and are either partly or completely economically dependent on them and therefore do not need to work. Given the racial and class dimensions of wealth accumulation and earning capacity in the US and UK, the 'successful' intensive mother is therefore more likely to be white and middle-class.

In *The School for Good Mothers*, the callousness and inequality of socially validated conceptions of good and bad motherhood is most obviously signified by the fact that the incarcerated mothers—who are largely stressed, overworked, and poor rather than neglectful and uncaring—are parted from their children for a year to teach them to mother in the state approved manner. However, Chan uses another trope to further highlight the cruelty of the government-led program. While they have only minimum phone contact with their own children—and phone privileges can easily be withdrawn—the mothers must form a bond with a lifelike AI doll who has been constructed to resembles their own child. The incarcerated mother must practice 'good' mothering on the dolls while repeating the phrase 'I'm a bad mother but I'm learning to be good'. They are constantly told that 'empathy is the cornerstone of our programme' despite the trauma inflicted on them and their children. As the dolls contain sophisticated monitoring devices that reflect the mothers' interactions and emotional responses to them, feelings of sadness and loss regarding their own child, i.e. responses that would normally be expected and approved of in a loving mother—are viewed as signs of their inability to bond.

Aside from setting the mothers up for inevitable failure, the philosophy of the correctional center also reflects the way in which sociocultural expectations of mothers are no longer largely confined to keeping children secure, fed, and healthy, but have expanded to the policing of maternal feeling. The mothers are constantly policed for any signs of dangerous maternal ambivalence or indeed any heightened emotions that are not directed towards the welfare and happiness of the (AI) child. In Chan's novel, the inmates are constantly told that 'mothering isn't about sense, it's about feeling' while also being instructed to follow a strict set of rules and regulations. Chan thus brilliantly captures the paradoxes of what Helen Reece describes as 'positive parenting' and Tracey Jensen as 'sensitive parenting' (*Parenting* 85–144) in which mothers must be spontaneous and fun-loving, while also constantly reflecting on their own parenting practices through the critical lens of the childcare expert. In the correctional center, any minor lapse in attention is recorded and used against the mothers. Mothers who continue to pine for their own children and do not show sufficient attachment to the dolls, are punished. Yet attachment to the dolls, whose only real purpose is to police the mother's behavior, is also dangerous. The AI dolls are sophisticated, sentient beings, but the instructors take a sadistic pleasure in devising tasks in which they are physically and emotionally damaged and tormented to test the mother's ability to calm and comfort them (such as hitting them and subjecting them to sexual attention). The dolls are also programed to display undesirable societal biases, prejudices and behaviors, so the white dolls display racist attitudes and the male dolls are aggressive to females. The mothers are then tested on their ability to curb these negative tendencies, which have been *directly* programed into them by state agencies rather than the mothers themselves. In this sense, the novel illustrates the way in which the unforgiving contemporary rhetoric of intensive mothering is defined by all-consuming responsibility without power, attached to the view that—as Chan's mothers are told directly—'if you can fix mothers, you can fix society'.

Chan's novel thus echoes Jacqueline Rose's recent analysis of sociocultural attitudes in her essay, in suggesting that mothers become 'licensed objects of cruelty' (2) who are called upon to do the considerable work of repairing the human damage caused by bigotry and social inequality.

Conclusion: Beyond the 'Mommy Wars'

In conclusion, the recent novels by Yoder, Whitehouse, and Chan use established literary forms, tropes and generic features—the Todorovian fantastic, the domestic noir and the dystopian horror story—to indict the treatment of mothers in the US and UK and explore the particular forms of maternal discrimination and oppression that neoliberal sociopolitical structures and attitudes produce. While the first wave of twenty-first century maternal writing varied in its attitude towards the new parenting orthodoxies, recent novels addressing maternal experience are united in their thematic concern with the patriarchal structures of maternal exploitation, despite their different generic references and sociocultural contexts. Although they examine the lives of a broad range of maternal subjects, they emphasize the socio-economic restraints on all mothers, rather than scapegoating and castigating 'perfect' (compliant white middle-class) mothers for perpetuating oppressive stereotypes and ignoring the experience of poorer and ethnic-minority mothers. This distinguishes them from comic mom's lit and cultural forms that promote the faux 'bad moms' stereotype. All three also register the protagonists' desire to experience more collective modes of mothering by highlighting the beneficial effects of female bonding. Taken as a whole, the work of Yoder, Whitehouse, and Chan thus constitutes what Raymond Williams termed a shifting 'structure of feeling' around the issue of modern motherhood in the US and UK, in which the atomized experiences of dissatisfaction and anger, associated with the maternal memoir or domestic crime novel, begin to evolve towards a collective sense of injustice.

Notes

1. See e.g. Mendes; Chamberlain; Blithe and Neal; Gilmore; Dey & Mendes; Eisele et al..
2. See Quiney; Cain; Garrett *Writing*; Henriksson et al.
3. *Nightbitch* conforms to Tzvetan Todorov's definition of the fantastic rather than the marvellous as the reader is left in a state of 'hesitation' and uncertainty as to whether the transformation should be perceived by the reader as figurative or actual.
4. See e.g. Hays; Maushart; Wolf; Douglas and Michaels; Warner; Asher; Badinter; Orgad; Glaser; Brearly.
5. See e.g. Gillies; Tyler; McRobbie; Jensen *Parenting*.
6. See Gillies; McRobbie; Jensen *Parenting* 115–142.
7. Early critics of 'mommy-blogging', such as Morrison, suggest that it provides a radical and perhaps more authentic space outside of dominant expectations

of motherhood. However, more recent analysis suggests that it now functions more commonly to reinforce rather than challenge normative ideas of mothering and is often tied to commercial imperatives.

8. See e.g. Quiney; Cain; Fine; Garrett *Writing*; Di Ciolla and Pasolini.
9. See Garrett 'Novels and Children' 202; Littler 179–205; Orgad 42; Harris.
10. Ros Gill's 2014 article on the culture industries demonstrates the disparity between the ethos of egalitarianism in creative arts employment and the statistical evidence that white men still tend to occupy the higher paid roles.
11. See e.g. Egan; Masad; Knight; Peake-Tomkinson; Feeny.

Works Cited

Abrams, Abigail, and Nik Popli. "How Overturning Roe v. Wade Could Affect Every American," *Time,* 12 May 2022, p.7, https://time.com/6176180/overturn-roe-transform-america/. Accessed 25 November 2023.

Agarwal Pragya. *(M)otherhood: On the Choices of Being a Woman.* Canongate, 2021.

Agarwala, Rina, and Jennifer J. Chun. "Gendering Struggles against Informal and Precarious Work." *Political Power and Social Theory*, vol. 35, 2018, pp. 1–28, https://doi.org/10.1108/S0198-871920180000035001.

Asher, Rebecca. *Modern Motherhood and the Illusion of Equality.* Harvill Secker, 2011.

Badinter, Elisabeth. *The Conflict: How Modern Motherhood Undermines the Status of Women.* Henry Holt and Company, 2006.

Blithe, Sarah J., and Mackenna Neal. "Communicating Gender Advocacy." *The Routledge Handbook of Gender and Communication*, edited by Marnel Niles Goins, et al. Routledge, 2020, https://doi.org/10.4324/9780429448317.

Brearly, Joely. *The Motherhood Penalty.* Simon & Schuster, 2022.

Briscoe, Constance. *Ugly.* Hodder and Stoughton, 2006.

Cain, Ruth. "'Just What Kind of Mother Are You?': Neoliberal Guilt and Privatised Maternal Responsibility in Recent Domestic Crime Fiction," in *We Need to Talk About Family: Essays on Neoliberalism, The Family and Popular Culture*, edited by Roberta Garrett et al. Cambridge Scholars, 2016, pp. 289–313.

Casey, Emma, and Rupa Huq. "Biscuits and unicorns: shifting meanings of domestic space in a post-lockdown world," *Journal for Cultural Research*, vol. 26, no. 1, 2002, pp. 24–38, https://doi.org/10.1080/14797585.2021.1989315.

Chamberlain, Prudence. "Affective temporality: towards a fourth wave." *Gender and Education*, vol. 28, no. 3, 2016, pp. 458–64, https://doi.org/10.1080/09540253.2016.1169249.

Chan, Jessamine. *The School for Good Mothers.* Penguin, 2022.

Cummings, Kelsey. "'But we still try': affective labor in the corporate mommy blog," *Feminist Media Studies*, vol. 19, no. 1, 2019, pp. 38–52, https://doi:10.1080/14680777.2017.1382548.

Cusk, Rachel. *A Life's Work: On Becoming a Mother*. Faber and Faber, 2001.

Dey, Adrija, and Kaitlynn Mendes. "'It started with this one post': #MeToo, India and higher education," *Journal of Gender Studies*, vol. 31, no. 2, 2022, pp. 204–15, https://doi.org/10.1080/09589236.2021.1907552.

Di Ciolla, Nicoletta, and Anna Pasolini. "The Violent Mother in Fact and Fiction." *Domestic Noir*, edited by Laura Joyce and Henry Sutton. Palgrave Macmillan, 2018, https://doi.org/10.1007/978-3-319-69338-5.

Douglas, Susan, and Meredith Michaels. *The Mommy Myth: The Idealisation of Motherhood and How it Has Undermined All Women*. Free Press, 2004.

Egan, Elisabeth. "*The School for Good Mothers*, by Jessamine Chan." *New York Times Book Review*, 9 January 2022, p.12, https://www.proquest.com/magazines/school-good-mothers-jessamine-chan/docview/2617702265/se-2.

Eisele, Olga, et al. "The politicising spark? Exploring the impact of #MeToo on the gender equality discourse in Australian print media," *Australian Journal of Political Science*, vol. 57, no. 4, 2022, pp. 309–327, <https://doi.org/10.1080/10361146.2022.2045900>.

Eisenmann, Tom. "Why Start Ups Fail: it's not always the Horse or the Jockey." *Harvard Business Review*, May–June 2021, https://hbr.org/2021/05/why-start-ups-fail. Accessed November 2023.

Eng, Viviane. "The PEN Ten: an interview with Jessamine Chan," *Pen America*, 2022, https://pen.org/the-pen-ten-jessamine-chan/.

Enright, Anne. *Making Babies: Stumbling into Motherhood*. Jonathan Cape, 2004.

Feeny, Madeleine. "The School for Good Mothers by Jessamine Chan: A Handmaid's Tale for the Squid Game Generation." *The Telegraph*, 21 February 2022, https://www.telegraph.co.uk/books/what-to-read/school-good-mothers-jessamine-chan-review-handmaids-tale-squid/.

Fine, Laura. "Sexual Violence and Cultural Crime in the Country Noir Fiction of Bonnie Jo Campbell," *Critique*, vol. 60, no. 5, 2019, pp. 515–26, https://doi.org/10.1080/00111619.2019.1612838.

Garrett, Roberta. "Novels and Children: 'Mum's lit' and the public mother/author." *Studies in the Maternal* vol. 5, no. 2, 2013, pp. 1–28, https://doi.org/10.16995/sim.25.

—. "Austerity Culture and the Myth of the Mumpreneur." *Mothering and Welfare: Depriving, Surviving, Thriving*, edited by Karine Levasseur et al. Demeter Press, 2020 pp. 99–114, https://doi.org/10.2307/j.ctv16pn3d9.9. Accessed 30 Nov. 2023.

—. *Writing the Modern Family*. Rowman & Littlefield, 2021.

Gill, Rosalind. "Academics, Cultural Workers and Critical Labour Studies." *Journal of Cultural Economy*, vol. 7, no. 1, 2014, pp. 12–30.

Gillies, Val. *Marginalised Mothers: Exploring Working-Class Experiences of Parenting*. Routledge, 2006.

Gilmore, Leigh. "#MeToo Storytelling: Confession, Testimony, and Life Writing," *Biography: An Interdisciplinary Quarterly*, vol. 45, no. 4, 2022, pp. 417–37, https://doi.org/10.1353/bio.2022.a910378.

Glaser, Eliane. *Motherhood: a Manifesto*. Fourth Estate, 2021.

Harris, Ella. "Compensatory Cultures: Post-2008 Climate Mechanisms for Crisis Times." *New Formations*, vol. 99, 2019, pp. 66–87.

Hays, Sharon. *The Cultural Contradictions of Motherhood*. Yale University Press, 1996.

Henriksson, Helena Wahlström, et al. *Narratives of Motherhood and Mothering in Fiction and Life Writing*. Palgrave Macmillan, 2023.

Hunter, Andrea. "Monetizing the Mommy: Mommy Blogs and the Audience Commodity," *Information, Communication & Society*, vol. 19, no. 9, 2016, pp. 1306–20, https://doi:10.1080/1369118X.2016.1187642.

James, Al. "Platform Work-lives in the Gig Economy: Recentering Work–Family Research," *Gender, Work & Organization*, vol. 31, no. 2, 2024, pp. 513–34, https://doi.org/10.1111/gwao.13087.

Jensen, Tracey. "'Mumsnetiquette': Online Affect within Parenting Culture." *Privilege, Agency and Affect*, edited by Claire Maxwell and Peter Aggleton, Palgrave Macmillan, 2013, pp. 127–45, https://doi.org/10.1057/9781137292636_8.

—. *Parenting the Crisis: The Cultural Politics of Parent Blame*. Policy: 2018.

Jensen, Tracey and Imogen Tyler. "'Benefits broods': The Cultural and Political Crafting of Anti-welfare Commonsense." *Critical Social Policy*, vol. 35, no. 4, 2015, pp. 470–91.

Knight, India. "The School For Good Mothers by Jessamine Chan: A 21st Century Handmaid's Tale," *The Times*, 20 February 2022, https://www.thetimes.co.uk/article/the-school-for-good-mothers-by-jessamine-chan-review-a-21st-century-handmaids-tale-3jhj7z5hm.

Littler, Jo. "Desperate Success: Managing the Mumpreneur." *Against Meritocracy Culture, Power and Myths of Mobility*. Routledge, 2017.

Lockman, Darcy. *All The Rage: Mothers, Fathers and the Myth of Equal Parenting*. Harper Collins, 2019.

Masad, Ilana. "In 'The School for Good Mothers', Parental Mistakes have Terrifying Consequences," *The Washington Post*, 6 January 2022, https://www.washingtonpost.com/books/2022/01/06/school-for-good-mothers-book-review/.

Maushart, Susan. *The Mask of Motherhood: How Motherhood Changes Everything and We Pretend that it Doesn't*. River Oram Press, 1999.

McRobbie, Angela. "Feminism, the Family and the New Mediated Maternalism." *New Formations*, vol. 80–81, 2013, pp. 119–37.

Mendes, Kaitlynn. *Slutwalk: Feminism, Activism and Media*. Palgrave Macmillan, 2015.

Meyer, Anneke and Katie Milestone. "The Lonely Cloud: Intensive Parenting and Social Media in Neoliberal Times." *We Need to Talk About Family: Essays on Neoliberalism, The Family and Popular Culture*, edited by Roberta Garrett et al. Cambridge Scholars, 2016, pp. 177–98.

Morrison, Aimée. "'Suffused by Feeling and Affect': The Intimate Public of Personal Mommy Blogging," *Biography: An Interdisciplinary Quarterly*, vol. 34, no. 1, 2011, pp. 37–55, doi:10.1353/bio.2011.0002.

Orgad, Shani. *Heading home: Motherhood, Work, and the Failed Promise of Equality*. Columbia University Press, 2019.

Peake-Tomkinson, Alex. "The Parent Snatchers; *The School for Good Mothers* reviewed." *The Spectator*. 2 April 2022, https://www.spectator.co.uk/article/the-parent-snatchers-the-school-for-good-mothers-by-jessamine-chan-reviewed/.

Pearson, Allison. *I Don't Know How She Does It*. Chatto & Windus, 2002.

Pelzer, Dave. *A Child Called It*. Orion, 1995.

Prushinskaya. Anna. *A Woman Is a Woman Until She Is a Mother*. MG Press, 2017.

Quiney (Cain), Ruth. "Confessions of a New Capitalist Mother: Twenty-First Writing on Motherhood as Trauma." *Women: A Cultural Review*, vol. 18, no. 1, 2007, pp. 19–40.

Reece, Helen. "The Pitfalls of Positive Parenting." *Ethics and Education,* vol. 8, no. 1, 2013, pp. 42–54.

Rich, Adrienne. *Of Woman Born: Motherhood as Experience and Institution*. Virago, 1977.

Rose, Jacqueline. *Mothers: An Essay on Love and Cruelty*. Faber and Faber, 2018.

Sears, William and Martha Sears. 2001. *The Attachment Parenting Book: A Commonsense Guide to Understanding and Nurturing Your Baby*. Little, Brown and Company, 2001.

Steedman, Carolyn. *Landscape for a Good Woman*. Rutgers University Press, 1987.

Tyler, Imogen. "'Chav Mum, Chav Scum': Class Disgust in Contemporary Britain." *Feminist Media Studies*, vol. 8, no. 1, 2008, pp. 17–34.

Walker, Alice. *In Search of our Mother's Gardens*. Weidenfeld & Nicolson, 2005.

Warner, Judith. *Perfect Madness: Motherhood in the Age of Anxiety*. Penguin, 2006.

Wegener, Claudia et al. "Motherhood in Social Media: Phenomena and Consequences of the Professionalization of Mothers and their Media (Self-) Representation." *Feminist Media Studies*, vol. 23, no. 7, 2023, pp. 3222–38.

Whitehouse, Anna. *Underbelly*. Orion, 2021.

Wolf, Naomi. *Misconceptions: Truth, lies, and the Unexpected on the Journey to Motherhood*. Anchor Books, 2003.

Yoder, Rachel. *Nightbitch*. Harvill Secker, 2021.

6

Terror as Usual: Gender-Based Violence and Women's Work in Cherie Jones's *How the One-Armed Sister Sweeps Her House*

Leighan Renaud

Content Note: This chapter engages with fictional representations of physical and sexual violence.

It has long been understood that in the Anglophone Caribbean many families and communities are matrifocal in nature. The simplest definition of matrifocality is mother-focused, and in the Caribbean this often means that women, in their roles as mothers and mother-figures, are central to the organization and running of community life. In her chapter, 'The Double Paradox', Janet Momsen articulates the notion that a matrifocal-lived reality in the Caribbean coexists alongside patriarchal hegemony, and she outlines the paradoxes of 'patriarchy within a system of matrifocal and matrilocal families; and of domestic and state patriarchy coexisting with the economic independence of women' (45). These paradoxes manifest in a singular attitude towards mothers and mother-figures in the region, wherein their work is simultaneously revered and denigrated.

Alongside the patriarchal ideologies upheld in Anglophone Caribbean countries, despite (or perhaps because of) the matrifocal nature of these communities, is a culture of normalized violence, and gender-based violence (GBV) continues to be a major concern. The UN Women's 'Caribbean Women Count: Ending Violence Against Women and Girls Data Hub', which collected data from five Caribbean islands, found that, on average, 46% of women interviewed had experienced at least one form of violence in their lifetime, and that up to 55% of them (dependent on island) had been victim to intimate partner violence (IPV) specifically ('Ending Violence against Women and Girls Data Hub'). GBV, indeed, interpersonal violence more generally, is a critical issue in the region, with academics, policymakers and creatives working to address it across various platforms. In academia, there have been decades of scholarship that has worked to understand the roots of this violence. In their book *Writing Rage: Unmasking Violence through Caribbean Discourse* (2006) Paula Morgan and Valerie Youssef argue that 'violence is an inevitable result of extreme male insecurity'; that insecurity being a product of local and regional economic, environmental, and cultural precarity (18).

Because, as Morgan and Youssef suggest, 'violence has been woven into the social fabric of modern Caribbean societies from their inception,' violence becomes part of the daily routines of people in the region (10). This routine of violence does not just include the interpersonal, but the institutional and neo-colonial, and I argue that an example of this is the tourism industry. Kevin Edmonds notes that, due to the network of externally-owned hotels and hospitality businesses, the Caribbean 'leads the world in tourism "leakage" with an estimated eighty per cent of the money spent by tourists ending up leaving the region via foreign owned hotels, operators, airlines, imported food and drinks etc' (138). The Caribbean region is one of the regions across the world most reliant on tourism for economic stability. That so much of the money made from the industry does not stay in the region is a form of neo-colonialism and, I would argue, an act of violence. Noel B. Salazar describes the 'violence in everyday tourism practices' as 'terror as usual', and I want to suggest that in the Caribbean, tourism's 'terror as usual' is compounded by the 'terror as usual' of GBV (704).

It is the fictional representation of 'terror as usual' and the way that it affects women's work that this chapter seeks to consider through an exploration of Cherie Jones' debut novel *How the One-Armed Sister Sweeps Her House* (2021). The novel tells interwoven and intergenerational stories about three women and the impacts of violence—domestic and criminal—on their lives in 1980s' Barbados. Two elements of the narrative that are particularly striking are the banality and mundanity with which GBV is described; and the way that domestic and sexual violence occur on the same beach that houses wealthy tourists, thus casting Caribbean tourism as its own form of violence. This chapter will explore representations of interpersonal and institutional violence. By focusing on the characters of Lala and Wilma, two women from the same family who are victims of IPV, I will consider the way in which the novel engages with the effect that intergenerational cycles of violence has on Lala and Wilma's ability to do the work associated with mothering (that is, both paid and unpaid labor within and outside of the home space), as well as consider how Jones uses domestic labor as a narrative device. I will consider the representation of

GBV as 'terror as usual' as supporting Momsen's claims of a double paradox reality for women in the Caribbean, who simultaneously have agency and are pivotal to the running of households whilst also being victims of a patriarchal need for control and domination that can result in violence.

Though *How the One-Armed Sister Sweeps Her House* is Jones's debut novel, she is in fact a prolific short story writer as well as a practicing corporate lawyer. This chapter is interested in the fictional representation of domestic and institutional violence in the Anglophone Caribbean and seeks to make visible the work it creates for the women who are victim to it. However, this chapter also wants to make visible the advocacy work Jones participates in through the writing and publishing of this novel. In an interview with Suroor Alikhan, Jones explains that she started writing this narrative as a short story in 2008 before realizing it needed to be a novel. Jones goes on to talk about her own experiences of violence and expresses an understanding that violence against women in the Caribbean is cyclical and rooted in patriarchal definitions of gender: 'we are reconsidering how we define gender and our assumptions about gender performance and looking at how these assumptions contribute to domestic violence' (Alikhan n.p.).

Cherie Jones considers herself, first and foremost, a writer. Thus, it has to be through her writing that she campaigns against GBV in her community. The novel, therefore, is a material example of the work that violence creates and so, whilst this chapter is concerned with literary representations of women's work and violence, I want to explicitly make visible the advocacy work that Cherie Jones has done and continues to do through the publication of this novel.

Violence and Domestic Work

The action of *How the One-Armed Sister Sweeps Her House* (henceforth referred to as *One-Armed Sister*) focuses on Mira, Wilma, and Lala (called Stella by her grandmother) as their lives are upheaved by violence in late twentieth-century Barbados. Mira is a mixed-race, white-passing Barbadian woman whose white British husband is murdered during a home invasion. The murder is perpetrated by Adan, the abusive husband of eighteen-year-old Lala. Lala and Adan live in a run-down house on the other end of Baxter Beach, which is known for the 'luxury villas' owned and rented by wealth tourists (140). The action of the novel centers largely on the relationship between Adan and Lala after the accidental death of their baby girl (unnamed at the time of her death, and so referred to by her parents as Baby), killed after being dropped on the floor by the couple during an argument. Wilma is Lala's grandmother, herself a survivor of an abusive marriage to an older man named Carson. Through Wilma's narrative we learn that her only daughter Esme was raped by Carson at the age of fourteen and subsequently gave birth to her only daughter—Lala—who Wilma raises.

The narrative is non-linear and largely written in the third person, with the perspective shifting between characters across the course of the novel. One chapter is written from the perspective of Esme in 1968, the year she is brutally murdered by her new husband. The chapter details all of the things Esme 'will tell her daughter about love when she is grown' (229). For example, given the chance, Esme would have told her daughter 'that the marriage proposal of a bad man is an initiation to lose your way,' because, amongst other reasons, 'for women of her lineage, a marriage meant a murder in one form or another' (237–239). There is a distressing understanding from all women in the family that violence is cyclical. Unfortunately, in the case of Esme, this realization comes posthumously and far too late.

Wilma certainly understands that violence against the women in her family is cyclical and intergenerational, though she rationalizes it in quite different terms. When being questioned by the police after the death of Baby (afraid of being wrongly accused of murder, Lala, Adan and their friend Tone conspire to make it seem that Baby was kidnapped and killed by an unknown third party), Wilma speaks openly about hers and Lala's lives, in the hopes that it helps to explain the current tragedy. Wilma reveals that she was only fourteen when she married thirty-four-year-old Carson at the behest of her mother, and that his subsequent rape of her resulted in the birth of their only child Esme, a chilling mirroring of Esme's story. The narrative details:

> She assumes it is a curse, says Wilma, this way the Wilkinson women have with men, this ability to so bewitch a man that he becomes besotted. A grown man cannot help himself, she explains, in the presence of a young Wilkinson girl. This is the way it has been for generations ... If she had to trace her lineage beyond the ancestors the Black Power people find, she imagines that she would find Delilah, the woman who was the downfall of Samson ... Most Sundays, says Wilma, she prays for the Samsons of the world. (98)

This passage is interesting for a number of reasons. Firstly, it suggests that Wilma is highly aware of the intergenerational cycles of violence that have befallen the women in her family. But, instead of blaming abusive men, she places the blame on the attractiveness of the Wilkinson women, perhaps as some misguided attempt to reclaim a level of power. She aligns herself with the biblical figure of Delilah, who is typically understood as a villainous character, a 'femme fatale' who subverts traditional gender roles and 'offers a grim warning to audiences about the dangers of women's unregulated sexual and social agency' (Blyth 496). By aligning herself and the other women in her family with Delilah, Wilma suggests that there is something dangerous about the agency of a young woman in Barbados, and mistakenly takes some responsibility for her own victimization. In *Violence in Caribbean Literature: Stories of Stones and Blood* (2015), Veronique Maisier connects the prevalence of matrifocality and the centrality of mother-figures in the region to the infantilization of Caribbean men. The 'maternal need to protect,' Maisier argues, results in Caribbean women excusing and taking responsibility for men, 'whether these men are their sons, companions or lovers,' thus perpetuating cycles of violence and a culture of silence around GBV (89). In the double paradox of matrifocality coexisting with patriarchal ideology, Wilma feels a mother-like responsibility towards her husband, despite being twenty years his junior, and is subsequently made to feel partly responsible for the patriarchal violence she falls victim to.

Whilst the non-linear narrative emphasizes the cyclical nature of violence against the women protagonists of *One-Armed Sister*, the occasional use of the second person serves as a captivating narrative device that highlights the urgency of the novel's subject matter. In his book *Unnatural Voices: Extreme Narration in Modern and Contemporary Fiction* (2006), Brian Richardson argues that second-person narration 'is a playful form, original transgressive and illuminating . . . always conscious of its unusual status' (18–23). Richardson argues that the use of the second person 'threatens the ontological stability of the fictional world . . . the protagonist/narratee is quite distinct from the actual or implied reader; nevertheless . . . this distinction can be collapsed whenever the "you" could refer to the reader as well as the protagonist' (20). Jones's use of the second person certainly plays with the distinction between protagonist and reader, and the sporadic interjection of this voice in the narrative serves to immerse us in the violence of her fictional Barbados in a manner that is visceral and oftentimes disturbing. The novel's third chapter is written entirely in the second person and offers the reader a keen insight into the psyche of Lala as she attempts, whilst lying next to her sleeping husband, to rationalize the reasons she stays with Adan. She goes back and forth with herself as she tries to forgive Adan's absence at and after the birth of the baby: '[y]ou don't grudge him that, three days ago, you had to take a taxi all by yourself, from Baxter's general, to bring you and Baby home . . . How many of the women on the ward came home to nobody? is what you ask yourself when you open back Adan's front door' (27–28).

This chapter in the novel is the first to indicate that Adan abuses Lala. This truth unfolds itself slowly over the course of the chapter, which culminates in him raping Lala despite her being newly postpartum. In a manner similar to that of Wilma's testimony to the police wherein she asserts a level of agency despite being the victim of abuse, Lala also tries to maintain that she has some level of control and power in the relationship, with the repeated refrain 'you is woman enough' (28) and '[y]ou is your own woman' (29). The use of the second person in this chapter, a narrative mode we might best associate with genres such a cookbooks and self-help books, suggests that Lala is trying to convince herself of something not yet material. The word 'is' is seemingly replaced by 'maybe' as the chapter draws to a close. The narrator says, '[m]aybe it is time to accept that this man is not the laughing giant you meet riding a unicycle . . . Maybe there is a reason that this is a man whose name you sometimes can't remember,' (33) demonstrating the way that Lala's confidence, both in her husband's capacity for goodness and her own power, diminishes as soon as Adan wakes up.

Adan's presence in the house disrupts the routines Lala establishes as a new mother, demonstrating the way that routine violence, and this 'terror as usual', impacts women's work and creates a new type of domestic work. Lala is described taking Baby for morning walks, '[setting] off down the beach, staying on the part of the sandy soil held together by the roots of the coconut trees, so that the wheels of the pram do not find themselves stuck' (29). Adan, still in hiding after committing murder, comes to find Lala on her morning walk and bring her back home, afraid that she might draw attention to his presence in the community. Despite trying to convince herself that she is her 'own woman,' Lala concedes when she notices Adan's face 'beginning to cloud over, like rain, so you go with him because Baby just born and little for her age and you don't want him to frighten her with what he will do if you don't go' (32). The threat of violence overrides Lala's maternal instincts to take Baby for daily walks, and following Adan home becomes the course of action in Baby's best interest.

Richardson argues that the use of 'you':

> radically alters the tone of the work and provides a unique speaking situation for the narrator, one that does not occur in natural narratives

> and consequently one that continuously defamiliarizes the narrative act. Its usage can engender a heightened engagement between reader and protagonist (28).

In *One-Armed Sister*, the use of second person encourages the reader to connect and identify with Lala whilst simultaneously throwing them off balance. Given the predominance of the novel's third person narrator, 'you' puts the reader in unfamiliar narrative territory, and this destabilization echoes the unsteadying effect of domestic violence. The narrative 'you' provides an opportunity to understand the subtle ways that violence, and the threat of violence, impact Lala's ability to say no. The chapter ends with Lala unable to assert her 'no' when Adan initiates sex, 'because like the wave that crests and falls and disappears somewhere beneath the wooden floorboards, he is out of reach. Somehow beyond you, woman or not' (34). All of Lala's previous assertions of her womanhood as affording her agency vanish upon the realization that, regardless of who she is, her husband will always be an abusive man.

The banality and mundanity with which violence against women is described in *One-Armed Sister* is as sobering as it is affective, and acts as a fictional embodiment of the normalization and culture of silence surrounding GBV in the region. A report by academics at the University of Huddersfield concluded that the reasons behind the prevalence of domestic violence in Barbados and the Eastern Caribbean are 'deeply entrenched in cultural and behavioural norms' (Jones et al. 23). One respondent quoted, named in the report as Olivia, says, 'I guess I grew up with DV. There was not that fancy name to it at the time. I only knew that my father used to beat my mother and if we cried he would beat us too ... It came to a point that you actually got used to it' (23). The notion that violence in the home is something that is so commonplace it doesn't have a 'fancy name' is certainly evident in *One-Armed Sister*. The narrative recounts instances of violence with the matter-of-fact tone one might associate with making a shopping list or some other routine household chore, suggesting that violence is simply another type of housework. Lala describes Adan's cutlass that lives next to their bed, a looming reminder of his violent power over their marriage. Lala describes it as the 'same cutlass he used to cut coconuts for her while she was pregnant, the one he holds to her neck on bad days' (111–12). The cutlass reminds her of both marital kindness and violence. Both acts are described in the same sentence, and there is no shift in tone from one act to the other, reinforcing the notion that the threat of violence is simply an everyday occurrence.

Lala tries to remember the details of the first time Adan hits her but is unable to do so (145). As the 'finer details' find themselves out of focus in the aftermath of the slap, Lala brings the house into focus in an attempt to 'seek order in the things around her' (145). The narrator describes Lala busying herself with housework:

> Lala had started with the bed that first morning she was boxed. She had removed the fitted sheet, the flat sheet and the two pillowcases and washed them, taken down the curtains from the window behind the bed and washed them too . . . washed the dishes and the curtains until her hands were grey from prolonged exposure to blue soap. (145)

The description of Lala's cleaning is more vivid and precise than any description of violence. The wounds she receives are usually written about in terms of the sensations she feels as a result (for example, she describes a particular attack as a 'sort of numbness' where she imagines her bones breaking with the 'explosive pop-pop of fireworks' (119).) In contrast, the description of Lala cleaning of the house is a clear and ordered view of events that conflicts with the non-linear, polyphonic narrative of the novel.

Accounts of violence in Wilma's life are told exclusively in the third person, and though Jones does not employ a second-person voice to recount any of Wilma's experiences, it is told through both Wilma and Lala's perspectives, and moves between past and present tense at various points in the novel, creating a feeling of zooming in and out of moments in Wilma's life. These narrative choices have a double effect in that they simultaneously gesture towards the urgency of Lala's story and also offer a familial historicization of the events of the novel by demonstrating that Wilma's abuse may have contributed to the way that Lala internalizes a normalization of domestic violence.

Chapter 11 is named 'Wilma' and starts with its titular character talking to the police in the Summer of 1984, after Baby's death. The chapter starts in the present tense:

> 'When Wilma Wilkinson is asked by the police, right there on Baxter's Beach, to tell them what she knows about her granddaughter, Lala, she decides to tell them the story of conquerors. She does not tell the story about how her granddaughter ran off with a giant who beats her. She tells the police instead that Lala is from a line of landowning women who do not need a man to survive' (84).

The Wilma of 1984 is concerned with outward appearance and is aware of how a patriarchal society is quick to cast judgment on any woman who does not subscribe to the values that society prescribes for them. She continues by making it known to the police that 'any tragedy that befalls Lala is one of her own making' (84). This chapter's opening paragraph demonstrates some of the ways that GBV in the region remains unspoken about. For poorer communities in the region, pride becomes a currency, and it is more important that Wilma maintains the fallacy of independence in her lineage than publicly recognizes the pattern of victimization that the women in her family have suffered. These generational cycles of violence create work for Wilma—the work of maintaining a public façade that denies the existence of any such violence.

Chapter 11 then moves back in time to October 1965 and, employing the past tense, the narrative focuses on a need for order and cleanliness in the wake of domestic violence, as articulated by Wilma's need to tidy after learning that Esme has been raped by her father, Carson:

> Wilma Wilkinson was a woman of order. So there was nothing unusual about her calmly cleaning her workroom while her daughter waited stoically on a three-legged stool, bits of blood and sick marbling the collar of her dress . . . A clean house is a clear head is what Wilma always said . . . Wilma packed away the newly cut patterns for an empire-waist dress, rolling the brown-paper templates for bell sleeves and a gathered skirt carefully . . . Common pins were notoriously easy to lose and nearly impossible to find again. She stacked and re-stacked a rainbow array of folded fabric . . . She found the stacks of fabric disconcerting if she did not fold and store them by colour, grouped into the many shades of every hue of the rainbow. (89–90)

Wilma tidies her workroom, and the narrative then details her thinking about which chicken to kill and cook for dinner, right before fourteen-year-old Esme enters the room, having just been raped by Carson. Wilma recalls it is Molly Marshall's dress she is working on 'with an unusual diligence' at the time, and that this 'must have been why she hadn't felt anything move in her spirit while Esme was being raped' (91). The narrative device of zooming in on the details of the everyday at such a horrific moment and Wilma's ability to recall these things are suggestive of the level of trauma felt by both Esme and her mother. The reader witnesses Wilma take responsibility for the attack, blaming it on her inability to 'sense' something wrong whilst undertaking paid labor. This scene is also interesting in that the reader witnesses abuse from the perspective of someone who has also been abused by the same person. By focusing on the work she is doing, the order of the workroom, which chicken to kill for dinner, Esme's attack becomes absorbed into the mundanity of daily domestic work—another instance of the terror-as-usual that Wilma has lived through. And Wilma's response certainly supports the understanding that domestic violence is an expected part of daily life. The narrator says, '[only] when the worktop was clear of sewing detritus did Wilma tend to Esme' (92). As she tends to Esme's wounds, the narrator describes the chickens clucking in the background, suggesting that the post-rape care of her daughter is simply another chore to get done that day, one that comes second, in fact, to maintaining the cleanliness and order of her workroom.

Wilma tends to her daughter with the same diligence we imagine she would use when dressmaking. She takes 'special care not to touch her forehead, searching softly for the sore lump at the back of her scalp. She found it, something to be worked around in future' (93). At first glance, once might easily accuse Wilma of coldness towards Esme during this scene—certainly, Esme determines her mother's response to be inadequate. However, I think that Jones makes it quite clear that Wilma's response is a pragmatic one that has been informed by years spent living through domestic terror. Wilma removes Esme from the house and has her live with her aunt because this is the only way that Wilma can ensure her daughter does not have to endure Carson's terror again. Esme, however, does not interpret Wilma's actions as protective, but feels that her mother chooses a life with Carson over her child. The double paradox of Caribbean matrifocality means that, whilst women are central within the household, patriarchal ideology and violence still maintain their control. Thus, whilst it may seem that Wilma has control over her home, and this is certainly the image she presents to the world, Carson's campaign of domestic violence and terror mean that she is limited in the autonomy she is able to wield. Removing Esme from the home is the only way she is able to exert any authority over her husband, but unfortunately this act of love is misperceived by Esme as maternal abandonment.

Through the characters of Esme, Lala and Wilma, *One-Armed Sister* demonstrates the ways that GBV in the Caribbean is cyclical and intergenerational. The shifting narrative perspectives, from second to third person narrator and between past and present tense, offer a kaleidoscopic perspective that captures the dizzying effects of living under a daily threat of violence. Both Lala and Wilma are described as paying very careful attention to their domestic work in the face of violence. Cherie Jones positions this additional work as a coping mechanism for both characters; a way for them to maintain and exercise a small amount of control over their lives in a violently patriarchal community.

Violence and Tourism

In *Consuming the Caribbean: From Arawaks to Zombies* (2003), Mimi Sheller discusses the many ways that, post colonization, Europe and North America have continued to exploit the Caribbean region—its peoples as well as the natural environment—for the purpose of consumption. Sheller contextualizes contemporary Caribbean tourism within a long history of conquest and exploitation in the region, and argues that, '[following] in the footsteps of the explorers, the planters, and the armed forces, the tropical "holiday in the sun" became a new safe means of consuming the Caribbean environment' (61). Sheller continues by suggesting that the picturesque 'paradise' image of the Caribbean first conjured by nineteenth century travel narratives 'continues to be a form of world-making which allows tourists to move through the Caribbean, and to see Caribbean people simply as scenery' (62). Coupled with the idea of the Caribbean environment existing only for tourist consumption is the rise of luxury tourism that has seen the installation of many internationally owned hotels across the Caribbean region, and often at the expense of both the environment and the local people. The tourist industry, in selling a utopic, paradisical version of the Caribbean works tirelessly to remove the tourist from the realities of local life. As such, the local is forced to render themselves invisible in order that the tourist economy continue to thrive.

One-Armed Sister joins Nicole Dennis-Benn's *Here Comes the Sun* (2016) as a twenty-first century novel that directly engages with negative impacts of Caribbean tourism. Both novels contribute to debates around exploitation of service workers, and the sex tourism economy in the Anglophone Caribbean. Where *One-Armed Sister* differs from *Here Comes the Sun* is that is much more explicit about positioning luxury tourism as another form of patriarchal violence that causes harm and creates work, not only for the feminized land, but also the feminized local. Jones's representation of this in the novel is incredibly nuanced: whilst Wilma and Stella are both visibly victimized and simultaneously rendered invisible within their paid service work, this work also offers them the possibility of liberation from the domestic violence to which they are also victim.

Adan and Lala are described as living in a dilapidated beach hut at one end of Baxter's Beach, and at the other end of this beach are the luxury holiday homes: 'Adan's house is at the very end of a stretch of beach without a calm, clear bar for bathing' (140). There is no opportunity, on this end of the beach, to enjoy the sea safely, which echoes the manner in which international investors choose prime locations for hotels and holiday homes, which ultimately impact local peoples' ability to enjoy their homeland freely. The narrative continues to describe the area, including a description of the ruins of a fish market: '[this] village died in the birthing of the big houses, because rich tourists who visit for a few months in a year do not wish to suffer the stink of a market in order to purchase food each day' (140). There are echoes, in this passage, of Jamaica Kincaid's description of the 'ugly tourist' in *A Small Place* (1988). To Kincaid, the tourist in the Caribbean is ugly because their desire to escape the 'banality and boredom' of their everyday life necessitates the disruption of the everyday life of local people (20). Cherie Jones's tourist wants to enjoy the luxurious and exotic landscape without having any material reminders of the life and work that was there before them and which will remain when their holiday ends. Because the tourist is offended by the smells of the food that they will later consume happily, an entire local economy, as embodied by the fish market, is forced to shut down. Local people are forced to renegotiate their own ways of being for the benefit of temporary visitors. This is one of the violent ways that tourism can be thought of as a form of neo-colonialism. The narrative moves on to describe the 'ruins of a nearby public bath . . . [long since] overrun by a colony of sea-grape bushes that have flourished to become colossal in proportion' (Jones 140). In a reversal of events, in the case of the public bath, nature intervenes and turns it into an unusable ruin, presumably before the tourist industry can do it anyway.

The natural environment's interventions against luxury tourism are reiterated in Tone's morning walk down the beach where he describes the sea as smelling of 'stewing moss, sargassum seaweed and the putrefying guts of beached fishes.' (139) It is meaningful that Tone, a sex worker with a history of being sexually assaulted by a male tourist whilst a teenager, experiences the beach in this way. Far from being a 'stroll on the stretch of pink powder reproduced in the magazines,' (139) Tone experiences the Caribbean beach, which has been exploited for tourist consumption, as a site of death and decay. Similarly, the narrator describes the coconut trees outside of Adan's house in equally disturbing terms. The narrator declares:

> [these] are not the trees of postcards, not the type you tie your hammock to and lay under with a good book and a rum punch. These

> trees throw shadows with claws onto the steps and sometimes, when the wind is high, they throw coconuts you have to dodge for fear they could kill you.' (111)

These direct comparisons between the tourist vision of the beach and the coconut tree, and their threatening and rotting realities, suggest that *One-Armed Sister* is heavily concerned with the way that tourism, in its bid to sell paradise for international consumption, compels the natural environment and the local people to betray themselves for the sake of the economy.

Tammy Ronique Williams argues that tourism 'reinforces an unequal balance of power between the West and host nations, so that many locals, especially in poorer areas . . . are often condemned to a life of servitude in the tourism sector' (193). This is certainly true for both Wilma and Lala who, in the service of tourists and wealthy homeowners, render themselves invisible so that they might make a living. Lala braids tourists' hair on Baxter's Beach to support herself, and it is something she takes great pride in, not least because it allows her to develop a small amount of savings (though Adan steals this money midway through the novel). After the death of Baby, to help with the costs of her funeral, the narrator describes Lala approaching the beach:

> with a vengeance with her mayonnaise jar of plastic combs and her little pack of beads, but no one comes to have their hair braided . . . the women who might have chosen the beauty of braided hair no longer trust Lala with their heads (213).

If, as Sheller argues, the idea of the Caribbean as a paradise to consume necessitates the tourist regarding local people as no more than scenery, then Lala's very public tragedy, made more public by repeated police questioning, renders her humanity too visible for the tourist. Her humanity, then, renders her an inadequate worker for the tourism industry. The violence of this neo-colonial institution punishes Lala's visible personhood by taking work away from her. Domestic violence stops her from working a job that she describes as giving her peace (32). Even before the death of Baby, because he is afraid of police attention after committing murder, Adan forbids Lala from leaving their home with Baby to braid hair on the beach. He reasons with his wife, 'you know I don't want nobody seeing me walking 'bout the beach just so' (32). The threat of violence for disobeying her husband, coupled with the pervading patriarchal ideology that positions Adan as familial breadwinner, forces Lala into a financially vulnerable position, meaning that her chances of ever gaining liberation from her abusive marriage are weakened.

Wilma is described as having multiple jobs whilst raising Esme and Lala, including seamstress, chicken seller and, during Lala's teenage years, a domestic worker for 'a madam called Mrs Kennedy in one of the big houses on Baxter's Beach' (179). As with Lala, violence at home limits Wilma's ability to fulfil her duties in paid employment, and Carson creates work as another way of exerting control over his wife. The sections of the novel that take place in July 1979 are told from the perspective of thirteen-year-old Lala and provide insight into Wilma's working life. At this time, Carson is aged and unwell, and Wilma is his primary caregiver. The narrator describes the events of a morning at home before Wilma leaves for work:

> Carson farts from the pantry off the kitchen . . . The stench that follows is familiar. Lala knows that Wilma will wash Carson by wheeling him into the backyard, cutting the clothes off him with her sharp, sharp scissors and turning the garden hose on him . . . 'You is one dirty old man is wah!' she protests. 'You mean you ain't know yet to find the potty Carson?'. . . Wilma showed [Lala] how, if promised a beer for keeping the bed clean, there would be no such spontaneous soiling of himself. (176 – 178)

The narrator suggests that, despite Carson being so 'old and feeble and cannot remember his own name sometimes' (180), he is still alert enough to spite his wife and force her to clean up after him. This spite is a form of violence—perhaps the last form of violence Carson is capable of.

Carson's violence in this scene is reiterated by the narrative decision to, once again, zoom in on the minute details of the housework Wilma is preoccupied with, and describes Wilma's preparing breakfast: 'Wilma drops the hose, rushes in, replaces the apron before lifting the saucepan with her bare hands (because Wilma is a woman of order and the apron comes first), burns her fingers, drops the little copper pot' (178). Detailed descriptions of domestic work function throughout the novel as a narrative device that draws attention to the reader's attention to everyday violence being experienced by the protagonists by over-detailing the everyday work that is happening around it. This narrative device is incredibly effective and is a welcome rejection of gratuitous descriptions of gendered violence without detracting from the important work of raising awareness of the issue.

The careful listing of events once Wilma has finished cleaning Carson, and her need to do things in a very particular order, even if it means burning herself, is reminiscent of the scene following Esme's rape, and once again highlights that domestic order becomes a way for Wilma to cope with the terror she lives with. She passes this desire for order on to Lala, almost pre-emptively, as if understanding the generational nature of the violence she suffers, equipping Lala early with the tools to survive. Wilma also gifts teenaged Lala with a doll on which she can practice braiding hair: 'Wilma has noticed how Lala turns the hair on her dollies into elaborate braided creations, how she experiments with her own hair when Wilma will let her' (176). In this act, Wilma offers Lala an opportunity to practice a craft that is all about patience, order, and minute detail. Order and detail become ways for Lala and Wilma to survive violence in the home, and they also become skills that they utilize in their paid work.

Once Wilma finishes cleaning and feeding her husband, she makes her way to Mrs Kennedy's house with Lala for eight hours of paid domestic work. Mrs Kennedy is described telling Wilma the chores she needs to complete for the day:

> Wilma will clean the house in preparation for Mrs Kennedy's party and Wilma will bake a cake that Lala would kill for and Wilma will remember to ask the gardener to cut the pink roses to decorate the table because they are Mrs Kennedy's favourite and she will serve green banana pickle because it is Mrs Kennedy's favourite. (182)

Again, we see the listing of domestic work in this scene, though to a very different effect. The repetition of 'Wilma will' coupled with 'Mrs Kennedy' serves to reinforce the troubling power dynamics at play between house mistress and domestic worker. The lack of punctuation in the passage—namely the lack of commas—add a sense of mounting pressure to the demands being placed on Wilma. There is no space for Wilma to pause and take in the requests. Rather, there is a breathless, unceasing expectation that Wilma will serve Mrs Kennedy to the highest standard. The demand for a cake that 'Lala would kill for' and the green banana pickle she loves so much suggest that Mrs Kennedy expects that Wilma treat her better than she would her own family, because she barely recognizes their humanity. This is further emphasized by Mrs Kennedy greeting Lala 'as if she is some little child' (182). The infantilization of Lala coupled with her lack of concern about the 'little issue at home' (181) that causes Wilma to be late to work suggest Mrs Kennedy's quiet and outwardly polite dismissal of their humanity. On an island like Barbados, with its history of slavery and colonial exploitation, the class, gender, and racial dynamics at play between Wilma and Mrs Kennedy are emblematic of the longer history of the labor exploitation of Black women.

The neo-colonial tourist economy demands that the realities of local people in *One-Armed Sister*, their traumas and their triumphs, be made invisible whilst they are in service of the tourist. This insistence that the locals render themselves unseen is a form of violence that demands the additional work of creating and maintaining a façade. This is evident in the novel through descriptions of Lala and Wilma, who continue (or try) to work through instances of domestic violence. Cherie Jones offers a unique layer of nuance to her representation of violence in the Caribbean in that, though she is deliberate in casting luxury tourism as harmful, also suggests that it offers Wilma and Lala small moments of freedom. The tourism industry provides Lala the opportunity for peace as she braids hair whilst watching the sea. It gives her the chance to save money so that she might continue to dream about a future free of violence. For Wilma, this work affords her opportunities to create the order and tidiness she craves, as well as allowing her to maintain the semblance of financial freedom that she takes great pride in. Neither Wilma nor Lala is able to achieve any fully realized sense of freedom in their lives in Baxter's Beach. Nonetheless, it is interesting to consider what tourism does offer them, and what it takes away from them. If the cost of financial independence, and the opportunity to start life anew elsewhere is their individuality and their visibility, then the cost is too high, and the violence is irreparably damaging.

Conclusion

How the One-Armed Sister Sweeps Her House is so named for the parable Wilma tells Lala at the start of the novel. It is a cautionary tale that Cherie Jones describes as a story 'to illustrate how community norms and values circumscribe and dictate the parameters within which we recognize, value and judge women, and how inherently patriarchal some of these norms and values are' (Alikhan n.p.). Underpinning this novel is an unwavering critique of patriarchy and the way it manifests as violence in the lives of the novel's female protagonists. Violence creates work for Wilma and Lala. The novel details the additional labor created for women living under threat of IPV. Descriptions of housework act as a narrative device to signal the threat or occurrence of violence. Housework is also represented as a coping mechanism, a way to create order and regain a sense of control when living under a regime of 'terror-as-usual'. This chapter is also intentional in its framing of luxury tourism in the Caribbean as another form of violence that creates a different kind of work. Lala and Wilma gain paid employment because they live in a tourist location, but they are also tasked with the work of making themselves unseen so that they might partake in this service industry. And whilst their paid work affords both women a sense of hope for another kind of future, the violence of the sector exacts too high a toll.

Finally, I conclude with an appreciation of this novel as a material outcome of the work Cherie Jones herself has had to do in the face of violence. This novel is an example of literary activism against a culture of normalized GBV in a region that has, itself, continued to be the victim of (neo)colonial exploitation and violence. Having conceived of the idea for this novel in 2008, the long road to its publication in 2021 suggests careful, meticulous work undertaken by Jones to ensure this story was told correctly. The result is a beautifully controlled novel that employs a number of affective narrative strategies that demonstrate the cyclical nature of violence in Barbados. Violence created work for Cherie Jones, and that work culminated in a thoughtful novel that explores the realities of living through 'terror-as-usual' in the patriarchal, neo-colonial Caribbean.

Works Cited

Alikhan, Suroor. "Raising Issues of Domestic Violence: An Interview with Cherie Jones," *Talking About Books,* 14 September 2022, https://talking-about-books.com/2022/09/14/raising-issues-of-domestic-violence-an-interview-with-cherie-jones/.

Blyth, Caroline. "Queering Delilah with Critical Theory and Gendered Bible Hermeneutics," in *The Oxford Handbook of Feminist Approaches to the Hebrew Bible*, edited by Susanne Scholz, Oxford University Press, 2020, pp. 494–507.

Dennis-Benn, Nicole. *Here Comes the Sun*. Liveright, 2016.

Edmonds, Kevin. "An Elusive Independence: Neocolonial Interventions in the Caribbean," *International Socialism: A Quarterly Review of Socialist Theory*, vol. 146, 2015, pp. 123–143.

"Ending Violence against Women and Girls Data Hub." *Caribbean Women Count*, UN Women, https://caribbeanwomencount.unwomen.org/.

Jones, Adele, et al. *Twenty-one lessons: preventing domestic violence in the Caribbean*. University of Huddersfield, 2017.

Jones, Cherie. *How the One-Armed Sister Sweeps Her House*. Tinder Press, 2021.

Kincaid, Jamaica. *A Small Place*. Farrar, Straus and Giroux, 1988.

Maisier, Veronique. *Violence in Caribbean Literature: Stories of Stones and Blood*. Lexington Books, 2015.

Momsen, Janet. "The Double Paradox," in *Gendered Realities: Essays in Caribbean Feminist Thought*, edited by Patricia Mohammed, University of the West Indies Press, 2002, pp. 44–55.

Morgan, Paula and Youssef, Valerie. *Writing Rage: Unmasking Violence Through Caribbean Discourse*. University of the West Indies Press, 2006.

Richardson, Brian. *Unnatural Voices: Extreme Narration in Modern and Contemporary Fiction*. Ohio University Press, 2006.

Salazar, Noel B. "The unbearable lightness of tourism . . . as violence: An afterword," *Journal of Sustainable Tourism*, vol. 25 no. 5, 2017, pp. 703–709.

Sheller, Mimi. *Consuming the Caribbean: From Arawaks to Zombies*. Routledge, 2003.

Williams, Tammy Ronique. "Tourism as a Neo-Colonial Phenomenon: Examining the Works of Patullo and Mullings," *Caribbean Quilt*, vol. 12, 2012, pp. 191–200.

PART III

THE EMPLOYMENT OF FORM

7

Scrappy Time: Domestic Work and Adrienne Rich's Literary Fragment

Lindsay Turner

Chantal Akerman's storied 1975 film *Jeanne Dielman: 23 Quai de Commerce 1080 Bruxelles* contains a funny glitch. The film follows its protagonist, a middle-aged housewife, over the course of several monotonous days of more-or-less routine housework. Each morning, before her son rises, Jeanne makes coffee in a kitchen where there's a small table with only one chair. Each morning, her son joins her in the kitchen to eat the breakfast she has laid out. When he is in the kitchen, and at all other times in the film, there are two chairs at the kitchen table. When I saw the film for the first time on a big screen, I was mesmerized by this discrepancy. I ran through all the possibilities: does Jeanne move the chair? Is it perhaps sitting beside her son's futon bed, holding his watch and a glass of water? It is not. The explanation for this glitch must be this: Akerman has filmed all the morning scenes sequentially—that is, the actress Delphine Seyrig makes coffee for day one and makes coffee for day two, and these acts are shot in one session, at which time there is one chair at the kitchen table. Next, Akerman has filmed all the breakfasts at once, at which time, two chairs. And so on, for all the repeated scenes in the film: these must have been shot all at once, then spliced and edited into days.

This makes sense for filmmaking expediency. There would be very little point in working any other way. But this glimpse into the film's inner workings fascinates me because it reveals something about what domestic labor does to time. On the one hand, the film is distinctly about the deadening continuity of domestic work. Until the end of the film, which I won't spoil, Jeanne Dielman exists in a kind of suspension of routine, carried along by the monotony of each day—a day which, we are given to assume, is basically exactly like all the days before it. On the other hand, though, these days are composed of repeated pieces of time, almost modular in nature, such that they can be taken apart and pieced back together in film production. All days are alike, but all days are disjointed. Time is both ongoing to eternity and stopped and restarted with each new task.

Jeanne Dielman appeared nearly ten years after the US poet Adrienne Rich's book *Snapshots of a Daughter-in-Law* (1963), but the two works are similar both in theme and in form, and in this essay I want to think about the particular temporal quality illustrated by Akerman's film by turning to Rich's work. For feminist thinkers and feminized workers alike, time poses conceptual and material challenges that are formidable, if not insoluble. How do we understand the time of housework, domestic work, or reproductive labor? How do we live the impossible temporal demands of waged or salaried work combined with the work of care in all its forms? There is very little in literature that can solve the material problem of time and feminized work: for that, we need robust social policies, better distribution of resources, and socialized childcare, among other things. But there is the potential that thinking about literary form can help conceptualize the time this work takes. In what follows, I lay out a theory of 'scrappy' form and 'scrappy' time. By 'scrappy,' I mean two things. The first is formal and literary: like Akerman's days, Rich's poems are often composed of scraps and fragments, the literary nature of which might be usefully recast in light of feminized work. The second thing I mean by 'scrappiness' is the way we use the word colloquially to mean resilient, tough, little but strong, unassuming but persistent, modest but abiding. In the scrappy time of domestic work, poetry—literary and artistic work—becomes itself scrappy: it persists, and in doing so, helps model ways of working and being. Moreover, at present, scrappy time conditions more than just domestic work. It structures a variety of very different spheres of labor today. Poetry, I argue, can help us feel what this time is like, and can help us see new and potentially valuable connections between these spheres.

On Adrienne Rich

Adrienne Rich was born in 1929 and died in 2012; her first book was published in 1951 and her last in 2010. Because Rich was not just active but actually prolific for over a half century—not just any half century, but the half century that saw a whole set of massive social changes (shifts in gender roles, changes inspired by decolonial movements worldwide, economic and cultural globalization)—her work provides a well-appointed window into poetry's relationship to changing ideas of gender and labor. In particular, and in keeping with this volume's transhistorical aspirations, Rich's work is shaped by and reflects back almost the entire history of the feminist movement in the US, from the early stirrings of feminist discontent at the heart of the traditional family in the repressed and repressive 1950s through the woman's liberation movement of the 1960s and 1970s, with its strains of lesbian separatism and awakening race and class consciousness, to the wider intersectional and more flexible ideas of feminism after the 1970s, as well as a critique of the co-option of certain feminist energies by neoliberalism in the 1980s and following. Indeed, Rich's work anticipates some, though importantly not all, of the strains and controversies that run through feminist debates today: she emphasized the importance of intersectional thinking, including race and class as well as gender, stressed the role of structures, institutions, and governments in protecting the welfare of women and children and against increasing austerity policies, addressed mass incarceration, and foregrounded the problem of US hegemony and its accompanying powers of environmental and social destruction as particularly detrimental to the lives of women in the US and abroad. Farm workers, private jets, media deception—it is all here, with one notable omission.

I want to pause briefly over this omission in order to make a point that, though not strictly necessary to my essay, needs to be made in any essay on Rich at this particular moment in history. In her poetry or her prose or her many speeches and addresses, over the course of her life, Adrienne Rich addressed nearly every issue that it would be possible for a feminist to address, not shying away from prescient or 'touchy' subjects: rape and sexual violence, police brutality, Zionism. Yet Rich—to my knowledge, and the knowledge of existing scholarship—never committed any views on trans identities to print, either in prose or in poetry. Certainly her early commitments to a lesbian separatist feminism, which included a period during which she discouraged or prohibited men from attending her readings, involved a degree of essentialism; just as certainly poems starting as early as 'Diving Into the Wreck' (1973) include exploration of an androgyny far outside of gender essentialism, and much later poems ('Axel Avákar,' for example, Rich's 'fictive poet, counter-muse, brother') work explicitly to form relationships of solidarity on lines other than gender. Rich's only involvement with trans identities was a devastating one, from the point of view of contemporary trans-inclusive feminism: Janice Raymond's 1979 transphobic *Transsexual Empire: The Making of the She-Male* both quotes Rich and thanks her for having 'read the manuscript through all of its stages and provided resources, creative criticism, and constant encouragement' (ix).

Was Adrienne Rich transphobic? There is no real way to answer this question. There is certainly no way to answer it in the negative. Yet for a poet of Rich's range and interests not to have weighed in against the transphobia and the violence against trans women that was as rampant in her day as it is in ours, if less visible from a mainstream point of view, is an unacceptable omission *by Rich's own standards.* Rich is, to put it mildly, merciless to herself in her reflections; in essays such as 'Blood, Bread, and Poetry: The Location of the Poet' and 'Split at the Root: An Essay on Jewish Identity' and 'A Poet's Education,' Rich wrestles with her whiteness, her privilege, the world she was brought up and into and the decades of feminism she traversed. Consistently, Rich is not content to be judged by the standards of the present (even if the standards of her own present moment had included transphobia, which they did not). In 'Blood, Bread, and Poetry,' for instance, Rich frames the kind of poetry she wishes to write as part of a 'long conversation with the elders and with the future (and yes, I do live and work believing in a future)' (245). Or, in 'North American Time':

> Everything we write
> will be used against us
> or against those we love.
> These are the terms,
> take them or leave them.
> Poetry never stood a chance
> of standing outside history [. . .]
> We move but our words stand
> become responsible
> and this is verbal privilege.

In other words, it is from the standards of *our* present by which Rich explicitly asked to be read. Given this, the fact that few, if any, scholarly works on Rich grapple with her silence here is all the more unacceptable—Holladay's biography, for instance, mentions Raymond five times and relies on her direct email correspondence to characterize Rich's relationship with her partner Michelle Cliff without identifying her as anything other than Rich's friend and fan, mentored and supported by Rich, and a feminist scholar. Yet if I am in this essay to hold Rich up as having offered a model for thinking about women's work—and if I believe, as I do, in thinking about *work* as constitutive of gender, or in other words, thinking of gender as a set of actions and performances, socially conditioned rather than essential and innate and biological, it would be going against these views and against the trans-inclusivity that is necessary to any real feminism not to flag the problem of Rich's non-expression of solidarity with trans women or to note the contradiction in using her example.[1] It would also, paradoxically, be going against Rich's own injunction to be, indeed, 'more merciless to [her work] than history,' to quote a line from the poem to which I will shortly turn. I think there is enough to gain from Rich's work, and enough to love in this work, to merit raising the issue, especially since it has been the subject of such official neglect and such resounding silence, before moving on.

Scraps and Fragments

Adrienne Rich's poetic work has not all been formally scrappy. The formal shift from her strictly metrical early work to the fragments and open forms of her later work is one hallmark of the poet's career. Rich's first collection, *A Change of World* (1951), might use its title to harken difference and futurity, but the book—which won the prestigious Yale Younger Poets award when Rich was twenty-one years old and a senior undergraduate at Radcliffe College—is very much a product of Rich's cultured, upper middle-class upbringing in the comfortable suburbs of Baltimore and of her Ivy League education. W.H. Auden infamously praised the collection for its neatness and order; Rich's poems, he wrote, are 'neatly and modestly dressed, speak quietly but do not mumble, respect their elders but are not cowed by them, and do not tell fibs' (278). But if her early work is orderly and studied, marked by a white, male literary inheritance and the mastery of that formal tradition, her later work (starting with the collection *Snapshots of a Daughter-in-Law,* her third, published in 1963) gets looser, more radical in both form and politics both. For most readers of the work, the formal shift is linked to feminist politics. Poet Marilyn Hacker, for example, writes: 'To read a woman poet using and subverting the modernists' collage / quotation / fragmentation techniques—so often employed in a mockery of women—in a project of specifically womanly and mordantly feminist inquiry was a heady pleasure' (16).

Hacker's use of the possessive 'modernists'' reflects the most common way to think about fragmentation, at least in literary study in English. Fragmentation as a literary technique is seen as the purview of High Modernists such as Joyce, Pound, and Eliot. This kind of fragmentation is vaguely mimetic of social fragmentation and the decline of shared cultural values that accompanied the era of speed, standardization, and world war. According to the *Princeton Encyclopedia of Poetry & Poetics*, for instance, the fragment is used 'to reflect the disjointedness of the psychological experience and convey a sense of general disorder' (Cushman et al. 506). In roughly contemporaneous philosophical terms, we might also think of the fragment in the work, most notably, of Walter Benjamin, whose *Arcades Project* (1999), as well as his focus on the Parisian arcade as a ruin, a site of fragmentation itself, offers a view of the fragment that is both representational and forward-looking. For Benjamin, the fragment is a Messianic creature; that is, it exists on its own, as it is, and will come to take its place in the whole only in the future. It is not necessarily the sign of the failure of completion or the presence of destruction but a historical marker, a constitutive element of contemporary ways of being and knowing.

But here it might be useful to make a distinction between the 'scrap' and the 'fragment,' and between Modernist quotation and other forms of collage, to use Hacker's terms, although I do not aim here to differentiate 'scrap' from 'fragment' in any material way. Instead, the difference is contextual and historical. If 'fragment' carries with it the legitimizing associations of philosophy and the inheritance of certain strains of European Romantic as well as Modernist thought, 'scrap' is decidedly 'lower' in its cultural resonances: think 'to scrap' as a verb, or 'scrap-heap,' or—again—'scrappy' as both diminishing and admiring qualification. More importantly for our purposes, the distinction is also gendered. The poetic and philosophical legacies of the 'fragment' are assuredly male. 'Scrap,' on the other hand, and especially as a material artifact, has a history that is feminized, not only in its association with textiles and fabrics but also in the tradition of the scrapbook, a pastime that arose in the mid-nineteenth century and was—and is, still—heavily feminized. The object of the scrapbook, itself arising from the much longer history of the commonplace book, was in fact not only the purview of women, yet as Bartholomew Brinkman points out in his study of scraps, print culture, and literary Modernism, '[w]hile all types of scrapbooks were produced by both women and men, the discourse surrounding scrapbooking—evident in periodicals and other popular publications of the period—was overwhelmingly gendered feminine' (18), especially when this scrapbooking came to include poetry. Scrapbooks were—and are—for compiling the sentimental and the familial. In them we are mostly likely to imagine, at least, finding materials coded feminine, from the inspirational quotation culled from a magazine (likely a women's magazine) to the detritus of homemaking and child-rearing (a ticket stub from a first date, a lock from a first haircut). Even the tools and motions of making a scrapbook—cutting out, piecing together, scissors and glue—belong to the register of feminized labor.[2]

There is no record of Adrienne Rich having kept a scrapbook, although her father transcribed her childhood writings into a notebook, and she did keep a journal. Yet the way she positions her own formal shift into 'fragments' (her word) has nothing to do with modernism or philosophy and everything to do with the material conditions of her own life and work. In her 1972 essay 'When We Dead Awaken: Writing as Re-Vision,' she describes one of the poems in question, 'Snapshots of a Daughter in Law,' written in the 1950s and dated 1958–60: 'The poem was jotted in fragments during children's naps, brief hours in a library, or at 3 a.m. after rising with a wakeful child. I despaired of doing any continuous work at this time,' she writes, 'yet I began to feel that my fragments had a common consciousness and a common theme' (24). Useful as Hacker's framing of Rich in relationship to modernism is, it is clear that Rich's deployment of the fragment comes less from a deliberate attempt to intervene in male modernist fragmentary poetics than it does out of the temporal pressures of domestic labor and the labor of reproduction.

Rich's use of the poetic fragment, and her description of her own work, involves a certain intimacy, even inseparability, of poetic form and of gendered domestic and reproductive labor. To understand poetry in this way means moving beyond the formal baselines set by readings of white male canonical established poets, by which poetic making occurs far away from the pressures of class, race, gender, and geography that condition other sorts of labor. In other words, Rich's point here is not necessarily to be anti-modernist, any more than the fragment itself was ever only the business of Anglo-European modernism. Instead, this version of the poetics of the fragment is closely tied to the material experience of a certain form of life and work.

But in addition to seeing this version of the fragment as a form that is complexly and intimately linked to gendered reproductive and domestic work, the fragment—at least in this version of Rich's work, in 'Snapshots of a Daughter-in-Law,'—also reveals something specific about the experience of this work: the way it unfolds in time, or does not unfold, but gets stuck. Returning to Rich's own language for her turn to the fragment, 'I despaired of doing any continuous work at this time, yet I began to feel that my fragments had a common consciousness and a common theme,' is illuminating. First, Rich speaks of these fragments not as cultural relics outside of her but as if they were part of her organic self—'*my* fragments.' The 'consciousness' and 'theme' that hold them together are what is outside of her, external to her, almost in a reversal of the modernist paradigm. And because she is speaking of the poem 'Snapshots of a Daughter-in-Law,' we know that both consciousness and theme here are the work of gendered domestic and reproductive labor.

'Snapshots of a Daughter-in-Law' begins with a second-person description not of the daughter-in-law but of the mother-in-law, 'once a belle in Shreveport / with henna-colored hair, skin like a peachbud,' depicted in stagy conflict with the title figure: 'Nervy, glowering, your daughter / wipes the teaspoons, grows another way.' Across its ten sections, the poem presents scenes of irregular length and point of view that hang together—barely—by threads of domesticity, femininity, and work. Section two, for instance, gives a decidedly Akerman-like portrait of a woman whose mental state is unraveling against a backdrop of numbing feminized chores:

Banging the coffee-pot into the sink
she hears the angels chiding, and looks out
past the raked gardens to the sloppy sky.
Only a week since They said: *Have no patience.*

The next time it was: *Be insatiable.*
Then: *Save yourself; others you cannot save.*
Sometimes she's let the tapstream scald her arm,
a match burn to her thumbnail,

or held her hand above the kettle's snout
right in the woolly steam. They are probably angels,
since nothing hurts her anymore, except
each morning's grit blowing into her eyes.

The poem's fifth section, given here in its entirety, extends this work—and also the implication of its deadening, fossilizing effects—into the arena of feminine beauty:

Dulce ridens, dulce loquens,
she shaves her legs until they gleam
like petrified mammoth-tusk.

Immortalized in these snapshots, above all, is the endless labor of the upkeep of both the body and the house, described intimately and damningly as it, along with gendered expectations for knowledge and behavior, destroys both mother-in-law and daughter-in-law and the relationship between them.

Fragmented by labor, the poem describes versions of that labor: labor that does not end, labor that numbs and dulls and petrifies. When Rich states that 'she despaired of doing any continuous work' at the time she composed 'Snapshots of a Daughter-in-Law,' it's clear that she means poetic work. But the reason she can't 'do any continuous work' is not because she cannot work, but because as the mother of three young sons she is very definitely doing another kind of work, *continuously*, to the point that it prevents her from doing any 'continuous' writing. The word 'continuous' is worth dwelling upon: it is, in part, what the poem illustrates, and it is what discussions of such work repeatedly emphasize. The time of domestic labor—of housework, of child-raising, cooking, cleaning, etc.—continues to vex. Part of the point of the Wages for Housework movement of the 1960s and 1970s was exactly the endlessness of reproductive work: the fact that it would be impossible to pay women hourly wages for the work they do *all the time*. The point of demanding a wage was less a demand for payment than a critique of the system that depends on such vast unpaid work and an attempt to make it visible in its immensity as work.[3] Taking a more expansive view of this work in all its contemporary complexity—as reproductive labor is both waged and unwaged, unevenly distributed and compensated along lines of gender, race, class, and geography—it becomes all the more obvious that no one has been very good at solving the problem of its temporal expanse, socially or technologically. The turn to austerity politics worldwide post-recession means that problems of time and uneven distribution are getting worse. In any case, the reproduction of human life is a constant and ongoing process. In the words of Simone de Beauvoir, it is Sisyphean (474), comprised of endless repetitions.[4] You do the dishes or someone does the dishes or no one does them until you have no more dishes and something has to be done about it. In order for life to continue, there is no not doing.

And yet something else emerges from Rich's own account of her life at the moment of her formal shift. Contained in her language of continuity and continuousness is a paradoxical insistence on the discontinuous, ragged, and fragmented nature of time and work, or what Rich calls 'the discontinuity of female life with its attention to small chores, errands, work that others constantly undo, small children's constant needs' ('When We Dead Awaken,' 23). The US writer and feminist thinker Tillie Olsen, in a similarly frustrated account of trying to balance reproductive work and literary production, points to the quality of care work as being constantly 'interruptible, responsive, responsible.' 'It is distraction, not meditation, that becomes habitual [in domestic work];' she writes, 'interruption, not continuity' (18). De Beauvoir, too, emphasizes the tension of motion and stasis, with the image of the housewife running-in-place. This is a strange, tense, strained temporality: a continuous time yet a time made up entirely of interruptions; a constant state of discontinuity; a stilled permanent motion; a monotony that is also unstable, unpredictable, and contingent on the needs and desires of others.

It is in the face of this kind of time that a certain kind of poetic fragment emerges for Rich. It is important to emphasize that this kind of fragment is not mimetic of fragmented time: that is, it is not supposed to suggest or represent the experience of discontinuous time, as the most superficial formalist reading might have it. This kind of fragment is also not synecdochical: it does not stand in for some experience of the whole, and we are not supposed to be able to put the fragments together to form a whole, or work back from them to some whole, because there is no 'whole,' continuous, forward-running experience of gender or labor to which to work back. Instead, experience of the whole *is* the experience of fragments, their 'common consciousness and theme,' or the constant fragmented time of work. And finally, the fragment is not quite purely indexical. It is not just that the fragment is the material trace left on the work of art by the work of care, and not only that Rich's form of poetic language comes out of and is shaped by her work, although this true of enough of Rich's poem, and important to understand: the fragment represents a refusal to concede or to compromise as a poet, and the scrappy determination to keep up with the work of writing even when it seems like all the time is filled with a different kind of work.

But the fragment also emerges in Rich's poetry as a formal element linked to something fundamentally *different* from continuously discontinuous time of work in which it is written. The fragment reveals or limns the jagged edges of that time: it shows the gaps and the interstices inherent in it in which a certain form of writing can be done. This writing is itself a very different form of work, a form of work that can offer critiques and visions, and that dreams ('grows another way')—even if it does not immediately effect—a totally different time (among other things). Indeed, Rich emphatically emphasized the need for writing to explode the conditions under which it takes place; 'nothing can be too sacred for the imagination to turn into its opposite,' Rich wrote, and 'you have to feel free to play around with the notion that day might be night, love might be hate' ('When We Dead Awaken,' 23). The poetic fragment bears the formal imprint of the time of work from which it emerges, as an index; it tells us, in its content, about that time; and finally—in this particular poem, at least—it bears with it the possibility of a certain world, place, and way of working.

Rich would later worry over the poem that was her entry into fragmented form, 'Snapshots of a Daughter-in-Law,' as being too literary in its allusions and tone, but the end of the poem, its final section, is a concrete example of what it might mean to break out of present time:

Well,
she's long about her coming, who must be
more merciless to herself than history.
Her mind full to the wind, I see her plunge breasted
and glancing through the currents,
taking the light upon her
at least as beautiful as any boy or helicopter,
        poised, still coming, her fine blades making the air wince

        but her cargo no promise then:
        delivered
        palpable
        ours.

The image itself is interesting—a strange and perfect prophetic conflation of ship, ship's figurehead, and helicopter—but so is the way time works in this section of the poem, which hinges between present and future. The word 'well' serves not only as conversational opener for the section but also to mark the beginning of a breakout of something else, a temporal differentiation, as in—'well, time for a change of subject.' The phrase 'she's long in coming,' similarly, keeps us poised on the knife-edge between present and future: she *is* long in coming means she hasn't come yet. In the phrase we can read both a past time of impatience that is still the present time, plus a future that is the end of impatience but is not here yet. The same goes for 'poised, still coming' in the eighth line: the gesture is towards a future that is close but not yet present.

The poem fragments even further as it approaches its end, and the temporal knife-edge gets thinner. Even as the poem ends with the fullness of fulfilled promise, and the certainty, the materiality, and the felt-ness of the possession of the figure's revolutionary cargo ('palpable, ours'), we still have the temporal marker 'then' ('no promise then'). More than a rhetorical signal, this word implies that the coming landing or delivery or fulfilment is still something that happens only in the future—*then*, not now. In other words, even as almost every bit of Rich's language indicates the full presence of the future, she still holds us back. We're still in the present, the time of the fragment. The fragment's cargo is not here yet. Certainly, what the as-yet undetermined cargo of the fragment contains is important, but so is the time towards which the fragment gestures. For the sort of worker who 'wears herself out marking time [and] simply perpetuates the present' (504), to use de Beauvoir's words again, a first problem is to imagine a breakout of the isolation of labor, and also to imagine a time that exists beyond the time of labor—to start to crack or even 'explode' that time, in Benjaminian terms. In Rich's work, we see a version of the poetic fragment that aims for a different discontinuity, striving towards a time outside the continuous–discontinuous present that is increasingly the time in which we work now.

Work and Time

Stirring as I find this ending, though, I also find it difficult to move from these lines to any larger claim about fragments, poetry, or reproductive and domestic labor. The poem's insights seem momentary—a flash vision of a future that emerges out of the present. But there are a few ways that this poem, and this new version of the poetic fragment, might illuminate our present. The first is in the tension the fragment carries along with it, of holding two very different and conflicting kinds of work together and attempting to perform them simultaneously.

The problem of the simultaneity of labor has been around, philosophically and materially, for a long time. Even Plato, we can recall, objected to the poet's presence in his Republic on the grounds that the poet muddies clear divisions of labor, representing himself as someone who knows more about (say) commanding a battle or seafaring than he actually does. More germane here is the conflict between creative work and reproductive and domestic labor voiced by Rich, Olsen, and other women and caretaking writers before and after them. Virginia Woolf concludes *A Room of One's Own*, originally delivered as lectures in 1928, with an acknowledgment of the 'many other women who are not here to–night, for they are washing up the dishes and putting the children to bed' (113). Olsen's *Silences* wrestles fundamentally with the problem of the voids, absences, and silences left in literary history by women who were too occupied with other work to write. Angela Garbes describes the impossibility of writing while taking care of her two daughters in the US during the COVID-19 pandemic and quotes the playwright Sarah Ruhl on the difficulty and the necessity of performing these two specific kinds of work in tandem: 'I appear to need to be alone in order to make things; it appears necessary to my survival' writes Ruhl. 'And yet my children appear to need me, always; it appears to be necessary for their survival. And yet for me to feel my sanity, these two practices, of motherhood and making things, so primary, need to feel as though they are compatriots' (Ruhl 157, quoted in Garbes, 41).[5]

On a first level, then, Rich's work gives a form that is at once inextricably tied to domestic and reproductive work but that somehow manages to hold domestic and reproductive up in tandem with this other kind of work—poetic work. Rich, and many others, give us work that tells us, in both form and content, what it *feels like* to be doing conflicting kinds of work today. But again, the problem of the simultaneity of labor, and of the discontinuous–continuous and scrappy time of work, extends beyond the home *per se*. Rich exemplifies the figure of the white US housewife—a figure that has in some cases been wrongly seen, in turn, to exemplify the problem of undervalued domestic and reproductive labor, and that has served as the lens through which the conflict between reproductive work and literary work has sometimes been seen (in Olsen and in Woolf, for example). But of course, for many women and many caretakers globally, the structures of domestic and reproductive labor are different. In some examples, this work is performed communally, not privately, outside the structure of the nuclear family. In many cases, it is performed—especially by women of colour and women from the Global South—both in the home and outside the home, for pay, for other families. In some cases, it is only performed outside the home. Finally, it is not inevitably or naturally a burden: as bell hooks reminds us, the work of homemaking can also be the creation of a 'site of resistance,' a space 'to resist racist domination and oppression' (47).

Looking at the particular scrappy temporality of care work provides an opportunity to widen the lens and see the work of gendered reproductive and domestic labor not as a particular—and particularly awful—kind of labor but as one that is linked to other kinds of work. For better or worse, this temporal model turns out to be a useful one for thinking about work today, which tends for all but the luckiest workers to be some combination of endless, piecemeal, contingent, double or triple, unstable, and monotonous: I am thinking of gig workers, contracted workers, subcontracted workers, migrant workers, and all those workers whose labor is not divided into eight-hour workdays, or even workdays at all. In part, this is what Jonathan Crary has slightly but not totally hyperbolically characterized as '24/7 time,' which 'renders plausible, even normal, the idea of working without pause, without limits' (10).[6]

But for the gig worker, as for the housewife, as for the woman taking care of her family and someone else's too, unlimited work does not mean that time is undifferentiated. We could think about the ride-sharing driver or other members of the gig economy, constantly interrupted at home—or at work—by the call for more work. We could think about the impossible temporal juggling of someone who works multiple 'full-time' jobs or the people—historically and still women of color—who do their own domestic and reproductive work and do that work for others. We could think about the state of discontinuity produced in workers' lives by all sorts of exploitative jobs, the kind that come and dry up at any minute;[7] or, finally, we could and probably do think about the constant, worrying simultaneous hum of the impossible demands of care work on almost all people who work in other places and times, in other ways.

Just as no amount of literary work can solve the problem of gendered domestic and reproductive labor, neither will it be able to render the lives of all of those who are overworked and undervalued materially more livable, although there are arguments to be made for creativity and imagination of the kind demonstrated by 'Snapshots of a Daughter-in-Law.' But I am suggesting that literature, here, helps us perceive something important about the time, or the temporality, of working—it can give it a form, it can show us what it feels like to work this way, or it can make us feel it. Might perceiving a common temporality—and more importantly, feeling it—turn the weird, failed, endless, ragged time of some kinds of work into a site of solidarity, of connection between different kinds of laborers?[8] Might bringing a 'valued' kind of work—the making of a poem—into close contact with historically and presently undervalued kinds of work lead to the revaluing of the latter? For this kind of experience, located and felt in specific moments, scraps of poetry might be a place to start.

Notes

1. For a similar activity-based redefinition of essentialized gender, see Angela Garbes's *Essential Labor: Mothering as Social Change,* in which Garbes describes 'mothering' as 'an action that includes people of all genders and nonparents alike' (9). Garbes also cites Alexis Pauline Gumbs, China Martens, and Mai'a Williams's anthology *Revolutionary Mothering: Love on the Front Lines,* writing of mothering as 'the practice of creating, nurturing, affirming, and supporting life' (9).
2. Brinkman spells out a similarly shaped argument about a 'scrappy poetics' in the work of Marianne Moore, although with different ends. Rather than viewing Moore's 'scrappy' collage work as 'a direct extension of the visual

avant-garde,' Brinkman suggests that 'Moore developed [a 'scrappy' poetics] that is largely indebted to the scrapbook as a popular and 'feminized' alternative to this formulation—an alternative that calls into question the major assumptions of the historical avant-garde' (107). This view, in turn, lets us see the modernist collage poems of writers such as T.S. Eliot, Ezra Pound, and William Carlos Williams in a new genealogical light (140). For full histories of scrapbooking and their relationship to gender, and to gendered labor, see Ellen Gruber Garvey's book *Writing With Scissors.*

3. The immensity is as vast today as it was in the 1960s and 1970s, if not more so; Garbes cites a 2019 study that estimates the economic value of the sum total of all the hours of care work performed by women globally, if paid at a US minimum wage, at 10.9 trillion dollars for the year 2019 (52; see Gus Wezerek and Kristen R. Ghodsee, 'Women's Unpaid Labor is Worth $10,900,000,000,000,' *New York Times,* March 5 2020, https://nytimes.com/interactive/2020/03/04/opinion/women-unpaid-labor.html). As a point of comparison, for astronomical figures, the US military budget for 2019 was around $686 billion, and the national debt in 2023—a figure broadcast in running electronic numbers on a billboard near my house as a demonstration of its immensity—was around $32 trillion. Even if, for an individual woman occupied with raising only her own children, the work is, of course, finite, the amount of care work required globally is quite literally coeval with life itself.
4. 'Few tasks,' de Beauvoir writes, 'are more similar to the torment of Sisyphus than those of the housewife; day after day, one must wash dishes, dust furniture, mend clothes that will be dirty, dusty, and torn again. The housewife wears herself out running on the spot; she does nothing; she only perpetuates the present; she never gains the sense that she is conquering a positive Good, but struggles indefinitely against Evil. It is a struggle that begins again every day' (474).
5. See Anne Boyer's *Garments Against Women* for another instance of conflicting and mutually exclusive kinds of work—for Boyer, 'writing' and 'not writing'—performed, tensely, together. I grapple with this simultaneity, or near-simultaneity, in my essay "Writing / Not Writing: Anne Boyer, *Paralipsis*, and the Model of Literary Work.'
6. See Sarah Kessler for an account of the development of the gig (app-based) economy in the US around 2014, with the rise of platforms such as Uber and TaskRabbit. If these companies provided quick opportunities for labour that were attractive for the freedom and flexibility they promised, Kessler shows how just as quickly, this model of working became 'not a solution but a problem in need of one' (110). 'Just as the gig economy is an extreme version of the economy-wide trend away from direct employment,' Kessler writes, 'so too—with its total lack of safety net benefits—was it an extreme version of the increasing insecurity felt by even the directly employed portion of the middle class' (184).

Even though it has been sometimes seen as the face of 'work today,' it is worth remembering that such instability and such seeming boundlessness has historically characterized the work of women (domestic workers, sex workers) and people of colour (agricultural workers, for instance): I am thinking, for instance, of Saidiya Hartman's descriptions of the Black women in 1930s Harlem who made up the 'paper bag brigade,' waiting each day in the old slave market of the Bronx 'for Bronx housewives to buy their strength and energy for an hour, two hours, or even for a day at the munificent rate of fifteen, twenty, twenty-five, or if luck be with them, thirty cents an hour' (Ella Baker and Marvel Cooke, quoted Hartman 301).

7. See M. Ty for a useful discussion of some characteristics of precarious work at present, including 'flexploitation' and the 'permatemp' worker.
8. As Joseph Entin remarks in his book on precarious labour, film, and literature, 'solidarity is not only an abstract, dispassionate principle, but also a visceral relation, a feeling experienced in the body, in specific moments and dynamics of engagement or action' (163).

Works Cited

Auden, W.H. Forward to *A Change of World*. New Haven: Yale University Press: 1951. Reprinted in *Adrienne Rich's Poetry and Prose*, edited by Barbara Charlesworth Gelpi and Albert Gelpi. Norton Critical, 1993, pp. 277–279.

Benjamin, Walter. *The Arcades Project*, translated by Howard Eiland and Kevin McLaughlin. Belknap Press, 1999.

De Beauvoir, Simone. *The Second Sex*. Translated by Constance Borde and Sheila Malovany-Chevallier, Vintage Books, 2009.

Boyer, Anne. *Garments Against Women*. Ashsahta Press, 2015.

Brinkman, Bartholomew. *Poetic Modernism in the Culture of Mass Print*. Johns Hopkins University Press, 2016.

Crary, Jonathan. *24/7: Late Capitalism and the Ends of Sleep*. Verso, 2014.

Cushman, Stephen, et al., eds. *The Princeton Encyclopedia of Poetry and Poetics*. 4th edn. Princeton University Press, 2012.

Entin, Joseph B. *Living Labor: Fiction, Film, and Precarious Work*. University of Michigan Press, 2023.

Garbes, Angela. *Essential Labor: Mothering as Social Change*. Harper Wave, 2022.

Garvey, Ellen Gruber. *Writing with Scissors: American Scrapbooks from the Civil War to the Harlem Renaissance*. Oxford University Press, 2012.

Gumbs, Alexis Pauline, et al., editors. *Revolutionary Mothering: Love on the Front Lines*. PM Press, 2016.

Hacker, Marilyn. "*Snapshots of a Daughter-in-Law*: The Young Insurgent's Commonplace Book." In *Field: Contemporary Poetry and Poetics* 77, 2007, pp. 16–20.

Hartman, Saidiya. *Wayward Lives, Beautiful Experiments: Intimate Histories of Social Upheaval*. Norton, 2019.

Holladay, Hilary. *The Power of Adrienne Rich*. Doubleday, 2020.
hooks, bell. "Homeplace: a site of resistance," in *Yearning: Race, Gender, and Cultural Politics*, South End Press, 1990, 41–49.
Kessler, Sarah. *Gigged: The End of the Job and the Future of Work*. St. Martin's Press, 2018.
Olsen, Tillie. *Silences*. The Feminist Press at CUNY, 2003.
Rich, Adrienne. *Adrienne Rich's Poetry and Prose*, edited by Barbara Charlesworth Gelpi and Albert Gelpi. Norton Critical, 1993.
—. "Snapshots of a Daughter-in-Law: Poems 1954–1962." 1963. W.W. Norton, 1967.
—. "When We Dead Awaken: Writing as Re-Vision." *College English*, vol. 34, no. 1, 1972, pp. 18–30.
Turner, Lindsay. "Writing / Not Writing: Anne Boyer, *Paralipsis*, and the Model of Literary Work," *ASAP / Journal,* vol. 3, no. 1, 2018, pp. 121–142.
Ty, M. "Beckett and the Character of the Unchosen; Or, the Time of Precarity." *the minnesota review* 85, 2015, 132–143.
Wezerek, Gus and Kristen R. Ghodsee, "Women's Unpaid Labor is Worth $10,900,000,000,000," *New York Times,* March 5 2020, https://nytimes.com/interactive/2020/03/04/opinion/women-unpaid-labor.html.
Woolf, Virginia. *A Room of One's Own*. New York: Harcourt, 1981.

8

Cheap Talk: Conversation, Gender, and Labor in *Talking to Women*, *The Pumpkin Eater*, and *The Golden Notebook*

Helen Charman

In 1964 the British writer, factory worker, and erstwhile aristocrat Nell Dunn published *Talking to Women*, a book composed of interviews with nine of her peers: Pauline Boty, who was twenty-five; Kathy Collier, twenty-six; Frances Chadwick, twenty-seven; Edna O'Brien, thirty-two; Emma Charlton, twenty-nine; Antonia Simon, twenty-six; Suna Portman, twenty-four; Paddy Kitchen, thirty-one; and Ann Quin, twenty-nine. (Dunn herself was twenty-eight at the time.) The interviews are almost universally engaged with a canonically feminist problem: how to distinguish between domestic labor and professional work.[1] This divide can, of course, also be characterized as one between private and public life, which in turn raises the question of whether such a thing exists as a 'private life' at all. In Dunn's book, something culturally coded as not only private but trivial—a conversation between women over a drink at the end of the working day—is afforded the status of historical and literary method. Despite its frequent centrality to working rhythms, women's conversation—gossip, or chat—has historically been considered a leisure practice, its quantity read as being in inverse proportion to its significance. The proverbial 'cheapness' of such talk has resulted in the implicit valuation of projects like Dunn's below other forms of literary expression. Yet in the dual context of both the Women's Liberation Movement (WLM), which dominated the decade that followed the publication of *Talking to Women*, and the contemporary trend for 'rediscovering' forgotten literary works by women, such understandings of value have begun to shift.

Feminism is often conceived of as being in some way generational, with its first, second, third, and fourth waves: each new generation is accused of either forgetting or following in its mothers' and grandmothers' footsteps.

Although this tactic of separation paints too simplistic—or perhaps too ordered—a picture, it is true that the WLM, generally dated to the first National Women's Liberation Movement Conference held at Ruskin College, Oxford in 1970, has become partially synonymous with the second generation of British feminism itself. *Talking to Women*, then, is a text positioned on a boundary, and in its careful chronicling of the internal weather of a handful of British women it anticipates changes that were to become more concretely politically legible in the years that followed. The most obvious way in which it does so is in its focus on work, which was central to the first four demands of the WLM, decided at the Ruskin conference: equal pay, equal educational and job opportunities, free contraception and abortion on demand, and free twenty-four-hour nurseries. These demands, alongside a further three that emerged later, aim to reform the state, seeking to mitigate the inequalities, as theorists of social reproduction have taught us, caused by the uneven division of labor within the home (Bhattacharya; Forrester). The second way in which Dunn's text appears to anticipate the feminist structures of the decade that followed is in its method: the exposure of feelings through free associative speech, rooted in the relatively new mode of oral history and, in its emphasis on pre-existing social bonds between the speaker and the interviewer, prefiguring the new practice of 'consciousness-raising'. Throughout the 1970s, consciousness-raising or 'CR' groups met and discussed aspects of their lives—housework, marriage, abortion, sex, birth, depression—and, through this discussion, articulated the political dimensions of these personal experiences (Charman). Talking, as many veterans of the WLM maintain in their recollections of that period today, changed everything.[2]

This chapter uses Dunn's text as scaffolding for a consideration of the relationship between the representation of women's talk and the changing aesthetic modes of the British novel in the post-war period. Drawing on theoretical histories of gendered, classed and racialized silence, particularly in relation to the construction of the literary canon and the legacies of the psychotherapeutic consulting room, I want to consider talk—conversation, gossip, chatter—in relation to other kinds of feminized labor, to literary labor, and to the conventions of literary language itself. I want to begin, as Dunn does, by looking backwards. The epigraph to *Talking to Women* comes from a surprising source: George Eliot's *Daniel Deronda* (1876), a novel which is often held as having opened up a rift in novelistic structure more generally. Raymond Williams, writing in 1970, categorized it as a text signaling a transition between two different social worlds, in which a protagonist's 'divided consciousness of belonging and not belonging' can only be resolved through 'an emigration, at once resigned and hopeful, from what had originally been offered as a decisive social world' (87). This 'emigration' is an act that traverses the boundaries of both the nation state and the family, tracing the divided consciousness of the protagonist—in this case, Deronda—along the already-fragmenting lines of communal identity that entered the next century. In considering the expression of 'divided consciousness' in novels written in the thick of the twentieth century, I will read the destruction of Williams's 'social world' as an opportunity for renewal through the formation of new relationships. These relationships, constructed from the bonds formed by feminist talking, are reliant on a psychoanalytic form of attention: the 'raising' of consciousness requires, at least in part, a striving to understand the subconscious structures of this earlier circumscribed social world.

Central to this understanding of the subconscious is the articulation of it. The primary comparative work of this chapter is between two novels published in 1962, positioned, like *Talking to Women,* on the edge of a profound change: Penelope Mortimer's *The Pumpkin Eater* and Doris Lessing's *The Golden Notebook*, both texts which foreground their protagonist's nervous breakdown with a social isolation and an increasingly unstable reliance on verbal expression. Rather than considering, as critics like Lisa Maria Hogeland have done, the insights of the 'consciousness-raising novel', I want to consider what the preconsciousness-raising novel has to tell: to what does it give voice? How, in the absence of the interlocutors that feminist kinship would provide, does the work of articulation become an individual occupation, and what remains occluded?

Private Joys

Oral history was something that Dunn would return to several times throughout her varied career: *Living Like I Do* (1977) gathered interviews with men and women who were living in alternative domestic arrangements, and 1991's *Grandmothers* compiled ten conversations about having grandchildren. In *Talking to Women*, her first offering in the genre, the method itself is as central as the content it produces. In this sense, it mirrors the prominence of 'talking cures', both in formalized therapeutic settings and in the practice of consciousness raising, in the cultural imaginary of the period. Out of print for many years, *Talking to Women* was 'rediscovered' by the independent feminist publisher Silver Press in 2018. In the introduction to that new edition, the novelist Ali Smith writes that:

> Talking, naturally (as well as talking naturally), is one of the central preoccupations of *Talking to Women.* Its common theme is the radical necessity of giving and having voice. Its interviewees admit and repeat both desire and difficulty in just, well, talking. While they do, something fundamental shifts in the act of the book: the possibilities of talk, and what talk means, shift as we read it. (vii)

Central to these shifts is the collapsing of boundaries between 'talking', 'communication', and the language of literary expression: 'Do you find communication a problem?', Dunn asks Kitchen; 'Yes,' she replies, at the beginning of a twenty-two-page-long interview, 'I'm not very good at talking' (171). Writing, in particular, is a prominent unifying factor between language and work. Although the book, particularly in the material released around its republication, was billed as one with a socially diverse group of subjects, there is a predictable skewing of the sample towards writers: O'Brien, Quin, Kitchen and Dunn herself were writers. (Others, like Boty and Simon, were artists.)

In this context, Dunn's insistence on the importance of 'privacy' is intriguing, not least in her surprising decision to root this in a longer lineage of literary production. In the 1964 preface to the book she compares the project of recording women's feelings about their lives to the advice given by Daniel Deronda to Gwendolen Harleth: she should reconcile herself, he thinks, to singing for '"private joy" instead of the public ear' (XIV). Over fifty years later, in the afterword to the new edition, Dunn returns to this reference point: what she remembers of these conversations, she writes, is 'the intense pleasure'. 'This was the 1960s,' she continues, 'a time of huge belief in freedom and self-fulfilment. A time indeed for the "private joys" of life' (211). Dunn's choice of allusion is curious not just for its irony—these are conversations that are going to be published—but for its context. In Eliot's novel, which is often categorized as one chiefly concerned with its dual plots—its protagonist's identity and corresponding vocation, and the unhappy domestic tragedy of Gwendolen—this is a moment of profound disappointment for Gwendolen, who has been hoping to make a career of singing for the 'public ear'. An eldest daughter whose formerly affluent family have fallen on hard times, she marries the abusive aristocrat Henleigh Mallinger Grandcourt in order to avoid having to secure employment as a governess. A complex and wilful character, she has lofty ambitions, which might be characterized as the very 'freedom and self-fulfilment' that Dunn eulogizes: 'Gwendolen,' the "meek governess", Miss Merry informs the reader early on, 'will not rest without having the world at her feet' (39). Eliot's narrator and, in the sense of the broader plot that consigns Gwendolen to a profoundly miserable fate, Eliot herself, take a dim view of Gwendolen, as is true of many of her young female protagonists, especially the beautiful and/or romantically ambitious ones: 'Gwendolen's confidence,' we are told, 'lay chiefly in herself. She felt well equipped for the mastery of life'; she believes in her ability to 'manage her own destiny' (40). Such hubris renders her ripe for a fall.[3]

Gwendolen's hopes of singing professionally are first dashed by the musician Herr Klesmer, who tells her that she should have started training earlier: now, she can only hope to become 'mediocre'. This conversation leaves Gwendolen thoroughly miserable, having, 'for the first time since her consciousness began', a 'vision of herself on the common level [. . .] treated like a passenger with a third-class ticket, in spite of private objections on her own part': this is a moment that we might expect a reader like Dunn to understand as a coming to the beginnings of a gendered consciousness, rather than one related to either self-fulfilment or freedom (262). Deronda, in counseling her later that she should imitate his decision to 'make it a virtue to be content with my middlingness', declares that 'We should have a poor life of it if we were reduced for all our pleasure to our own performances' (411). On the surface, this is a good point: it is true that we cannot all be talented singers. It is easier, however, to make a virtue of your 'middlingness' if you are a gentleman of means, rather than a young woman desperately seeking a path to financial independence amongst the very limited options available to her.

Both of these interactions are made worse, for Gwendolen, by the elevation of two other women in comparison to her: Catherine Arrowpoint, to whom Klesmer has scandalously become engaged, and Mirah Lapidoth, the young woman Deronda has taken under his wing and will eventually marry, who he refers to as one of the 'few' who can provide public pleasure through art and music. In Dunn's book, as well as in a wealth of feminist literature from the 1960s and 1970s, of which there was an enormous amount, written, illustrated, mimeographed, stapled, and distributed across the country, it is observed over and over again that the insights of the WLM had enabled women to talk to each other as if for the first time: they were able, finally, to exist in solidarity, rather than competing as enemies or rivals. Also frequently repeated in the literature, even when it is explicitly antipathetic toward Freud himself, is the centrality of the articulated unconscious to the feminist political project. The liberation of women would, in theory, ensure that men, women, and children would be free to understand their own feelings, their own consciousness;

Sheila Rowbotham, writing in 1979 phrased it thus: 'How do we conceive and imagine a completely different society, involving not only change in the external structures but an inner transformation of our consciousness and our feelings?' (119). Consciousness raising was one possible answer, although some, like the feminist psychoanalyst Juliet Mitchell, cautioned against the reification of feelings alone: although women—always, under capitalism 'the chief repository of feelings'—were 'thus among the first to gain from the radical "capture" of emotionality from capitalist ideology for political protest movements,' to express an emotion had to be understood as the beginning rather than the end of a process. 'Emotions,' she wrote in 1971, 'cannot be "free" or "true" in isolation: they are dependent today on a social base that imprisons and determines them' (*Woman's Estate* 38). In other words, any attempt to remove feelings from their sociopolitical context limits both our understanding of them and the possible, radical forms these emotions might take in the future (Charman). 'Giving voice' to these feelings in writing, then, was one path toward understanding women's lives and women's labor as fundamentally political in their construction and conception.

The events of *Daniel Deronda* take place between 1864 and 1866: Gwendolen, alas, is around a century too early for *Spare Rib* magazine and a local consciousness-raising circle. She is also too early, although only by a decade, for psychoanalysis, although Eliot appears at times to be anticipating its insights, as Jacqueline Rose's virtuosic reading of the novel's opening scene in *Sexuality in the Field of Vision* (1986), demonstrates. For Rose, Gwendolen functions as the 'spectacle of femininity'—we are compelled to look at her from the very first line, 'Was she beautiful or not beautiful?—and as such she structures the novel's crisis of representation, in which the 'relentless scrutiny of the woman' exists as a brutal, 'logical' response to the failure of omniscient realist narrative (112; 108–109). In *Daniel Deronda,* this works itself out—or rather, doesn't—in the radical splitting of the story: the initial primacy of Gwendolen in the novel means her body can become the ground on which Eliot tests out her splintering knowledge, before casting her off from the marriage plot's final resolution. Gwendolen ends the novel—and, in Williams' and Rose's account, marks the end of the Victorian novel as a form more generally—silenced: unable to work as a singer and able only to communicate with Deronda, her sole confidant for most of the narrative, via letter. In this context, then, Dunn's emphasis on 'private joy' remains a perplexing one. Yet, if the work of a writer is, to return to Ali Smith's observation about *Talking to Women,* to 'give voice', then where does Eliot—who described her social realist novels as 'experiments in life' (*Letters*, vi, 216–17)—give voice, in the paradoxes of Gwendolen's unfulfilled relationship between her own voice, her ability to work, and her own desires, to prevailing orthodoxies about ambition and gender? In its use of *Deronda* as an ambivalent framework for a mock therapeutic historical method, Dunn can be productively understood as striving to perform feminist history from below, something the historian Hannah Proctor has linked to the psychotherapeutic recovery of 'lost' voices. In this way, we can see a clear link between the social function of texts like Dunn's—recording women's relationships to their feelings and to their labor—and the 'psy' disciplines themselves: psychoanalysis is concerned with what is unspoken or unspeakable, something feminist readings of Freud's case histories have specifically centered in their aim to recover traces of women's voices (Mitchell, *Psychoanalysis and Feminism*; Showalter).

Baby Talk

Central to the wider project of women's liberation, especially that conceived by writers like Mitchell and Rowbotham—both key figures of the New Left who endeavored to merge socialist and Marxist theory with feminist thought—was to identify the domestic as inseparable from the socioeconomic: it also, as Stephen Brooke has pointed out, had its roots in more practical critique of the 'central ambiguity of modern women's lives: the tension between their reproductive and productive roles' (187). Marital isolation was a central concern: the angel in the house—certainly not something Gwendolen could have been identified as—required renewed attention. Maternal feelings, and their relationship to domestic work, were a particular point of contention, something impossible to disentangle from the fight for abortion provision. There was a growing understanding, as Adrienne Rich articulated in 1976 in *Of Woman Born* that gestation had historically been 'a form of forced labour' (158): without reliable and safe contraception or abortion, pregnancy cannot truly be 'chosen'. *Talking to Women* was published three years before the landmark 1967 Abortion Act, which, although it did not legalize abortion *per se*, introduced a series of circumstances in which pregnancies could be terminated lawfully in England, Scotland and Wales, up to twenty-four weeks.[4]

Women's talk was literally productive in its centrality to the procurement of terminations before the 1967 act: the act of gathering information about methods, risks, abortionists, and fees was one cloaked in gossip, disguised in the euphemisms of idle chatter. It was also ameliorative: in discussing their experiences of such a common process, women were able to identify the imperative toward shame that abortion engendered as a social tool rather than a moral absolute. In the interviews in *Talking to Women* that mention abortion, a frequent reference point is Penelope Mortimer's 1962 novel *The Pumpkin Eater*, an unsettling portrait of a woman who is almost constantly pregnant until she is persuaded to undergo a sterilization by her unfaithful and controlling husband. In Mortimer's rendering, the desire to be continually pregnant or breastfeeding is an ambiguous one, at times understood, including by her psychiatrist, as a way of dealing with the shame of sexuality, and at others as her own profound and radical attempt to fully control her body, which is frequently objectified and pursued by male characters. Writing in 1987, Roberta Rubenstein observed that Mortimer's novel had been almost entirely ignored by critics: this remains true almost two decades later, although more attention has been given to Harold Pinter's film adaptation, which was directed by Jack Clayton and released in 1964 (Rubenstein, 58). *The Pumpkin Eater* positions a woman's body and its performance of maternal labor exactly on the boundary of the public and the private, with the problem of 'giving voice' to complicated feelings and desires, alongside the question of value and use. Mrs Armitage, its protagonist, spends most of the novel alone with only her children for company: in its title, the novel engages with domestic containment as well as the associations of infant speech development in its invocation of the English nursery rhyme 'Peter Peter Pumpkin Eater', which provides the novel's epigraph: 'Peter, Peter pumpkin eater, / Had a wife but couldn't keep her; / He put her in a pumpkin shell / And there he kept her very well'.

Speech, repeatedly, professionally and personally, fails Mrs Armitage. The novel opens in what we assume to be a psychiatrist's consulting room, where the very idea of curative speech is being problematized: 'Well,' Mrs Armitage is saying, 'I will try. I honestly will try to be honest with you, although I suppose really what you're more interested in is my not being honest, if you see what I mean.' She goes on to describe a 'wool drawer' that her mother had when she was small, and the 'pointless' task of tidying it she was assigned 'whenever it was a wet afternoon.' The psychiatrist sees exactly what she means: 'You would like to be something useful,' he said sadly. 'Like a tea cosy' (7). A few pages into their conversation, Mrs Armitage begins to get frustrated with the line of questioning: 'I thought I was supposed to lie on a couch and you wouldn't say a word. It's like the Inquisition or something'. The doctor corrects her assumption: 'I'm not an analyst, Mrs Armitage' (10). What he is, the novel initially encourages the reader to believe, is the latest in a long line of paternalistic authority figures who restrict her agency: both actual fathers, who we see arrange her marriage as a kind of trade deal struck for boarding school fees and property, and other medical professionals. The family doctor, when he visits the house after her first nervous breakdown—the reader learns from the perspective of Mrs Armitage the eavesdropper—discusses her desire for another child with her husband over a drink: if she wants one, he says, 'Then why doesn't she have one? When this little storm's over, probably just the thing. She drops those babies like a cat, you know – it's a pleasure to watch' (37). So far, so simplistic: we can see the lines being drawn between the aggressors (men) and Armitage, the victim. Rapidly, however, Mortimer complicates the picture: not only does Armitage herself describe her abandonment of previous husbands, rather than the other way around, but she disputes the expected diagnoses: although her husband has 'no use for Freud', which he describes as 'all that cock', he would 'unhesitatingly say that I longed all my life for a husband like my father: practical, positive, a man with a work bench, reliable;' a description we recognize, even believe, before it is dispelled: 'But then, my father was not like this. His reliability was invented by Jake' (47). In fact, this fantasy of reliability is more accurately a fantasy of Jake's own relationship to himself. To his wife, whose constant pregnancies he seems to find emasculating in its erasure of him from the center of her attention—'where do *I* come in?,' he asks—he functions, psychically at least, like another infant:

> He craned up to kiss me. Like a child, with puckered mouth and closed eyes, he waited. I looked at him carefully. I thought of my other husbands, decent, adult, unselfish men from whom I had escaped while escaping my childhood – each one an insufficient parent, readily left alone. They seemed to watch me while Jake waited for his maternal kiss. Now it's your turn to suffer, my girl. Now it's up to you to do the forgiving and forgetting. Now it's your turn to refuse freedom or give it out inch by inch. (31)

This vision of Jake as a child, and of herself as a parental figure in her marital relationship, echoes some of the insights about marriage and its negotiations shared in *Talking to Women* and in the feminist press in the decades that followed, in magazines like *Red Rag* and *Spare Rib* but also in more surprising places, like Vicky Seddon's industrial reportage during the 1984–85 miner's strike: Cath Cunningham from Fife told her that 'mining women in particular have a protective attitude to their husbands;

when you get married or go to stay with someone you take on the role of mother' (45). But Armitage, crucially, has nobody to talk to about this particular state of affairs. The relationship with the psychiatrist has ended abruptly: he tells her he is going on a three-week skiing holiday, and she—abandoned—never makes another appointment. She compares this revelation of the falsehood of the relationship, its financial basis, to a salesman leaving a free sample, before blaming him explicitly for her sterilization: 'I heard later that he had broken a leg ski-ing, I thought then, blaming him, that if he hadn't gone we might both have remained undamaged' (79). Without him, she really is entirely alone:

> I needed the outside world, but had no idea where to find it. For the first time I needed friends: there were none. Over-indulgence in sexual and family life had left us, as far as other relationships were concerned, virginal; we said we had friends as much as schoolchildren, busy with notes and hearts and keepsakes, say they have lovers. (122)

Without an interlocutor, and, crucially, without any friends, her self-knowledge can only ever be partially realized, her consciousness only fleetingly raised: at the beginning of the novel, when she realizes that Jake is having an affair with their live-in nanny, she recalls that she had in fact already known this before the point of discovery, that she had been aware of him holding both of their hands in the cinema ('keeping us both happy'): 'I knew you were. Perhaps I actually saw you were. But I didn't believe it' (28). Denial was, in many accounts, essential to the self-sacrifice that the condition of housewife required. The 'virginal' consequences of her 'over-indulgence' in family life, meanwhile, have resulted, at least by her psychiatrist's diagnosis, in a 'horror of sex without children', which is 'messy', and 'unproductive' (47). Indeed, Armitage's problems are to do with a lack of productivity. Not only is she isolated from other women and, therefore, the production of intimacy, but she is also denied the usual housewife's consolation for the lack of economic productivity that domestic labors provide: Jake is a successful screenwriter and they can afford to hire a cleaner. In the absence of the tasks she used to perform in her previous marriage, Armitage is consumed by apathy, 'I could dust the room or tidy the magazines now the house is empty. But why? It's somebody else's job' (34). The only mode of production that remains within her grasp is reproduction: to have another baby would put her body, as it were, to work, and the labors of gestation would be doubly purposive.

When this desire is thwarted, then, Armitage is experiencing a common act of reproductive coercion—although transposed onto a different class and race position than forced sterilization usually is—which is figured as a belated act of communication. After her abortion and sterilization, recovering in hospital, she discovers a letter from her husband's mistress, a revelation which manifests itself bodily: 'I went to the basin and was sick. I could feel the lips of my wound parting, as though my wound were laughing at me' (114). The wound, later, refuses to heal: her body 'my body, which had always done exactly what I wanted, turned spiteful' (122). Jake's mistress, Beth Conway, is also the victim of reproductive coercion, albeit from the opposite perspective. Her husband, once he discovers the fact that she is pregnant with Jake's baby, forces her to keep it, explicitly figuring the pregnancy itself as a punishment and the idea of a public birth as a humiliation:

> She's going to have this kid in a public ward and if there's any way of stopping her getting a whiff of gas, I'll find it. She's going to wipe its bottom and stare at its ugly mug for the rest of her young life. There's going to be no more movies, no more champagne, no more hair-dos, no more sexy clothes for my little Beth. This kid's going to kill her. I've told her that. (129)

There is no possibility of this shared experience forging a connection between the two women, however: the news of Beth's pregnancy is delivered to Armitage by an anonymous caller, and they never directly communicate. Their isolation, marked by this non-communication, denies them the comfort or even the liberation that their shared suffering could have provided, articulated in accounts of consciousness raising. In *Spare Rib*, one writer recalled that:

> We spoke of our families, childhood, friends, colleagues, lovers, our painful experiences, fears, secrets and happy times, our future dreams and plans . . . all of which sparked off talk on many other subjects. We were continually surprised, encouraged, and excited by the similarity of our experiences, and as this sharing went on many of us found the confidence to do things that really mattered to us, however trivial . . . Through consciousness- raising there is the realization that you are no longer alone. (Philpott, 585–587)

Armitage, denied this, has to find outlets for such articulation through her various paternalistic interlocutors. At the end of the novel, in bed with

Giles, one of her three former husbands, she is finally able to give voice to some of her rage, and, more crucially perhaps, her maternal ambivalence. He tells her, unsettled by her frankness, that she loves her children, and she replies:

> You sound like someone reciting a kind of creed. Supposing I told you that I didn't love the children, that I don't give a damn about the children? It might be true, you know. But for years you've relied on me to bring them up and provide love and cut their fingernails and teach them to tell the truth, as though it mattered. You've been free. Supposing I want to be free? (135)

The psychiatrist, who she has previously understood as the only person to whom she could speak anything approaching freely, comes under attack: the freedom he afforded, as he encouraged her to think about her feelings, was a transactional one, a manufactured intimacy:

> There must come a time in your life, mustn't there, when the most important thing to do is to find out who you really are, what you're really like. That doctor I went to . . . he made me angry, he wanted me to change. You know, he wanted to sterilize my . . . *attitude* to everything. (135–136)

Armitage, here, is positioned on the brink of something: the catharsis of this realization is a feminist one, anticipating the changes in conversation to come, but it has not yet found its vessel, or its outlet. There is no other woman in the room, and no movement, yet, to home it: these are private agonies.

Crazy Talk

In *The Golden Notebook,* privacy is not the problem. Doris Lessing, as Lorna Sage wrote in 1983, 'is not—despite the title of her essay on the art of the novel, "The Small Personal Voice" (1957)—a private or self-contained writer' (10). Its focus is not domestic or creative labor, but rather the work of political organizing, and the work of keeping the self together after the demise of the structures it previously existed within. This work, the work of self-sustainment, relies, like the more bourgeois concerns of *The Pumpkin Eater* and *Talking to Women,* on giving voice. Anna Wulf, its protagonist, suffering from writer's block and the general feeling that everything is 'cracking up' (27), alternates between talking her problems out—or trying to—with her friend, Molly, in five omnisciently narrated sections of the novel entitled 'Free Women', paying to talk to a psychoanalyst she shares with Molly, Mrs Marks, and writing in four different notebooks: black, recounting her time in the then-named Southern Rhodesia; red, her time in the Communist Party; yellow, the end of a relationship; and blue, documenting her feelings and her dreams.

None of Anna's vocalizing works. In the traditionally realist 'Free Women' sections, Anna and Molly converse in a 'tone' that, ironic and matter-of-fact, provides the illusion of emotional communication whilst blocking it completely: 'if I'm not careful,' Anna writes, 'Molly and I will descend into a kind of twin old-maidhood, where we sit around saying to each other, Do you remember how that man, what-was-his-name said that insensitive thing, it must have been in 1947 ...' (53). A little later, Anna describes the tone spatially, a container: 'I hate that tone, and yet we all lived inside it for months and years ... it was a self-punishing, a locking of feeling, an inability or a refusal to fit conflicting things together to make a whole; so that one can live inside it, no matter how terrible. The refusal means one can neither change nor destroy ...' (72). This way of speaking flattens out the textures as well as the extremities of Anna and—we assume—Molly's psychic lives: it is the opposite of consciousness raising, based as it is in a refusal to entertain that the personal might overlap with the political. (Molly praises Anna's work as being 'real', rather than 'little novels about the emotions' (61)). *The Golden Notebook* became a touchstone in the feminist movement of the decades that followed, and Lessing herself complained in a preface to the novel written in 1971 that it was being misread as a 'trumpet for Women's Liberation', with nobody noticing its central themes because 'the book was instantly belittled, by friendly reviewers as well as hostile ones, as being about the sex war, or was claimed by women as a useful weapon in the sex war'. It was a book that appeared to anticipate the zeitgeist to come, or, in Lessing's own words, it was not read in the 'right way' because it 'skipped a stage of opinion [...] written as if the attitudes that have been created by the Women's Liberation movements already existed' (9). This is particularly clear in the meta-fictional interlude of Ella and Paul in the yellow notebook: Ella is a writer with a job answering letters sent to the medical column of a women's magazine that are too personal for the male doctor to answer himself, and she diagnoses the festering gendered wound of suburban domesticity, a place where superficially 'everything's fine—all quiet and tame and suburban. But underneath it's poisonous. It's full of hatred and envy and people being lonely' (178). Paul, her lover—a neurologist—has what Sage calls 'an ironic recognition of the shape of things to come', asserting as their affair implodes that 'The real revolution is, women against men' (52).

One of Anna's frustrations with the 'tone' in 'Free Women' is made manifest in its foreclosure of any attempt to discuss their respective psychoanalytic experiences with Mrs Marks, or Mother Sugar as they jokingly call her: the first several pages of the novel revolve around Anna attempting to open the subject in the face of Molly's 'unspoken but clear determination not to discuss it' (27). The only aspect of the process that Molly is prepared to discuss is Anna's block, her tangible and diagnosable unproductivity, unable to see—as the reader will, eventually—that it is precisely this interpersonal inability to communicate, the urge to compartmentalize, that drives the blockage and Anna's eventual breakdown. Psychoanalysis, for Anna, allows her to articulate her emotional experiences, but acts, too, as a form of narrative containment. Mrs Marks, she complains to an unwilling Molly, is too beholden to archetypes: 'Mother Sugar used to say, "You're Electra", or "You're Antigone", and that was the end, as far as she was concerned' (27). In the blue notebook, which Anna describes as failing to be 'the most truthful of the notebooks' as she had expected, an extended conversation is recounted with Mrs Marks/Mother Sugar in which Anna identifies that her analyst's Freudian intentions—namely that she will be 'able to live more easily now than I did', accustomed to her ordinary unhappiness—have fallen short of the release she is seeking (412–413). This release is presented in textual terms: the work of psychoanalysis is the work of telling and interpreting stories, of naming things inside them: 'The pleasure of recognition, of a bit of rescue-work, so to speak, rescuing the formless into form. Another bit of chaos rescued and "named"' (414). Analysis of her dreams is failing in its very fictionality to enable Anna to unblock her ability to write fiction:

> But no sooner do you accomplish that, than you say quickly—put it away, put the pain away where it can't hurt, turn it into a story or into history. But I don't want to put it away. Yes, I know what you want me to say—that because I've rescued so much private pain-material—because I'm damned if I'll call it anything else, and 'worked through it' and accepted it and made it general, because of that I'm free and strong. Well all right, I'll accept it and say it. And what now? I'm tired of the wolves and the castle and the forests and the priests. I can cope with them in any form they choose to present themselves. But I've told you, I want to walk off, by myself, Anna Freeman. (414–415)

Telling stories, here, is the problem. *The Golden Notebook,* in its detailing of the psychic and social fallout of the mass exodus from the Communist Party of Great Britain after the Soviet Union's invasion of Hungary in 1956, has been described by Hannah Proctor and Larne Abse Gogarty as a kind of history from below, a departure from the external approach of 'conventional political histories'. Wulf diagnoses the Party itself with a historical malady: 'Nothing happened in our small, amateur and indeed ludicrous group,' she recalls of her time in Southern Rhodesia, 'that hadn't happened right back with the *Iskra* group in London at the beginning of the century, at the start of organized communism. If we had known anything at all about the history of our own movement we would have been saved from the cynicism, the frustration, the bewilderment' (85). Proctor and Abse Gogarty identify the history worth knowing, not as the kind that could be 'gleaned from examining the minutiae of political and organizational structures, strategies, logistics and decision-making,' but rather that of 'affective experiences and interpersonal dynamics': communist feelings.

There are comparisons to make between communism and feminism here. In 1970, the radical feminist Shulamith Firestone described the period between the first and second waves of feminism—the period into and about which Lessing was writing—as suffering from a 'blackout of feminist history' that kept 'women hysterically circling through a maze of false solutions' (30). The notebooks, her failed analysis, and her thwarted communication with Molly are perhaps all Anna's attempts to exit the maze. Anna, in her confrontation with Mrs Marks/Mother Sugar in the blue notebook, asserts that part of her chafing against the restraints of myth stems from the fact that 'there are whole areas of me made by the kind of experience women haven't had before [. . .] I believe I'm living the kind of life women never lived before' (415). In response, the analyst anticipates Firestone:

> In what way are you different? Are you saying there haven't been artist-women before? There haven't been women who were independent? There haven't been women who insisted on sexual freedom? I tell you, there are a great line of women stretching out behind you into the past, and you have to seek them out and find them in yourself and be conscious of them. (415)

To be conscious of them: to raise these figures like ghosts within your mind, and carry them with you. Anna, however, cannot achieve this without jeopardizing the integrity of her own subjectivity: 'it occurs to me,' she writes, a few pages later, 'that what is happening is a breakdown of me, Anna' (419). And so she disintegrates, multiple times and in multiple notebooks. But then she comes back: the novel ends twice, once with Anna—dispersed, discombobulated—taking Saul Green's instructions and writing out the first sentence of her novel, which is also the first sentence of *The Golden Notebook*, and then, for a final time, with the return to sanity, the 'Free Women' settling to a life of post-communist compromise, of marriage counseling and the Labour party, of ordinary unhappiness. Sage, echoing what Jacqueline Rose finds in *Daniel Deronda*, diagnoses this doubled denouement as Lessing's achievement of an 'impossible object', setting 'realist ends' against 'realist means' and, in the process, bringing 'the realist tradition to crisis point'. Lessing's novel, she writes, 'was a momentous book—a book *of* its moment, opened up to subconscious and subcultural imperatives which the realist perspective had structured and supressed' (55–56). On the dust jacket of the first edition of the novel, Lessing writes that it is 'an attempt to break form; to break certain forms of consciousness and go beyond them.' What happens next is nothing less than the work of giving voice to history, at the very moment of its occurrence. This requires in equal parts two forms of labor that, reproductive and crisis-ridden as they are, we can recognize as feminized: writing and talking.

Notes

1. I am using such national terms with a full awareness of their tendency toward generalization, especially in relation to feminist organizers in the north of Ireland, who often felt ignored and excluded. See, for example, Fairweather et al.; McWilliams. See also Charman.
2. For the most comprehensive collection of testimonies from those involved in the WLM, see Jolly.
3. Eliot herself had a highly complex relationship to the 'woman question' more generally, despite her close relationships with prominent figures campaigning for women's rights like Barbara Bodichon and Bessie Rayner Parkes, and her controversial decision to break convention and live with George Henry Lewes out of wedlock. See, in particular, Paxton; Beer. Ironically, Eliot largely succeeded—although at no small personal cost—in doing precisely what she accuses Gwendolen of: she had separated herself off from 'the common level' and was, to an almost unprecedented extent, the manager of her own destiny.
4. In 1965, Dunn's play *Up the Junction* was adapted into a BBC television film, directed by Ken Loach, and part of the influential *Wednesday Play* series that was later to premiere *Cathy Come Home* and other classics of the emerging kitchen-sink realism genre, which was instrumental in bringing more oxygen to the legalization debate.

Works Cited

Bhattacharya, Tithi. editor. *Social Reproduction Theory: Remapping Class, Recentering Oppression*. Pluto Press, 2017.

Beer, Gillian. *George Eliot and the Woman Question*. Edward Everett Root Publishers, 2018.

Brooke, Stephen. *Sexual Politics: Sexuality, Family Planning, and the British Left from the 1880s to the Present Day*. Oxford University Press, 2011.

Charman, Helen. *Mother State: a political history of motherhood*. Allen Lane, 2024.

Dunn, Nell. *Talking to Women*. Silver Press, 2018.

—. *Living Like I Do*. Futura Publications, 1977.

—. *Grandmothers—Talking to Nell Dunn*. Chatto & Windus, 1991.

Eliot, George. *Daniel Deronda*, edited by Terence Cave. Penguin 1995, repr. 2003.

—. *The George Eliot Letters*, ed. Gordon S. Haight, 9 vols. Yale University Press, 1954.

Fairweather, Eileen, et al. *Only the Rivers Run Free: Northern Ireland: The Women's War*. Pluto Press, 1984.

Firestone, Shulamith. *The Dialectic of Sex*. William Morrow and Company, 1970.

Forrester, Katrina. "Feminist Demands and the Problem of Housework." *American Political Science Review*, vol. 116, no.4, 2002, pp. 1278–1292.

Hogeland, Lisa Maria. *Feminism and its Fictions: The Consciousness-Raising Novel and the Women's Liberation Movement*. University of Pennsylvania Press, 1998.

Jolly, Margaretta, editor. *Sisterhood and After: An Oral History of the UK Women's Liberation Movement, 1968–present*. Oxford University Press, 2019.

McWilliams, Monica. "Struggling for Peace and Justice: Reflections on Women's Activism in Northern Ireland." *Journal of Women's History*, vol. 6, no. 4 / vol. 7, no. 1, Winter/Spring 1995, 13–39.

Mortimer, Penelope. *The Pumpkin Eater*. London: Penguin, 1962.

Mitchell, Juliet. *Psychoanalysis and Feminism: A Radical Reassessment of Freudian Psychoanalysis*. Allen Lane, 1974.

—. *The Longest Revolution: Essays on Feminism, Literature and Psychoanalysis*. Virago, 1984.

—. *Woman's Estate*. London: Penguin, 1971.

Paxton, Nancy L. *George Eliot and Herbert Spencer: Feminism, Evolutionism, and the Reconstruction of Gend*er. Princeton University Press, 1991.

Philpott, G. "Consciousness Raising: Back to Basics." *Spare Rib Reader*, edited by Marcia Rowe. Viking, 1982, pp. 585–587.

Proctor, Hannah. "Case Histories from Below: Class Struggle in the Psychoanalytic Consulting Room." *ICI Berlin*, 1 March 2022. Video recording, mp4, 44:04, https://doi.org/10.25620/e220301.

Proctor, Hannah, and Larne Abse Gogarty. "Communist Feelings." *The New Socialist*, March 2019. *New Socialist*, https://newsocialist.org.uk/communist-feelings-lessing-gornick/.

Rich, Adrienne. *Of Woman Born: Motherhood as Experience and Institution.* Virago, 1977.

Rose, Jacqueline. *Sexuality in the Field of Vision.* 1986. Verso, 2005.

Rowbotham, Sheila, et al. *Beyond the Fragments: feminism and the making of socialism.* Newcastle Socialist Centre, 1979.

Rubenstein, Roberta. *Boundaries of the Self: Gender, Culture, Fiction.* University of Illinois Press, 1987.

Sage, Lorna. *Doris Lessing.* Routledge, 1983.

Seddon, Vicky. *The Cutting Edge: Women and the Pit Strike.* Lawrence & Wishart, 1986.

Showalter, Elaine. *The Female Malady: women, madness, and English culture, 1830–1980.* Pantheon Books, 1985.

Williams, Raymond. *The English Novel from Dickens to Lawrence.* Oxford University Press, 1970.

9

Problems with Progress: Reading Transhistorically for Feminized Work in Buchi Emecheta's *Second-Class Citizen*

Ida Aaskov Dolmer and Emily J. Hogg

In Buchi Emecheta's 1974 novel, *Second-Class Citizen*, the protagonist Adah refuses to send her children away to live with a foster mother. Adah has recently migrated from Nigeria to London with her family, and the practice of employing foster mothers, the novel explains, is the norm for Nigerian migrant parents. This leaves her needing childcare in order to be able to undertake her paid employment as a librarian, but she finds that nursery waiting lists are very long: 'as every young mother who tried to place her child in a nursery could testify, there was no place for the children' (Emecheta 61). In the end, she hires a childminder, Trudy: a white woman who lives in a very underprivileged area in London. Adah has previously noted that, when it comes to foster mothers, 'no one wanted to know whether the house was clean or not; all they wanted to be sure of was that the foster mother was white. The concept of "whiteness" could cover a multitude of sins' (50). Her own experience with Trudy reveals the stark limitations of this attitude of racial superiority. Making an unexpected visit to Trudy's house, she finds her children's toys being played with by Trudy's own children, while hers are left with wildly unhygienic and dangerous playthings: 'Vicky was busy pulling rubbish out of the bin and Titi was washing her hands and face with the water leaking from the toilet' (58). Ultimately, Adah's son Vicky contracts viral meningitis. Trudy tries to claim that the illness must have been contracted earlier, in Nigeria—which she imagines as inevitably underdeveloped: 'He could have caught it from the water you drank at home, you know, before you brought him here . . .' (74). Adah knows this is ridiculous: 'What was it Trudy was saying about the child she had had in the best hospital in Nigeria, in the best ward, under the most efficient Swiss gynaecologist that the Americans could get for her as a member of their staff?' (74).

In this moment in the novel, different racialized narratives of progress in women's paid and unpaid work converge. The idea that a white English woman will provide superior care for a child is decisively undermined, and the notion that any problem must have originated before migration to England is rendered absurd by the obviously unsanitary conditions at Trudy's house. In addition, Adah faces a recognizably contemporary dilemma: what should a mother do when state-sponsored childcare is limited if not entirely unavailable, and she has a full-time job that is important to her not only financially but also in terms of identity, and which requires her to leave the home for most of the day? The novel was published in 1974 and is set in the early 1960s, and Adah's dilemma appears at first sight curiously out of step with the conventional historical narrative of this period and the position of women's labor within it. The struggle to balance career and unpaid reproductive work that Adah experiences is more readily associated with post-1970s neoliberal contexts than with this earlier period. Later in the novel, as we discuss in more detail below, this sense of temporal disjunction is further heightened when Adah encounters the discourses of the nascent women's movement. Having already experienced the 'freedom' to work outside the home, a freedom the feminists she reads about are beginning to fight for, she is skeptical about the extent to which employment can be associated with liberation. In its publication history, too, the novel seems to resist understanding in linear, chronological terms. It does not fit into the conventional account of the high points of Black British writing, being published, as Nicola Wilson has pointed out, in between the first major wave associated with Sam Selvon and George Lamming in the 1950s, and the efflorescence of Black British women's writing in the 1980s. And although Adah's story is also explored in another of Emecheta's works, *In the Ditch,* this was published before *Second-Class Citizen,* even though *Second-Class Citizen* is set before *In the Ditch.*

In recent years, a number of critics have called for more transhistorical forms of reading, approaches which highlight continuities and connections across different periods rather than primarily seeking to situate texts in the moment of their own publication.[1] Michaela Bronstein's *Out of Context: The Uses of Modernist Fiction,* moreover, shows how 'anti-historicist' (19) features can be found within works of literature; Bronstein analyzes the ways modernist works seek to imagine and contact an imagined future and argues that the 'formal features' of texts function as 'strategies for futureproofing' (19)—that is, as methods for engaging unknowable future readers. This chapter takes its starting point in the temporal disjunctions that characterize Emecheta's novel: the way that, though set in the early to mid-1960s, it explores a number of the issues thought to be characteristic of more recent labor conditions for women. We read the novel's prescient critique of these conditions through and alongside the narrative's own questioning of developmental narratives of progress, especially colonialist discourses about the position of women in Nigeria in comparison with Britain. In her experiences of labor, paid and unpaid, Adah appears out-of-time, and the novel also frequently stages its own resistance to linear, teleological narratives of progress. Attending to these aspects of the text, we find resistance to narratives of Western feminist progress accomplished through women's paid employment, and a model of an alternative way of narrating the history of women's work—as continuity and constant readjustment and revisiting crises and conflicts, rather than triumphant development.

Women, Work, and Progress

A basic conception of progressive development—the notion that human knowledge and experience is accumulating over time and improving individual and social life in a broadly incremental way—has been widely identified, and critiqued, as intrinsic to the modern view of history itself.[2] Postcolonial theorists have shown that colonialist epistemology is underpinned by developmental ideas: in *Time and the Other: How Anthropology Makes Its Object* Johannes Fabian points out and critiques the 'denial of coevalness' in Western anthropology in which difference is established between the Western scholar and the exotic Other by locating them at different positions along a process of progression that inevitably culminates in Western enlightenment and development. The West represents evolved modernity, and the Other represents unevolved pre-modernity. Queer theorists have relatedly argued that, as Carolyn Dinshaw puts it, queerness possesses a 'temporal dimension' (4): it opposes and disrupts the heteronormative life-course, its prescribed waypoints, and the broader notion of maximally productive linear progression it implies, upholds, and valorizes.

Developmental narratives of progress have also frequently shaped the way that the history of the feminist movement has been told (see McBean; Wiegman). According to Clare Hemmings, academics often pay lip service to notions of complexity and multiplicity, while tending in practice to subsume and unify discordant events into simpler story of feminism's development or failure. For a political movement intent on creating change, the significance of progress as a concept is easy to understand (without the idea that *something* might improve, why engage in activism at all?). Yet difficulties arise when progress is imagined as a singular, linear path that claims to encompass people of vastly different social positions and with contradictory experiences. In particular, the concepts of 'waves' and 'generations' retain a tenacious hold on the way that feminism's history is imagined and told, even though they have been widely critiqued for smoothing out contradictions and overstating coherence (see e.g. Browne; Hemmings; McBean; Roof). Such singular narratives have often produced coherence by placing white women at the center. It is often assumed, for example, that the feminist movement in Britain reached its apex in the late 1970s, because this was the case for the predominantly white Women's Liberation Movement. But Natalie Thomlinson points out that this general narrative is insupportable if 'the vitality of the Black women's movement in the 1980s' is considered (65–66). This is an issue of direct relevance for the reception of Buchi Emecheta's oeuvre. As Nicola Wilson has argued, 'the existence of Emecheta's published writing from the early 1970s is an important antidote to conventional narratives of literature and feminism in the UK during the second-wave feminist movement,' (307) which tend to suggest that a coherent, white movement became fragmented later in the decade because of emergent feminists of colour. Emecheta's writing, Wilson suggests, makes it clear that the critical discussion of marriage, housework, and childcare had never been the sole preserve of white feminists.

In popular media and political discussions of gender and work over the last half-century, fairly straightforward and linear progress narratives are clearly apparent. A common way of framing the dramatic social changes of the last fifty years suggests that women have been progressively liberated from the oppressive drudgery of housewifery to become independent wage-earners. As the Women's Budget Group wryly notes, for example, 'The Conservatives regularly remind us that there are more women in work than ever before and paid employment is often positioned as a key route out of poverty' (2). It is certainly the case that significant shifts in relation to gender and work have taken place in over recent decades in Britain. The brief flourishing of welfare state capitalism between the end of the Second World War and the end of the 1970s was predicated on its starkly gendered division of labor and naturalized assumptions of female domestic responsibility. Welfare policies, for example, as Eve Worth points out, were 'largely premised on the assumption that there would be one wage earner in a family and women were likely to be economic dependants' (94). From the 1970s onwards, many women entered the formal labor market; more and more professions became open to women; policies on sexual harassment and gender discrimination attempted to combat some of the barriers women face in the workplace, albeit with mixed results.

Undoubtedly, this shift brought the significant advantages of greater financial independence and a wider scope of opportunities and experiences for many women. Yet to present this simply or only as progress is misleading. First, working-class women and women of colour have historically not been absent from the formal labor market to the same extent as white middle-class women, and the types of work in which they have been over-represented have typically been low-paid and undervalued (see Davis). This complicates the notion that paid work, in and of itself, is somehow liberating and encourages a longer historical view of women's paid labor. Second, as Nancy Fraser has argued, neoliberal capitalism has made use of feminist campaigning around workplace equality, invoking the emancipatory potential of women's work as justification for 'depressed wage levels, decreased job security, declining living standards, a steep rise in the number of hours worked for wages per household [. . .] and a rise in female-headed households' ('Feminism, Capitalism and the Cunning of History,' 110). Where women's paid work has come to be seen as a symbol of gender equality, and work is framed as a central source of self-fulfilment, independence, and passion (see Weeks), the exploitative conditions of that increasingly precarious work have been more easily disguised. In addition, the entrance of more women into the labor market since the 1970s has not been accompanied in Britain with any comprehensive reorganization of the labor of social reproduction. The work of caring, cooking, and cleaning still must be done; ideologically it is still often associated with women (and empirically women still seem to do more of it than men do (Arber and Ginn; van Hooff)), but as housewife-ideology has become less compelling, more women are now socially and economically expected to undertake full-time paid work as well as maintaining the domestic sphere.

This phenomenon of women's immense responsibilities in both public and private spheres and the resulting time-squeeze is discussed in terms of the 'new sexual contract' (McRobbie), the 'second shift' (Hochschild and Machung), or the idealized cultural archetype of the 'supermom' (Orgad). For Nancy Fraser, though, the problems of the supermom and the housewife are two different manifestations of the same underlying problem. According to Fraser, all forms of capitalism contain a crisis tendency related to the work of social reproduction, the labor required to maintain and care for the current and future workforce ('Contradictions of Capital and Care,' 100). The capitalist drive towards endless, maximal accumulation tends to render social reproduction minimally important, even though it is a prerequisite for production itself. Different phases of capitalism imply, she argues, different crisis tendencies. A major crisis underlying the era of welfare state capitalism was its naturalization of 'heteronormativity and gender hierarchy' (ibid. 111) and the dissatisfaction, boredom, and eventually resistance it induced in the very women who were able to achieve the discursive ideal and devote themselves entirely to home and family (ibid. 108–112; 'Feminism, Capitalism and the Cunning of History,' 100–109). The crisis tendency of the contemporary moment is its failure to address social reproduction at all, leaving care and the foundational work of maintaining everyday life to be done in spare time that few people actually have ('Contradictions of Capital and Care' 112–115).

In this chapter, we read *Second-Class Citizen* in relation to narratives of women's progress through paid employment. Sam McBean has found in popular feminist literature 'a history of feminist conceptualizing of time as less linear and less generational' (4) than the one frequently found in theoretical and historical accounts of feminism, and which depends on 'a linear model of progress' (3). Like McBean, we turn to literature for alternative approaches to the time of feminism, but we do so here with a specific focus on the question of work.[3] We argue that the novel's attention to aspects of women's work experience sometimes considered distinctively neoliberal, as well as its own skepticism about the teleological development of women's workplace status, works to push beyond the idea that more paid work equals more liberation for women, and that liberation has consequently been increasing in linear fashion as women's workforce participation increases.

'Her Duty to Work': The Supermom's Second Shift in *Second-Class Citizen*

In Emecheta's *Second-Class Citizen*, Adah is the mother and main caretaker of four young children, and she performs the vast majority of the care work and housework in her family's ever-changing, precarious homes. In addition to this reproductive labor, Adah is employed as a librarian, and by the end of the novel she has begun to pursue a career as an author. As a result, much of the novel is concerned with Adah figuring out how to fulfil both her reproductive and productive duties. Adah's husband Francis is a student, and he outright refuses to help in any significant way with childcare, housework, or paid work, leaving Adah to be both the main breadwinner and homemaker of their family. This double duty means that Adah never seems able to find enough time to fully carry out or dedicate herself to all her work. Although she enjoys her 'first-class job' as a librarian, she is also concerned about leaving the children when she goes to work: 'what about her children? Who was going to look after them?' (49). The problem of time becomes very evident when Francis volunteers to take care of the children for a very short period; it feels for Adah like 'a stolen hour' (83) even though she spends this time doing even more housework and cooking for the family. The effort and sense of guilt implied by this conception of stealing time brings to mind the notions of 'time-debt' and 'time-famine', concepts especially salient for contemporary working mothers, as Arlie Hochschild has explored in *The Time Bind*.

Although the reader can recognize that it seems unfair that Adah must do all this work, both reproductive and productive, while her husband does next to nothing, through most of the novel this seems the natural course of things to Adah:

> Looking back at that time, she still wondered why she never thought it odd that she should be doing all the worrying about what they were going to live on, why she, and she alone, always felt that she was letting those she loved down if she stayed away from work, even for the sake of having a baby. The funniest thing was that she felt it was her duty to work, not her husband's. (104)

It is notable here that it is only later, and only with the benefit of hindsight, that Adah can see how unfair the household's division of labor is. This theme—the relationship between the experience of work and the way it is understood temporally—is one the novel explores throughout.

Towards the end of the text, the promise of progress through Women's Liberation arrives; we glimpse nascent second-wave feminist ideas as Adah reads about them: 'She had been reading a great number of women's magazines, and was surprised to read of mothers saying that they were bored just being housewives' (179). Here, the arguments made by Betty Friedan about 'the feminine mystique' are echoed, and the women in the magazines describe the discrepancies between the role that women are socially relegated to, the housewife-mother, and their suppressed desires to be educated on the same level as men and to work for pay outside the home, imagined as the road to gender equality and liberation. However, Adah does not understand this boredom and hidden desire: 'She was not that type of woman. [. . .] that was all she asked of life. Just to be a mother and a wife' (179). Adah has experienced what it is like to work the double duty of a working mother responsible for both earning enough money to provide for her family *and* being the main caretaker and homemaker, and she has realized, before this 'liberation' was accessible or framed as desirable to the general population of mothers and housewives, that this is an impossible balance to strike, especially for an immigrant woman whose access to well-paid employment is highly limited.

This is also a change for Adah. With her experience of being simultaneously homemaker and wage-earner, Adah now sees the ability to work in just one sphere, even if this is in the under-recognized and unpaid sphere of reproductive work, as the desirable path. Taking place at a time when the women around her call for access to paid work, Adah narrates another perspective on this relationship with and desire for work, and she can demonstrate that it is not a perfect or equal future or a path to feminist progress. Adah's perspective seems temporally out of sync with the women in the magazines; they protest for the experience she has already had, and which she knows to be exhausting and intensely difficult. The sense that a linear narrative of progressive development through time is being disturbed here is signaled when, on her first day at the library, a beautiful June day, Adah travels through London and sees that 'The trees had burst into green, ceasing to look like the naked, dried-up, juiceless old women they had reminded Adah of when she first landed in England. Now, everything was young, clean, moist and full of juice' (47). While the association between age and desiccation here is certainly problematic, it is notable that nature appears to be reversing its course: the aged become young on her first day at her job; time seems to run backwards as she pursues her career.

Migration Narratives and Subverted Progress

The apparent contrast between Adah's perspective on work and what is presented as the general view among women on the desire to work for pay, as presented via the inclusion of women's magazines, is simultaneously explained and further complicated by the story of migration at the heart of the novel. When Adah first arrives in London her husband Francis explains why the houses are so close to each other in comparison with the vast expanses in Nigerian villages: 'They build their houses like that here because land is not as plentiful as it is in Lagos. I am sure that builders of the future will start building our houses like that when Nigeria is fully industrialized. At the moment we can afford to waste land in building spacious verandas and back yards' (41). In his imagination of the future of Nigeria, Francis uses the template of London as a more developed, further progressed, and ultimately better and more desirable way of organizing space in the nation, and he theorizes that this must inevitably be the direction in which Nigeria is headed, thereby relying on the narrative of Nigeria as temporally 'behind' the UK in terms of development. However, to this Adah replies, 'We may never be as bad as this. Jammed against each other' (41). With her disdain for the claustrophobic and crammed buildings in London, Adah subverts the expected consensus that London's city development must ultimately have progressed further than and be superior to the Nigerian use of space that allows for large back yards and verandas—spaces that are deemed by Francis a waste of land. The notion that closely crammed and identical houses are the natural progression of, and more developed than, the spacious and detached houses in Nigeria is shown to be the result of the colonial relationship between Nigeria and London rather than reflecting how most people actually want to live, and the idea of London as unequivocally more progressed than Nigeria and as the future into which Nigeria must move is questioned and undermined.

The rejection of colonialist progress narratives, which is articulated through the discussion of domestic space, also shapes the novel's depictions of Adah's work-life. The novel's migration narrative and the intersection with the representation of feminist progress reveal how classed and racialized the narrative of progress regarding women's work is—Adah used to be perfectly able to balance productive and reproductive work with time to spare. While still living in Nigeria, although she was also the main breadwinner there, the situation was rather more relaxed: 'All Adah had to do was to go to the American library, work till two-thirty, come home and be waited on hand and foot, and in the evening be made love to' (28). The cause of this different experience of work seems mainly to be access to childcare and maids doing 'all the work in the house' (28).

Before living there, Adah imagines London and the UK more widely as a place of unending opportunity, 'like paying God a visit' (8). Indeed, the image of Britain as a civilized paradise is one to which the women in Adah's village are hooked, 'like opium' (15). However, once she and her family arrive in London, Adah's access to affordable domestic help and childcare all but disappears, leaving her to take care of her children according to British norms, in which 'she had to wash piles and piles of nappies, wheel the child round for sunshine during the day, attend to his feeds as regularly as if one were serving a master' (50). Having once employed maids herself, Adah now feels herself to be in the position of a servant, with her child the master. This echoes a familiar narrative in postcolonial literatures in which the colonial subject often imagines the empire's center, usually London, as a land of opportunity, a dream which is crushed soon after arrival when the migrant arrives in London and finds a less than warm welcome.[4]

When Adah first arrives in London and wants to apply for librarian jobs, Francis—who has been in the country for longer—shouts at her:

> You must know, my dear young *lady*, that in Lagos you may be a million publicity officers for the Americans; you may be earning a million pounds a day; you may have hundreds of servants; you may be living like an élite, but the day you land in England, you are a second-class citizen. So you can't discriminate against your own people, because we are all second-class citizens. (42–3, original italicization)

In this outburst, Francis not only maintains that Adah should be the one bringing money into the family, but also that she is supposed to do so with a job that is suitable to an immigrant woman and not aspire to a 'first-class job' such as working in a library. Although London is imagined as leagues ahead of Nigeria when it comes to wealth and opportunity, it also becomes very clear that once arrived in London ('the day you land'), Adah becomes classed as a migrant woman, a 'second-class citizen', which bars her access to the imagined wealth and opportunity.

Despite Francis's warnings, Adah does find a job as a librarian. But this produces its own difficulties; while working full-time at the library, Adah needs someone to take care of her children. It is at this point in the novel that the question of fostering is raised. Her husband refuses to take care of the children while she works and argues that they should follow the practice of most of the other Nigerian families they know in London by sending their children to live with a foster mother: 'No sane couple would dream of keeping their children with them [. . .] They say that in England Nigerian children have two sets of mothers – the natal mother, and the social mother' (50). Adah, however, feels that this is 'all right for the Nigerian wife who, for the first time, was tasting the real freedom of being a wife':

> She was free from the hindering influence of her kith and kin, she was free to work and earn money. Any type of work would do: cleaning, packing goods in a factory, being a bus conductor; all sorts of things. (50)

What makes her own situation different from that of the generic 'Nigerian wife', as she frames this difference, is that neither earning money nor being an adult separate from her family of origin is a *new* experience for her; she has already known this 'freedom' in Nigeria, and because this is not the 'first time' she experiences it, she has a different perspective on the relationship between work and mothering. Moreover, she suggests, she is a pursuing a career; she is not just working, jobs are not interchangeable for her: she's developing a career in a field she is passionate about.

The social position of women has long been bound up with colonialist discourses of progressive development, as Wardlow and Hirsch note: 'gender has been deployed discursively as a handy trope to exoticize various peoples who then become urgently in need of outside intervention to save them', with 'gender relations' frequently being used 'by a great number of people in very different places [. . .] as a means of locating themselves and others along a historical continuum, labeling themselves or others as more or less modern or traditional' (20–21).

What we find in *Second-Class Citizen* is a critique of the way women's work, specifically, is conceptualized within such developmental narratives. The novel combines, intersects, and critiques two progress narratives—the notion that the UK has progressed further than Nigeria, and the notion that doing paid work can be equated with women's liberation. By the end of the novel Adah has achieved a freedom in London that she *already had* in Nigeria: the ability to pursue a career she is committed to and to share childcare responsibilities. The temporal difference and denial of coevalness characteristic of colonialist representations, as well as the simplistic idea that paid work in itself is a measure of women's liberation, are thus complicated in Emecheta's novel as they are disturbed and negated by Adah's experiences.

Progress and Reproduction

Thinking about the history of women's work in the way suggested by Emecheta's novel means resisting what Sara Ahmed has described—primarily in the context of resistance to anti-racist and feminist criticisms—as 'overing.' Ahmed recounts moments in which she points out that something is racist or sexist, to which people will often respond 'that [they] thought I sounded "very 1980s," and that [they] thought we had "got over" identity politics' (179). In this way, Ahmed identifies 'overing' as a strategy used to reject protest against injustice with the claim that the objections being raised belong to a previous era of political, anti-racist, and feminist struggles. Overing reveals the influence of the model of progress, which assumes conditions must be continually improving; it takes for granted that the passing of time will necessarily produce more fairness and equality, and thus that feminist and anti-racist critique will become increasingly irrelevant. The clear connection between Emecheta's novel, published in 1974, and feminized work-lives in the 2020s shows that the set of problems posed by the concept of 'women's work' (the crisis of social reproduction, the dilemmas of love, passion, and exploitation, which both motherhood and career can elicit) are not over. The past, present, and future of feminized work exist in a complex and complicated relationship with one another.

In this sense, the novel invites readers to be skeptical towards progressive, developmental thinking more generally, and it is significant that it does so while also retaining a strong concern with children and parenting. Critiques of progress narratives have often argued that teleological social visions embody hope for the future in the ongoing reproduction of the family—'reproductive futurism,' as Lee Edelman terms it (2). Stephen Guy-Bray, glossing Edelman, writes that reproductive futurism denotes 'the narrowing of political and critical discourse effected by the fetishization of human reproduction,' which seeks to 'establish the perpetuation of the bourgeois family and of the complex of ideas associated with it as the standard against which all efforts must be evaluated' (38). Edelman's articulation of this position in *No Future* is the most famous and most controversial, but this association between notions of progressive development and reproduction can also be found in discussions of feminism. Robyn Wiegman argues, for example, that the popular notions of 'waves' and 'generations' work to render the history of feminism reliant on 'progressive understandings of time and indebted to reproduction as its implicit epistemology' (165). In such accounts, the problems associated with thinking of development as progressive are associated with—indeed, even thought to stem from—the imaginative centrality of cis-heterosexual reproduction.

A difficulty with this rhetorical framing, as Anca Parvulescu has argued, is that if 'The Child' as a figure is idealized, the material labor of social reproduction has been marginalized and devalued. According to Parvulescu, references to 'reproduction' in discussions of progress narratives typically represent 'a narrow concept of reproduction as procreative heteronormativity tethered to heterosexual sex,' which leaves 'untold the other story of reproduction: our daily reproduction in the service of capitalism' (89). In this sense, the same sense in which Marxist feminists use the term 'social reproduction,' we cannot choose whether or not to participate in reproduction: 'As long as we are not dead, however much we embrace the death drive, we are all married to reproductive futurism' (89). Reproduction (understood as the maintenance of the conditions of life itself) is the work that makes existence possible; to try and reject it is to ignore the foundation of social and individual being—our bodily health, our nourishment, the care that our inevitable vulnerability necessitates.

Parvulescu reads J.M. Coetzee's novel *Slow Man* against *No Future*, to show how the literary depiction of elder care can insist on the value and the inevitability of reproductive work in the more expansive sense, and thus challenge the idea that reproduction is primarily about children, child-rearing, and the reproduction of the cis-heterosexual family, literally and discursively, and thereby that reproduction is necessarily oriented towards the future. Yet what about children—and what of the conventionally feminized work of caring for them? As Parvulescu points out, there is an uneasy tension between 'The Child' and real-life children, between the symbolic and material registers here; in 'a transnational context,' she writes, 'few of us applaud the fact that some children do not seem to have a future' (91).

We argue that *Second-Class Citizen* makes a significant contribution to this discussion. As we have argued, this novel seeks to disrupt prevalent progress narratives about women and work. Yet at the same time, it does this while attending in significant detail to the labor of childcare and maintaining reproduction in all its guises as at the center of Adah's life. What we find in Emecheta's novel is a rejection of linear narratives about progress in women's work, but this is a rejection that does not bring down reproductive labor in the fall and does not subsume reproductive labor entirely into a symbol of teleological progress, but rather makes its distribution, its material realities, and its difficulties a center of narrative interest. In this way, *Second-Class Citizen* disconnects reproductive work from the idea of progress towards a necessarily better future made symbolic in the child, and it instead shows reproductive work to be indeed central to life but pointing towards both future and past at once.

Conclusion

The history of work, and especially the history of women's work, is often understood as a series of phases in which the generalized insecurity of passion-driven feminized neoliberal work follows the more routinized, masculinized Fordist era and its expectation that women be, or desire to be, housewives. What is crucial here is the way that, despite the precarity and insecurity of much contemporary labor, the transition from the era of Friedan's 'problem that has no name' to the era of the 'supermom' has often been understood as an unequivocable sign of feminist progress. That is, in line with the intense discursive significance of teleological progress narratives more generally, the *transformation* of capitalist social structure has been understood as unambiguous *improvement,* especially for women.

Second-Class Citizen presents a central character who, when it comes to her paid and unpaid work as well as to her status as a Nigerian migrant woman in London, is in multiple senses out-of-time. In paying attention to this aspect of the text, the novel can be read transhistorically as a prescient iteration of some of the critiques of the idealized 'balanced woman' made post-second wave feminism, as (white, middle-class) women came to realize that entering the workforce did not necessarily mean doing less work in the home, and as neoliberal developments meant that attachment to capitalist work became more and more all-consuming. Adah struggles with finding time to work enough to provide food, clothes, and a secure and comforting home for her family while also being required to actually cook the food, clean the home, and care physically and emotionally for her children and husband. Importantly, her struggles are narrated in contrast to her contemporary surroundings, in which women are just beginning to fight for the 'freedom' to do both. Emecheta's novel is thereby both a reminder of the inflated hopes of the idea of feminist progress in paid work, made even before women's paid work became a normative expectation for all, but it is also a reminder of the racialized and classed aspects of this liberation. In the novel, certain crises of reproductive work are not necessarily constrained to specific times, and they instead exist contemporaneously and differ in their degree of impact across social classes, races, and other social designations—it is because Adah is a highly educated Nigerian migrant to the UK that she becomes a 'supermom' *avant la lettre.*

Although, as Fraser argues, every 'historically specific form of capitalist society' has its own 'social reproductive contradiction,' these are general tendencies ('Contradictions of Capital and Care' 100). Emecheta's novel is a reminder of the granularity and distinctiveness of individual experience, especially minoritized individual experience, and the way it complicates such generalizing heuristics, even when they have considerable explanatory power. Reading the novel transhistorically reveals how such heuristics inherently cannot claim universality and that multiple crisis tendencies may temporally co-exist across social strata. It also speaks directly to current conditions: to read the novel five decades after it was published, after five decades of significant change in the gendering of labor, is to find a critique of some of the working conditions associated with contemporary feminized work. When this aspect of the text is considered alongside the novel's own explicit critiques of colonialist progress narratives, we can interpret it transhistorically: as a narration of feminized work that rejects the notion that movement into the future inevitably means progress or improvement. This is something that has particular value as the novel's future has become our present, and the hopes expressed by second-wave feminism have not all been fulfilled.

While many critiques of teleological narratives exist, Emecheta's novel is also significant because while it questions the notion of progressive development it does so while examining the feminized work of child-care. That is, it suggests that casting doubt on culturally pervasive progress narratives need not happen outwith the question of social reproduction. Instead of a direct equivalence between social reproduction and reproductive futurism embodied in the (white) heteropatriarchal family, the novel's attention to temporal complexity is articulated with and through the materiality of reproductive labor. To think with this novel about how work alters, how it might become fairer and more equitable, means not only rejecting the notion of predictable progressive development but also attending carefully to the work of mundane maintenance and routine care that has so often been feminized and made invisible.

Notes

1. For a full discussion of transhistorical reading, see the introduction to this volume. Felski, Hayot, and Coombs and Coriale have been particularly influential in our understanding of the approach.
2. This topic has been discussed very widely. Particularly important accounts can be found in Chakrabarty, Allen, Latour (especially pp. 188–194), Freeman among many others.
3. On literature's relationship with progressive accounts of feminism, see also 'Progress and Feminist Literary Criticism,' by Emily J. Hogg.
4. See for example John McLeod's *Postcolonial London* or, for accounts contemporary with the period represented in *Second-Class Citizen*, see the 1965 collection *Disappointed Guests: Essays by African, Asian, and West Indian Students,* edited by Henri Tajfel and John L. Dawson.

Works Cited

Ahmed, Sara. *On Being Included*. Duke University Press, 2012.

Allen, Amy. *The End of Progress: Decolonizing the Normative Foundations of Critical Theory*. Columbia University Press, 2016.

Arber, Sara and Jay Ginn. "The mirage of gender equality: occupational success in the labour market and within marriage." *British Journal of Sociology*, vol. 46, no. 1, 1995, 21–43.

Bronstein, Michaela. *Out of Context: The Uses of Modernist Fiction*. Oxford University Press, 2018.

Browne, Victoria. *Feminism, Time, and Nonlinear History*. Palgrave, 2014.

Chakrabarty, Dipesh. *Provincializing Europe: Postcolonial Thought and Historical Difference*. Princeton University Press, 2000.

Coombs, David Sweeney and Danielle Coriale. "V21 Forum on Strategic Presentism." *Victorian Studies*, vol. 59, no. 1, 2016, 87–89.

Davis, Angela Y. *Women, Race and Class*. Penguin, 2019.

Dinshaw, Carolyn. *How Soon is Now? Medieval Texts, Amateur Readers, and the Queerness of Time*. Duke University Press, 2012.

Edelman, Lee. *No Future: Queer Theory and the Death Drive*. Duke University Press, 2004.

Emecheta, Buchi. *In the Ditch*. Allison & Busby, 1972.

Emecheta, Buchi. *Second-Class Citizen*. 1974. Fontana/Collins, 1982.

Fabian, Johannes. *Time and the Other: How Anthropology Makes Its Object*. 1983. Columbia University Press, 2014.

Felski, Rita. "Context Stinks!" *New Literary History*, vol. 42, no. 4, 2011, 573–591.

Fraser, Nancy. "Feminism, Capitalism and the Cunning of History." *New Left Review*, vol. 56, March/April 2009, 97–117.

—. "Contradictions of Capital and Care." *New Left Review*, vol. 100, July/August 2016, 99–117.

Freeman, Elizabeth. *Time Binds: Queer Temporalities, Queer Histories*. Duke University Press, 2010.

Friedan, Betty. *The Feminine Mystique*. W. W. Norton, 1963.

Guy-Bray, Stephen. "No Present." *Sex, Gender and Time in Fiction and Culture*, edited by Ben Davies and Jana Funke. Palgrave Macmillan, 2011, pp. 38–52.

Hayot, Eric. *On Literary Worlds*. Oxford University Press, 2012.

Hemmings, Clare. "Telling Feminist Stories." *Feminist Theory*, vol. 6, no. 2, 2005, 115–139.

Hochschild, Arlie Russell. *The Time Bind: When Work Becomes Home and Home Becomes Work*. Metropolitan Books, 2001.

Hochschild, Arlie Russell, and Anne Machung. *The Second Shift: Working Families and the Revolution at Home*. Penguin Books, 2012.

Hogg, Emily J. "Progress and Feminist Literary Criticism: The 'New Eras' of Nadine Gordimer." *Influence and Inheritance in Feminist English Studies*, edited by Emily J. Hogg and Clara Jones. Palgrave, 2015, 49–65.

Latour, Bruno. *Politics of Nature: How to Bring the Sciences into Democracy*, translated by Catherine Porter. Harvard University Press, 2004.

McBean, Sam. *Feminism's Queer Temporalities*. Routledge, 2016.

McLeod, John. *Postcolonial London: Rewriting the Metropolis.* Taylor & Francis, 2004.

McRobbie, Angela. "Top Girls?: Young Women and the Post-Feminist Sexual Contract." *Cultural Studies*, vol. 21, no. 4–5, 2007, 718–37.

Orgad, Shani. *Heading Home: Motherhood, Work, and the Failed Promise of Equality.* Columbia University Press, 2019.

Parvulescu, Anca. "Reproduction and Queer Theory: Between Lee Edelman's 'No Future' and J.M. Coetzee's 'Slow Man.'" *PMLA*, vol. 132. no. 1, 2017, 86–100.

Roof, Judith. "Generational Difficulties; or, The Fear of a Barren History." *Generations: Academic Feminists in Dialogue*, edited by Devoney Looser and E. Ann Kaplan. University of Minnesota Press, 1997, 69–87.

Tajfel, Henri and John L. Dawson (Eds.), *Disappointed Guests: Essays by African, Asian, and West Indian Students.* Oxford University Press, 1965.

Thomlinson, Natalie. *Race, Ethnicity and the Women's Movement in England, 1968–1993.* Palgrave Macmillan, 2016.

van Hooff, Jenny H. "Rationalising Inequality: Heterosexual Couples' Explanations and Justifications for the Division of Housework Along Traditionally Gendered Lines." *Journal of Gender Studies*, vol. 20, no. 1, 2011, 19–30.

Wardlow, Holly and Jennifer S. Hirsch, "Introduction." *Modern Loves: The Anthropology of Romantic Courtship and Companionate Marriage*, edited by Jennifer S. Hirsch and Holly Wardlow. University of Michigan Press, 2006, 1–31.

Weeks, Kathi. "Down with Love: Feminist Critique and the New Ideologies of Work." *Women's Studies Quarterly*, vol. 45, no. 3/4, 2017, 37–58.

Wiegman, Robyn. "On Being in Time with Feminism." *Modern Language Quarterly*, vol. 65, no. 1, 2004, 161–76.

Wilson, Nicola. "Feminist citation in Buchi Emecheta's Early Fiction and Autobiography: Publishing race, class, and gender." *The Routledge Companion to Literature and Feminism*, edited by Rachel Carroll and Fiona Tolan. Routledge, 2024, 306–321.

Women's Budget Group. "Women, Employment and Earnings: A pre-budget briefing from the UK Women's Budget Group," 2020, https://wbg.org.uk/wp-content/uploads/2020/02/final-employment-2020.pdf.

Worth, Eve. *The Welfare State Generation: Women, Agency and Class in Britain since 1945.* Bloomsbury Academic, 2022.

Afterword: Women's Work Across Contexts

Christina Lupton

1.

The chapters in this collection collectively agree upon the tight economy of women's labor and care work. But how far do they agree on where and how writing fits into this economy? In some cases, it is clear enough that bookwork, a term usefully invoked by Lucie Duggan, belongs to the category of labor to be remunerated: as demonstrated by Nicola Wilson, Aki Hayashi, research assistant to Eduard Blunden, works for him in a transaction that is described straightforwardly enough in these terms. Nell Dunn's conversations with her friends and neighbors might, as Helen Charman points out, be less easily classified as work—yet the transcription and sculpting of those conversations into Dunn's collection *Talking to Women* can be. But what about the writing of Cherie Jones, author of the novel *How the One Armed Sister Sweeps her House*? Jones has pursued writing throughout her life, partly under the umbrella of her PhD in Creative Writing undertaken alongside her employment as a general counsel for a government agency in Barbados. In her analysis of Jones's novel, Leighan Renaud argues persuasively that we ought to consider this writing one of the jobs that domestic violence produces for women, who are left to clean up, on so many levels, the mess men have made. In a different vein, Leah Misemer argues that the creation and distribution of political comics models the kind of activity that should count as political work. Working and writing belong in these terms to the larger arena of effort in which woman push back against the world as it is, but not so obviously to the realm of professional work.

Being paid to write novels and for television allowed Buchi Emecheta to thrive as a single mother of five after the end of her marriage in 1965.

But in the darkest days of her life in London, writing was often the easiest of the tasks facing her as breadwinner and caregiver to five young children. For a brief period after the birth of her fourth child, when her husband is employed delivering mail, Emecheta's character, Adah, finds peace enough in being on leave from her job at the British library to write her novel: 'all Adah had to do every day was take three babies to the park for an hour or two, come home, give them their lunch, tuck them up to rest, and write *The Bride Price*' (173). Yet Adrienne Rich, publishing in New England in the same years as Emecheta began writing in London, found this same combination of childcare and writing almost impossible. Her early poetry won her accolades, but domestic responsibility stood painfully in the way of her doing more of it, depriving her of the pleasures of being alone and self-directed that seem to accrue to the writer. The 'scrappy' nature of her writing in these early years can, Lindsay Turner observes, arise inspirationally from such scenes of interruption and emotional conflict. But Rich and Emecheta, we could also argue, are both strong examples of women who perceive various forms of work (as teachers, social workers, mothers, librarians) as overshadowed by writing, an activity with its own gravitational pull; and an occupation whose pleasures mitigate rather than accrue to the pains of alienated labor.

2.

Of course, we do not need to decide exactly what work is to appreciate the light the chapters collected here shed on it. Perhaps obviously, there's no one task that qualifies as work *per se*. Sometimes gardening is work; sometimes it's recreation. The same goes for looking after a child, having sex, writing a poem, making a comic, lifting weights, drawing up a legal case, cooking a meal, reading a book. All of these activities can be laborious; but all can also provide an incentive to stop laboring. In addition, all of them, we might argue, can fall outside the work/non-work binary, as forms of endeavor hard to measure except as part of the process of becoming the person doing them. Thus, regardless of how difficult it can be to say what work is or is not, one thing we learn from these chapters is that, while many of the activities done consistently by women (including writing) are enjoyable, they are enjoyed best when they are offset by other kinds of activity. Would anyone choose to do anything—or everything—all of the time?

Frigga Haug, a theorist important in German Marxist feminist circles for many years, describes the good life as including four ways of passing time: paid work, reproductive work (this might involve caring for others, a home, or an environment), political work, and culture: the lifelong development of the self through learning. Ideally, she argues, a 16-hour waking day would be divided equally between all four of these modes.[1] Considering the equitable distribution of time in this light, she contends, would refresh both class and gender debates. This perspective suggests that it's the combining of different occupations and skillsets over the course of the day that matters. It also suggests that it's this combination of roles that women, or feminized workers, have both striven for and mastered, at least to a higher degree than people following more well-beaten career paths. Haug's approach might be helpful in extracting the positive sense in which feminized work has been understood, including by the editors and authors here, as suggesting a life of manifold activity and social responsibility—the sort of life that from a certain angle can seem like the only real existence worth fighting for. This is the upside of what I take Turner to be arguing for when she suggests the 'scrappiness' of Rich's poetry, written as mother to young children, might also be seen as a model for the way in which so many people are now working—by switching between tasks, none of which are tied securely to an old sense of professional identity.

Yet, there's also, a downside to working like this: the term 'scrappy' suggests so, along with the different arguments here by Emily J. Hogg, Ida Aaskov Dolmer, and Charlotte J. Fabricius, for the bad ways that work can feel feminized: by being endless, unseen, underpaid, unlikely to produce status or self-direction. If the switching between tasks in this feminized mode comes at the cost of having control of one's time, or having the chance to focus on the thing you care about most, or having time to rest, then it may not feel like much of an advantage. Perhaps, Audre Lorde suggests, women have mastered poetry 'which can be done between shifts, in the hospital pantry, on the subway, and on scraps of surplus paper' (116). But just think, as Varsha Panjwani's chapter asks us to do, of the novels women could have written if they had had the slabs of time men did, the people cooking for them, the rooms kept hushed and clean, the resources organized. Perhaps no one wants to do one thing all the time: but no one wants life to be sliced up too much either, or to be drawn from one activity too quickly to the next by necessity, or to be forced from their desk by hunger or a crying child before they have had time to get the lines down.

3.

Historically, women have deployed some fancy footwork in claiming that what they do ought to be recognized as work, while simultaneously urging models of the good life that are more porous for everyone to the upsides of care and creativity, and community. The Wages for Housework movement, for instance, has gone down in history for recognizing domestic work *as work*. Between 1972 and 1977, Selma James in England, Mariarosa Dalla Costa in Italy, and Silvia Federici in the US argued passionately for the consequence of recognition being that domestic workers should be paid by the state for their efforts on the domestic front. In many cases, the state pensions, parental allowances granted independent of tax credits, and single parents' allowances that rolled out at this time were the tangible results of those campaigns led by women.[2] But the larger conceptual aim of the Wages for Housework campaign was in fact to limit the work women did. The case for wages was calculated to move unsalaried labor (applied to everything from nursing an aged parent to servicing a partner's emotional or sexual needs) into the deficit column, thereby crediting women with the right to other kinds of activity. In *Wages Against Housework* (1975), Federici stresses this: 'To say we want money for housework is the first step towards refusing to do it, because the demand for a wage makes our work visible, which is the most indispensable condition to begin to struggle against it' (206).

The larger point here is that work in general should be reduced. No improvement of working conditions for those with salaries, the argument goes, could address the fact that for every child at school, and every man in the workplace, a woman was devoting hours of her life to getting them there. Dalla Costa reflects back on the fact that:

> it went counter to the perspective proposed by the institutional left, with its labour ideology that told women that adding another job to the work that they were already doing in the home was the only future path. We denounced this. To calculate women's work one should have started with the work they were already doing, housework, and, on that basis, one had to conceive of a major reduction of the workday. (Interview, 224)

This emphasis on limiting the workday gets lost if we remember the Wages for Housework as a movement advocating only the recognition of domestic or reproductive activity as work.[3] And it is that original point of the movement's objection to work that still resonates today with the more recent anti-work politics of Kathi Weeks, or with the radical suggestion that Sophie Lewis makes in *Full Surrogacy Now*, that pregnancy might be best reckoned with as a form of paid labor.[4]

This tactical move of naming domestic *work* was useful in the 1970s as a way of calling attention to women being prevented from doing the full roster of things that Haug names as proper to the well-lived and balanced life—most notably, as Federici agrees, the political and cultural activities that can only happen once the basic needs are met. Some of the authors in this collection—Renauld accounting for Jones's representation of GBV in Anglophone Caribbean communities; Panjwani in suggesting that women writers are even today defined by their lost opportunities—use this same tactic to suggest how childcare, domestic violence, and housework pile up as work. But to call these things work is only a small step in allowing women to leave their mark on the world in ways *other* than through individual or professional success. Labeling all effort work is one way to take the drudge of human life seriously; to make time and place for everyday tasks in the annuls of history. Yet the real problem—of how the person overburdened with domestic and care chores is ever to access the world as an artist, a lover, a citizen, a writer—is not a semantic one.

To describe women's activity only in the name of work can be, in these terms, too quick to concede to the work/not-work opposition that has failed to describe the life most of us want. The 'feminization' of work captures the painful hustle involved in combining financial survival with caring for others and writing a book; or the stress of monetizing one's care work or becoming an online influencer, as the characters in the novels described by Roberta Garrett are pressed to do. It might also suggest a certain kind of commitment to service that, as we learn in the Introduction, has been co-opted by post-Fordist capitalism as a positive attribute of the productive worker. But the feminization of *life* might, I think, describe even better the hope most humans nurture, of being able to act beyond those boundaries of work and leisure, for the sake of both one's own and one's community's pleasure and development. Within the realm of social psychology, Carol Gilligan, for example, has critiqued the ways that success has been measured by standard of individuation and competition that is by default male. Her 1990 study *In a Different Voice* pushes back against the stereotypes that split love and work, attributing care to the feminized realm and instrumental abilities to the male domain. 'Looked at from a different perspective,' she points out,

> these stereotypes reflect a conception of adulthood that is itself out of balance, favoring the separateness of the individual self over connection to others, and leaning more toward an autonomous life of work than toward the interdependence of love and care. (17)

Those three recent novels described by Garrett, where mothers who back away from professional ambition but are left to careen between caring for children and earning money as small-time entrepreneurs or home office workers, are exposés in this sense of the bias Gilligan explores. The problem is not so much that women themselves back away from individual models of success in favor of more other-centered lives, but that the post-Fordist ideal does not reward the prioritizing of collective or cultural development. Novels, and literature itself, is a complicated artifact of this unfairly divided world. In some ways literary production seems to rely on the most extreme forms of individuation and withdrawal from community: the novelist is even less likely to be with her children than the mommy-blogger. On the other hand, literature has a long history of creating and supporting real world communities and connections, which livestreamed accounts of a busy but alienated life at home seem to lack.

There are plenty of signs in this collection, and on its pages, of what such a literary life of care and connection might entail. Take, for instance the activities of publishing and distributing comics that Misemer describes as a feminist praxis. Or the feminist bibliography project Nicola Wilson has been a part of and out of which her research on Hayashi arises. Wilson opens her chapter by describing that project as valuable and challenging for those who were involved in its editing team, but as having escaped the metrics by which the work of British academics is currently being measured. There's testimony here to the collective life that research and writing can support, but which fails as academic output by the standards of the British University. One response to this mismatching of priorities is to suggest that everything we do—the collectives we form, the politics and the friendships we pursue—should be better recognized as work. But another is to insist that our institutional work, narrowly understood, must be properly paid and limited precisely so that activities, like collective writing and editing, can continue to galvanize other ways of life outside work. In 1999, Andre Gorz stated:

> Never has the irreplaceable, indispensable function of labour as the source of social ties, social cohesion, integration, socialization, personalization, personal identity, and meaning been invoked so obsessively since the day it became unable to fulfill any of these functions. (57)

His observation applies even more acutely to the recent failures of literature as a profession. We live now in a time where literary jobs are so scarce that work, even in its best sense, seems unlikely to save us or our relationship with the books we love. But this is not to say that literature might not still have a role as something else.

Here, the example of Karen Brahe, a Danish noblewoman who clearly put great effort into assembling, studying, and marking up the works in her library collection is salutatory. In Brahe's context, of seventeenth-century Denmark, there were almost no professional opportunities to handle books, certainly not for women. Yet the effort that went into Brahe's library was, Lucie Duggan shows, extraordinary and productive of all kinds of connections, within and across time. That endeavor was characterized partly by there being no market value, no pecuniary interest, attached to Brahe's effort. It can be worthwhile recognizing that Brahe, like the many women of her period who wrote, read, collected, annotated, circulated, and reviewed books, was able to do so precisely because she did not have to earn a living. I make this point less to validate Brahe in her class position, than to emphasize the space she had to cultivate her learning away from the market. For Turner, the model of women managing to write while shouldering a persistent domestic burden suggests their alliance with gig workers; for Roberta Garrett, the modern mommy-blogger is a part of the problem. But the example of Brahe shows how other women, removed from the immediate challenges of salaried work, have become leaders in combining bookwork and creative and community effort. This need not be a celebration of the book-owning, leisured classes: it can also be a positive model of what life might look like for more people if the bar for basic survival were met, for instance through universal basic income, or the kind of allowances once given to UK students and still given to all students across Scandinavia, or to academics to make collections like the one you are reading. The communities that Misemer describes, which are organized around the production and distribution of comics outside the marketplace are also models here of why having some kind of life after work is and has been so important to women's political life.

4.

As Hogg and Dolmer's chapter on Emecheta argues, examples of the lives led well by literary women can be found in the past as well as the future; in Europe as well as outside it. Emecheta's early life in Lagos in the late 1950s, where she was able, because of the extended household she lived in, to become a mother and study and work in a well-endowed library is one example. As Emecheta herself saw it, life in London for an educated woman with small children was in many ways much harder than the life she left behind in Nigeria. There is no logic that secures women a fair share of the bounty of modernity–a bounty associated, at least until recently, with the promise that we would all be working less as soon as automation set in and the wealth spread around. There is also no obvious correlation between the victories of rights-based feminism and the fairer distribution of common tasks like childcare and editing, and political organizing.

This collection comes out of Denmark, which is worth noting as the setting where many of the fights fought by and for women, inside and outside the workplace, have been won: healthcare, childcare, parental leave, and the division of childcare between men and women are at the very best end of the spectrum for what has ever been achieved in any country at any point in history. Statistically, the incomes of men and women in Denmark are also more-or-less even until the birth of a first child. Yet even in this context, women remain poorly represented in the higher echelons of most workplaces, and their incomes plummet empirically to become nearly thirty per cent less on average than men's once a child is born. Key areas of Danish society, including the STEM subjects and the creative industries, remain far more dominated by men than they are in equivalent national systems across Scandinavia.[5]

The introduction to this collection asks us to consider 'what feminized work *is*, what it feels like, what it *means*.' I have tried to give some sense of how that feeling might be translated positively, to suggest that effort of trying to imagine ourselves in the round—not as just as employees, but as children, retirees, patients, students, readers, collectors, lovers, parents. This way of looking at the world, other than in terms of individual, professional success, might be positively described as feminized. But it can also be associated with the ongoing success of more caring social systems. In Denmark, university grants, paid parental leave, state daycare, state healthcare, good retirement packages, and agreed limits to the working week mean that time away from work has been shared amongst men and women, and amongst rich and poor, more successfully than in most other national contexts. This is a reminder that the fight for a life worth living, one that has classically been valued by and associated with women, remains worthwhile. But the other kinds of inequality that remain palpable in the Danish context—in the workplace, in the creative industries, and at the level of income disparity more generally—might also serve as a reminder, as Dolmer and Hogg suggest, that history can flow backwards as well as forwards—and that it can sometimes, as Emecheta experiences, flow in both directions at once.

Notes

1. Frigga Haug, *Die Vier-in-einem-Perspektive. Politik von Frauen für eine neue Linke* (Argument Verlag, Hamburg 2008). There is currently no English translation of this text, but Haug has published versions of the argument as 'A Politics of Working Life' in *Learning and Work and the Politics of Working Life*, edited by Terri Seddon et al.
2. Toupin names two such campaigns: the proposed tax credits scheme in the UK in 1974, which would have made wage earners the only beneficiaries of state support for children, and the 1976 struggle in Toronto. In both cases, Wages for Housework campaigners defended family allowances and their direct payment to women (135).
3. In *Full Surrogacy Now*, Sophie Lewis describes this as an unfortunate 'tendency to literalistically misapprehend the Wages for Housework Campaign provocation' (76). One example would be the 2013 piece by journalist Kristin Wartman for the *New York Times*, writing about Selma James having campaigned to 'Pay People to Cook at Home.'
4. Weeks and Lewis both reference the Wages for Housework campaign explicitly in the studies listed here. In Weeks's case, she describes it as offering 'a critical standpoint from which the alienating and exploitative conditions of modern work can be critically interrogated' (15).
5. See, for example, https://innovationsfonden.dk/sites/default/files/2018-10/gender-diversity-in-denmark.pdf.

Works Cited

Dalla Costa, Mariarosa. Interview with Louise Toupin, *Wages for Housework: A History of an International Feminist Movement, 1972–77*. Translated by Kathe Roth. UBC Press Vancouver, 2018, 220–40.

Federici, Silvia. "Wages Against Housework" (1975). *Wages for Housework: The New York Committee 1972–1977: History, Theory, Documents*, edited by Silvia Federici and Arlen Austin. Autonomedia, 2017.

Gilligan, Carol. *In a Different Voice: Psychological Theory and Women's Development*. Harvard University Press, 1994.

Gorz, Andre. *Reclaiming Work: Beyond the Wage Based Society*. Polity, 1999.

Haug, Frigga. "A Politics of Working Life," in *Learning and Work and the Politics of Working Life*, edited by Terri Seddon et al. Routledge, 2010.

Lewis, Sophie. *Full Surrogacy Now: Feminism Against Family*. Verso, 2019.

Lorde, Audre. *Sister Outsider: Essays and Speeches*. Crossing Press, 2007.

Toupin, Louise. *Wages for Housework: A History of an International Feminist Movement, 1972–77*. Translated by Kathe Roth. UBC Press Vancouver, 2018.

Weeks, Kathi. *The Problem with Work: Feminism, Marxism, Antiwork Politics and Postwork Imaginaries*, Duke University Press, 2011.

Index

EU Authorised Representative:
Easy Access System Europe Mustamäe tee 50, 10621 Tallinn, Estonia
gpsr.requests@easproject.com

Printed and bound by CPI Group (UK) Ltd, Croydon, CR0 4YY
29/09/2026
02224981-0006